THE REPUBLIC OF GUPTA

THE REPUBLIC OF GUPTA

A Story of State Capture

PIETER-LOUIS MYBURGH

PENGUIN BOOKS

Published by Penguin Books
an imprint of Penguin Random House South Africa (Pty) Ltd
Reg. No. 1953/000441/07
The Estuaries No. 4, Oxbow Crescent, Century Avenue, Century City, 7441
PO Box 1144, Cape Town, 8000, South Africa
www.penguinrandomhouse.co.za

Penguin
Random House
South Africa

First published 2017

1 3 5 7 9 10 8 6 4 2

PUBLISHER: Marlene Fryer
MANAGING EDITOR: Robert Plummer
EDITOR: Bronwen Maynier
PROOFREADER: Lisa Compton
COVER DESIGNER: Gretchen van der Byl
TEXT DESIGNER: Ryan Africa
INDEXER: Sanet le Roux

Set in 11 pt on 15 pt Minion

solutions
Printed by **novus print**, a Novus Holdings company

MIX
Paper from
responsible sources
FSC
www.fsc.org   FSC® C022948

This book is printed on FSC® certified and controlled sources.
FSC (Forest Stewardship Council®) is an independent, international,
non-governmental organization. Its aim is to support environmentally sustainable,
socially and economically responsible global forest management.

ISBN 978 1 77609 089 1 (print)
ISBN 978 1 77609 090 7 (ePub)

For Zelda, my fortress

'The appearance of the law must be upheld.
Especially while it's being broken.'
– William Magear Tweed, *Gangs of New York*

Contents

Preface

When I learnt in the latter half of 2015 that the publishing of *The Republic of Gupta* would become a reality, I was filled with a great deal of excitement. As a journalist, I had become well accustomed to the confines one's words are subjected to when writing for newspapers or even online platforms. Finally, I thought, here is an opportunity to let rip on the wonderfully expansive canvas that is a 300-page book.

But soon, dark blots of trepidation began to mix with my excitement. What if the subject matter simply did not yield enough material to fill the pages? And were the Guptas really interesting enough to justify spending over a year researching and writing about them?

Despite being plagued by apprehensions, I got on with the task. My progress, frankly, was not the result of some noble display of internal strength. It was deadline-related paranoia that whipped me to the finish line. Much has been said about what inspires people to write, but the procrastinating author *knows* the deadline to be his or her cruellest master and most effective motivator.

And so it came to be that my earliest sentences grew into paragraphs, and paragraphs into chapters. As this book began to take shape, I realised that my initial fears over the subject matter were unfounded. In fact, it quickly became clear to me that there were more than enough issues pertaining to South Africa's most infamous business family that I could write about. This became particularly evident from March 2016 onwards, when the proverbial dam wall broke regarding the Guptas' influence over government affairs.

The challenge, it seemed, would rather be deciding what to include and what to leave out. In this regard, *The Republic of Gupta* seeks to unpack the most important developments involving the family. It is not intended to be a blow-by-blow summary of every single news event featuring them and their business empire. Instead, I have accompanied my discussion of the more pertinent Gupta-related news events with an in-depth exploration of other issues that did not find their way onto the front pages of newspapers. By combining the two approaches, I hope to give readers a broad yet thorough account of who the Guptas really are.

As I write this, the Guptas are very much a developing news story. New revelations and information about the family's doings have made their way into the press on an almost weekly basis since the start of 2016. This has made writing *The Republic of Gupta* somewhat tricky. I am well aware that relevant Gupta-related issues will surface after this book goes to print. Perhaps one day, when it appears that the Gupta saga has finally reached its conclusion, I might be tempted to write a sequel to the story.

During the process of sourcing new information on the family, I met with several individuals whose identities cannot be disclosed. The use of unnamed sources in journalism is at once indispensable and problematic. On the one hand, people often have legitimate concerns over their personal safety when divulging sensitive information that has a bearing on the rich and powerful. It goes without saying that such sources need to be protected at all costs. On the other hand, the use of unnamed sources raises concerns over the credibility of the information they provide. For this reason, it is of the utmost importance to determine the veracity of such information before it is stated as fact. Where it is not possible to do so, the journalist needs to consider carefully whether such unverified information should be made public at all. At the very least, unproved claims should be clearly labelled as being just that. This is a good ethos to be guided by while writing about a topic as controversial as the one tackled in *The Republic of Gupta*. I hope I have succeeded in doing so.

One of the people I met during my research is a former politician who had close ties with the Guptas. At one point during our conversation, I became the interviewee. The former politician wanted to know why I had decided to focus specifically on the Guptas. There are many other business-people who abuse their close ties with government officials for personal gain, he told me; why not focus on them too?

It was a fair question. President Jacob Zuma alone is closely linked to a wide network of tender moguls who seem to be disproportionately successful when it comes to securing big government contracts. There are many other senior government officials who maintain similar relationships with people in the private sector. Given Zuma's questionable stance on the bond between his party and those doing business with the state, it is no wonder that this symbiosis has become increasingly predatory in nature during his tenure as president.

It was Zuma, after all, who in 2013 told guests at the 101st anniversary gala dinner of the African National Congress (ANC) that 'a wise businessperson will support the ANC ... because supporting the ANC means you're investing very well in your business'.[1]

When he revisited the same topic in a speech at a dinner hosted by the ANC's Progressive Business Forum in October 2015, Zuma's message had morphed into something that was at once desperate and menacing. 'I always say to business people that if you invest in the ANC, you are wise. If you don't invest in the ANC, your business is in danger,' he reportedly told the audience.[2]

But it is not only Zuma's closest business buddies who have responded to the president's invitation with enthusiasm. There must be hundreds, if not thousands, of businesspeople who have positioned themselves to repeatedly benefit from state expenditure at every level of government. This includes national and provincial departments, state-owned entities, as well as provincial and municipal authorities.

What the former politician did not acknowledge, however, was the exceptional proximity to and influence over the highest echelons of government that the Guptas have apparently been allowed to establish. This sets them apart from other politically connected players in South Africa's business fraternity. There is no doubt in my mind that we are mostly in the dark about the shady dealings of some of these other tender barons, but the fact that we have been hearing so many tales of government officials being summoned to the Guptas' infamous Saxonwold estate suggests that the family has been exceedingly more aggressive in their 'lobbying' efforts. It is for these reasons that the term 'state capture' has become synonymous with the Guptas, and why a book such as this one would necessarily explore the issue of state capture by means of honing in on the Guptas' exploits.

I am indebted to the firebrand opposition leader Julius Malema and his Economic Freedom Fighters (EFF) for helping me come up with a title for this book. When Zuma appointed the obviously pro-Gupta Mosebenzi Zwane as the new mining minister in September 2015, it was the EFF and Malema who started to refer to this country as 'the Gupta Republic of South Africa'.[3] As we will see, the new mining minister's later actions would strongly support the EFF's claim that Zwane had from the outset been a Gupta appointee.

Zwane's promotion was not an isolated incident. Looking back at the events of 2016, and considering the myriad earlier indications of the Guptas' hold over those in power, it is now clear that a good deal of the government's most important decisions are not made at the Union Buildings or even at Luthuli House. Instead, all indications are that our very own Number One has transferred a signicant amount of the country's executive power to the residents of 1 Saxonwold Drive. It is from their fortified estate in one of Johannesburg's plushest suburbs that the country's de facto first family rule over a highly profitable fiefdom I like to call the Republic of Gupta.

PIETER-LOUIS MYBURGH
JOHANNESBURG, MARCH 2017

Introduction:
Unpacking state capture

If there is one positive contribution the Guptas have made to South African society, it would be the unique words and phrases that have entered our public discourse as a result of the scandals in which they have been involved.

Zuptas, a portmanteau that embodies the unholy alliance between the Guptas and the family of President Jacob Zuma, is a great example of the lexicographic treasure the brothers Ajay, Atul and Rajesh Gupta have so kindly bestowed upon us. And *Saxonwold shebeen* – that elusive watering hole former Eskom boss Brian Molefe referred to after he was implicated in the public protector's 'State of Capture' report – would not have been added to our political vocabulary had it not been for the Guptas.

But the most significant concept that has entered our collective consciousness as a result of the family's conduct is that of *state capture*. A brief exploration of what the term actually entails seems like an appropriate point of departure for a book about the Guptas of Saxonwold.

According to a World Bank policy paper, state capture is defined as 'the extent to which firms make illicit and non-transparent private payments to public officials in order to influence the formation of laws, rules, regulations or decrees by state institutions'.[1] Two of the policy paper's authors, Joel Hellman and Daniel Kaufmann, writing for the International Monetary Fund's quarterly magazine *Finance & Development*, further define state capture as 'a form of grand corruption' that is especially rife in some 'transition economies'.[2] In such economies, state capture sees 'so-called oligarchs manipulating policy formation and even shaping the emerging rules of the game to their own, very substantial advantage'.[3]

When there is evidence of the widespread occurrence of such practices in any particular country, one can start referring to it as a *capture econ-*

omy – that is, 'an economy in which a relatively small share of firms has managed to capture public officials at various levels of the state to extract concentrated rents and to purchase individualized provision by the state of under-provided public goods'.[4]

In the context of state capture, the rents mentioned above refer to 'privileged benefits from government'.[5] These rents can take the form of unusually high profits derived from owning licences and permits that can only be obtained from particular government entities, and which are needed by companies or individuals to partake in certain sectors of the economy. The Guptas, for instance, would have had to secure mining rights and environmental licences from the Department of Mineral Resources for the coal mines they operate. These rights and licences would have helped the Guptas' mining entities secure their coal-supply contracts from Eskom, South Africa's state-owned power utility. The profits derived from such contracts would therefore classify as rents. In other words, rents can include profits and other benefits that companies and individuals enjoy as a result of their relationship with government, benefits and profits they would not necessarily have managed to accrue in an open and competitive business environment. Rent-seekers may employ techniques and strategies associated with state capture to ensure that they successfully obtain such rents.

In and of itself, rent-seeking is not necessarily dubious or illegal. It is a form of lobbying by means of which companies and individuals 'try to obtain benefits for themselves through the political arena', explains Stanford University's David R. Henderson in *The Concise Encyclopedia of Economics*.[6] Such lobbying is a standard feature of the relationship between the state and the private sector, but that does not mean its negative connotations are unjustified.

The financial website *Investopedia* describes rent-seeking as the 'use of the resources of a company, an organization or an individual to obtain economic gain from others without reciprocating any benefits to society through wealth creation'.[7] The manner in which Gupta-linked financial services firms have clinched lucrative transaction advisory contracts from government entities springs to mind here. As discussed in this book, these contracts seem to hold few benefits, if any, for the state-owned companies and for the South African taxpayers who partly keep these entities afloat. According to *Investopedia*, 'Rent-seeking becomes a problem when entities engage in it to increase their share of the economic pie without increasing the size of the pie.'[8]

Rent-seeking is also associated with diminished competition, as well as the formation of monopolies. Because the returns generated from 'economic rents ... are higher than the normal profits obtainable by competing in the economic market place', as argued by *South China Morning Post*'s Richard Wong, rent-seekers often seek to stifle competition by 'lobby[ing] government to set up regulatory and legal barriers to market entry'.[9]

Another risk associated with rent-seeking and state capture is the possibility that the companies that secure disproportionate amounts of economic rents do not necessarily provide the best services that are on offer in the open market. In a paper for Weber State University in the US, John Mukum Mbaku notes that 'the rights to the artificial scarcity created by government regulation of economic activity are usually won or captured by the most effective and efficient rent-seeker and not necessarily by the most efficient entrepreneur or producer'.[10]

It is in the aggressive pursuit of government-granted rents that state captors and rent-seekers, along with their partners in government, can make themselves guilty of crimes such as bribery.

Unlike other forms of corruption, state capture offers reciprocal advantages to both the captor and the functionaries of the state whom they hold captive.

The World Bank distinguishes between administrative corruption and state capture. The former is associated with the 'grabbing hand' theory of government corruption, whereby corrupt payments and other forms of gratification 'accrue primarily to corrupt officials'.[11] Traffic officials demanding bribes from motorists may constitute administrative corruption.

Where state capture occurs, 'rents deriving from the capacity of firms to encode private advantages in the rules of the game as a result of bribes to public officials are shared by firms and the corrupt officials'.[12] A government tender that has been purposefully manipulated to benefit a particular bidder is a good example of this. In this case, the 'rules of the game' are bent by officials overseeing the tender process and who receive corrupt benefits, or a share of the rents, for doing so. The winning bidder's rents, in this case, will consist of the profits it generates from a contract it secured by manipulating the bidding process.

Most scholars who have written about the topic seem to be in agreement that such bending of the rules needs to occur in a systemic and sustained manner before a government or an economy can be accused of having been captured.

'State capture is not another name for corruption,' writes Andrej Nosko of the Open Society Foundations, an international collective of foundations that advocates for free, transparent and accountable governments across the globe. Nosko argues that 'while corruption reflects moral failure of individuals, state capture is a systemic failure which occurs in a country without functioning checks and balances by design'. Referring to a variety of countries in Eastern Europe that are 'emerging from authoritarian regimes', Nosko writes: 'What happens elsewhere due to poor controls happens intentionally in places like Bulgaria or Romania, where capture of the state institutions and important industry sectors defines reality.'[13]

South Africa is not a transition economy like the Eastern European countries that adopted capitalism only in the wake of the collapse of communism circa 1989, which have served as models for studies on state capture. But our drastic political transition in 1994 certainly brought about sufficient levels of flux for would-be captors to exploit. It is no coincidence that the first Gupta brother arrived in the country as the National Party government's political power was being transferred to the African National Congress.

More than two decades have passed since our transition to democracy. The Gupta-related developments that have dominated news headlines since the start of 2016 make this an opportune time to deliberate over whether state capture has become as 'pernicious and intractable' in South Africa as the World Bank's Hellman and Kaufmann found it to be in some of the former Soviet states they studied.[14]

It would be difficult to find someone more appropriate to contribute to such a discussion than Mcebisi Jonas, the then deputy finance minister whose revelations about an improper job offer he received from the Guptas ushered in a wave of concern over state capture in South Africa. Jonas claimed that the Guptas offered him the job of minister of finance in October 2015, on condition that he ensured the controversial multibillion-rand nuclear procurement programme went ahead.

Little over a month after these details were made public, Jonas wrote an article for *Umsebenzi*, the online magazine of the South African Communist Party (SACP), in which he argued that South Africa possesses positive characteristics that have prevented state captors from fully taking hold of government's levers of power.

Unlike the 'failed or failing states' where state capture thrives, Jonas argued, 'the South African state is able to exercise full administrative control over its territory; it is able to successfully maintain a monopoly over violence; and finally it is able to consistently provide public goods to its citizens'. He added that 'the robustness of our democratic and watchdog institutions', including our 'vibrant' and free media, ensures that the 'dirty laundry' associated with state capture does not escape public scrutiny.[15]

In the face of such transparency, would-be state captors in South Africa are often exposed before their devious schemes can come to fruition. Imagine what the Guptas could have achieved by now had it not been for South Africa's strong civil society.

But we should not rest on our laurels. State capture poses a 'grave danger' to South Africa in general, and to the ruling party in particular, warned Jonas. 'In its worst iteration, political office can become associated with possibilities for personal wealth accumulation, what is often referred to as the "commercialisation of politics". This could have the effect of changing the focus and practice of politics away from driving fundamental socio-economic transformation (as envisaged in the Freedom Charter) towards managing national and transnational business networks that service the wealth acquisition of [the] politically-connected elite.'[16]

I agree with Jonas's assessment of our strong safeguards against state capture. But I am not convinced that what he described as a worst-case scenario has not to a large extent already become the norm in South Africa. As an investigative journalist, I witness far too regularly how government spending achieves little else but the 'wealth acquisition of [the] politically-connected elite'.

Yes, state capture may not be so pervasive and ingrained in South Africa that it has seeped into every corner of our government's structures. But, as Transparency International's Maíra Martini writes in a dissertation on the topic, 'State capture can also arise from the more subtle close alignment of interests between specific business and political elites through family ties, friendship and the intertwined ownership of economic assets.'[17] Perhaps this definition of state capture best describes the so-called Zupta alliance.

Ongama Mtimka, a lecturer at Nelson Mandela Metropolitan University's Department of Political Studies and Conflict Transformation, argues that the 'alleged interference by the Guptas in the affairs of government' should be labelled 'predatory capture'. This, explains Mtimka, is 'a system in which one or a few individuals hold specific political figures ransom and bully their way to individual gain'.[18] Themba Maseko, the former head of the Government Communication and Information System (GCIS), can attest to such bullying by the Guptas. After he refused to help channel government funds to the family's newspaper, Ajay Gupta allegedly told him that he would be 'sorted out'. Mere months after this chilling threat, Maseko was forced to resign from his position at the GCIS.[19]

As we have seen with Maseko's story, as well as with those of other whistle-blowers, President Jacob Zuma or one of his kin is usually directly involved when the Guptas make their preposterous offers or threats to state officials. Unless Maseko and the others have for some reason banded together to spread lies about the Guptas – an implausible theory that the family and their allies have been trying to sell the country – all indications are that the Gupta brothers have been crafting their state capture plans with the explicit consent of South Africa's most senior government official.

In light of the above, perhaps *targeted capture* should be considered as a new entrant alongside the other subcategories of state capture. The Guptas seem to be most adept at targeting specific individuals in government for the purpose of making them party to their state capture schemes. A section of this book sets out how the Guptas seemingly cosied up with Zuma and his family long before he became president. One cannot help but wonder whether they somehow foresaw his rise to power and managed to get in on the ground floor. A more sinister possibility is that the Guptas played an active role in Zuma's ascent. Either way, the Guptas have been highly successful in their targeting of the Zumas.

The Guptas and their most-prized government captives (dare we call them possessions?) may deny it for all they are worth, but the family's interactions with senior government officials bear all the classic hallmarks of state capture. This is especially evident in the Zupta alliance.

The Guptas derive unprecedented advantage, power and influence from their relationship with the president and his family. And the latter derive ample gratification from their ties with the Guptas, mostly via Zuma's son Duduzane.

A variety of commentators who have watched in horror and disbelief as the unfolding Gupta saga played out in 2016 and 2017. have warned that the country is on the edge of a precipice as far as state capture is concerned.

'If the patronage politicians win the battle within the ANC and complete the capture of the state the country will slip from stagnation into the abyss,' wrote Co-Pierre Georg, a lecturer at the University of Cape Town's African Institute of Financial Markets and Risk Management, on *The Conversation* website.[20]

We can laugh at Molefe's imaginary Saxonwold shebeen. Even the word-splicing that gave us the Zuptas is worth a chuckle. But considering the implications of an ultimate victory for the Guptas and those like them, state capture may very well be the gravest problem South Africa is grappling with at the moment.

Prologue:
Rough landing

Tuesday 30 April 2013

The sky above Pretoria was a faint, lacklustre grey as Barry Bateman guided his car in a southerly direction on the congested N1 highway. The well-known radio news reporter, who had been awake before sunrise, felt a tingle of excitement at the prospect of what might await him at his destination.

As he neared the off-ramp that would take him to Air Force Base (AFB) Waterkloof, he noticed a fleet of luxury four-by-four vehicles impatiently muscling its way through the early-morning traffic on the northbound side of the freeway. A police car flashed its blue emergency lights as it led the convoy on its impertinent trek through the traffic. Another police car, its blue lights also ablaze, kept pace with the last of the SUVs, almost as if being lugged along in the convoy's slipstream.

The cavalcade embodied an unapologetic assertion of might and money. The expensive SUVs and their escort moved in menacing unison, too large and too loud to be ignored by any motorist who might block their passage.

To many of the road users around Bateman the scene was most likely familiar. The blue-light brigades of politicians travelling between Pretoria and its neighbour to the south, Johannesburg, are a common sight on the sixty-three-kilometre stretch of highway between the two cities.

Bateman too was accustomed to the sight, but on this particular day the cavalcade's presence drew his attention for a reason the other motorists would not have been aware of.

Glancing at the motorcade, Bateman reread in his mind a tweet directed at him the previous evening. A fellow Twitter user had claimed that wedding guests of the infamous Gupta family would be landing in a private aeroplane at AFB Waterkloof the following morning.

Bateman was well aware of the Gupta brothers Ajay, Atul and Rajesh. Reports of the trio's close ties to top government officials and the business benefits that flowed from them had become more frequent since 2010. In that year the *Mail & Guardian* newspaper had noted that 'concern is growing in political and business circles about the relationship between President Jacob Zuma and the Gupta family'.[1]

The suggestion, however, that even such valuable connections as those enjoyed by the notorious brothers could guarantee a feat like the one mentioned in the tweet seemed highly improbable to Bateman, if not ludicrous. He had even broadcasted his scepticism, tweeting back to the Twitter user that the landing of a private plane at a South African air force base was unlikely.

But journalists like Bateman are guided in equal measure by doubt and curiosity. As the blue-light convoy shrunk in his rear-view mirror, he allowed the latter sentiment to momentarily quell his cynicism. He had already told his radio station's head office in Johannesburg, where he had a meeting scheduled for later that morning, that he would first be making a quick stop at the air force base to check out a tip-off.

He harboured no expectation that he would again be walking straight into an event that would dominate the news agenda for the coming months, or even years. Less than three months earlier, on the morning of 14 February 2013, he had been the first journalist to arrive at the upmarket residential estate where Paralympic superstar Oscar Pistorius lived. The country, and indeed the world, would learn later that morning that Pistorius had shot and killed his girlfriend, the twenty-nine-year-old model Reeva Steenkamp.

Bateman's subsequent coverage of the court proceedings, both on radio and on Twitter, had turned him into something of a superstar in his own right. The day after the shooting he had a Twitter audience of just over 17 000. By 22 February, as Bateman was tweeting details of the athlete's bail application in the Pretoria magistrate's court, his Twitter following had dramatically risen to almost 123 000.[2]

But Bateman's thoughts were far from the awful events of Valentine's Day when he finally drove into the visitors' area outside AFB Waterkloof's main terminal building. It was just after 07:00. No one stopped him at the main entrance.

He parked his car and stepped out into a scene that one would expect to find at a small commercial airport near some popular holiday destination. The parking lot was buzzing with activity. Groups of people dressed in civilian outfits were coming out of the terminal building. Some lingered for a while; others headed straight to a fleet of white Range Rovers similar to the ones that had driven past Bateman earlier. The cars were parked in a line outside the building, waiting for their passengers to arrive. Other groups of civilians were getting onto buses idling nearby.

In the meantime bags, suitcases and other pieces of luggage were being carried to the waiting vehicles by what looked like ushers.

The relaxed, holiday-like atmosphere that clung to the newly arrived visitors was in sharp contrast to the air of officialdom brought to bear by the heavy police presence near the terminal building. Cars belonging to the South African Police Service (SAPS), the Tshwane Metro Police Department (TMPD) and Gauteng's traffic police unit were scattered throughout the parking area.

The reason for their presence at the base became clear with the departure of each convoy of white SUVs. Emergency lights flashed and sirens howled as police cars left the site, each with a cluster of luxury vehicles in tow. The traffic flow at the entrance to Waterkloof was being managed by traffic officers who had apparently been deployed at the base specifically for this unusual event.

Bateman had now left his car to walk around the parking area. He started taking pictures. In the background, on the opposite side of the terminal building, he could see and hear a helicopter slowly climbing into the air. The words 'Sahara Computers' were clearly inscribed on the side of the aircraft.

An Airbus A330-200, its tail and body bearing the blue and gold hues of the Indian airline Jet Airways, stood parked near the terminal building. Bateman assumed this was the civilian aircraft he had been tipped off about on Twitter.

Amid the numerous visual and aural distractions on offer to a curious journalist, Bateman's attention was eventually drawn to a familiar face.

Standing near the main entrance to the terminal building was Atul Gupta, the de facto ambassador of the Gupta business empire. His attire was that of a businessman who had been absolved of all boardroom burdens for the day, yet wished to maintain a modicum of formality. He wore his dark blazer unbuttoned, allowing his considerable belly to test his pink T-shirt's tolerance for stretching.

The businessman's plump cheeks were hard at work as he laughed and smiled with each new batch of travellers that wandered through the terminal's entrance. He also appeared to be assisting with the general logistics of the event, guiding some of the guests to the SUVs.

Bateman knew he had to approach Atul right there and then. He took out his phone and switched on the record button in advance, just in case. One never knows how an interviewee might react. No journalist wants to struggle with a cellphone's record function in the middle of a tense conversation.

Bateman walked up to Atul.

'Mr Gupta, it is Mr Gupta, right? I'm Barry Bateman, from Eyewitness News. How are you doing?'[3]

Atul beamed at the journalist with such enthusiasm that the upper hairs of his moustache threatened to creep into his nostrils.

'Hey Barry, how are you? Nice to see you man!' His voice resonated with enthusiasm, as if the journalist were a close friend he had not seen for a very long time.

But the pleasantries were short-lived. Bateman had not come to the base to exchange chit-chat with the businessman.

'Why are you using an air force base to bring your family in?'

Atul's moustache slowly receded from his nose. His cheeks, which a moment ago had bulged in a display of pure joviality, became slack as his broad smile faded.

'Are you interviewing me?' Atul's eyes darted to the cellphone in Bateman's hand. It was still recording.

'I would like to,' replied the journalist.

Atul indicated that he would be willing to give an interview, so Bateman tried to steer the conversation back to the issue of the wedding guests landing at the base.

'It's just interesting—,' he started.

'Don't be smart with me,' Atul interrupted. '*Ask* me. Don't try to start recording and be all smart,' he admonished.

Bateman badly wanted the interview. He decided to stop the recording as a show of good faith. It seemed to do the trick, as Atul agreed to continue with the conversation, but only after he had finished his responsibilities.

'I'll speak to you later,' he said as he moved away to attend to the needs of yet another group of newly arrived guests.

Bateman decided that it was time to break the news to South Africa without Atul's input. At exactly 08:26 he tweeted: '#GuptaWedding dozens of Gupta family members are arriving at Waterkloof Airforce Base from India on chartered flights.'

Bateman then went back to his car and started compiling a voice package for his radio station's upcoming news bulletin. At 09:00 listeners of 702 and Cape Talk, two of South Africa's most popular news and actuality radio stations, heard further details of the Guptas' brazen exploits at AFB Waterkloof.

After the news had been broadcast, Bateman kept his eyes peeled for Atul Gupta. He hoped to still get the interview he had been promised.

A while later, with the parking area now considerably emptier, Bateman spotted Atul alongside a group of people he could not identify. They were getting into one of the last vehicles on site.

Bateman approached.

'Listen, you promised me this interview, let's do this interview,' he urged the businessman.

'No, no, no, I'm in such a rush,' replied Atul, brushing off the request, although the earlier iciness in his voice had melted away. He was again beaming at Bateman. 'You and I must chat. I'm opening up a television station one of these days,' he said as he climbed into the car.

Bateman watched as the SUV drove through the base's main entrance and disappeared around the corner.

Months later, as the Gupta-owned television station Africa News Network 7 (ANN7) began airing its news content on South African television screens, Bateman would grin to himself at the thought of Atul Gupta's subtle job offer that morning at Waterkloof.

Bateman's news bulletin and tweets set off an immediate explosion of indignation and disbelief that seemed to echo across the country.

Before 10:00 that morning most of South Africa's major news outlets were informing their readers, viewers and listeners that a private plane carrying guests for the wedding of one Vega Gupta had landed at the base. Vega, the country would soon learn, was the daughter of Achla Gupta, the only sister of Ajay, Atul and Rajesh.

The would-be bride, who was twenty-three at the time, was to marry Aakash Jahajgarhia, a twenty-four-year-old businessman from India who had been working at the Jahajgarhia Group, a family-owned collection of companies with interests in the property-development and investment sectors. The wedding was set to take place at Sun City in the North West province, arguably South Africa's most famous holiday and casino resort.

But the first motorcades ferrying guests to the venue could hardly have reached their destination before the growing public criticism forced the first government entity to make an official statement regarding the incident.

Roughly two hours after the plane had landed, Siphiwe Dlamini, a spokesperson for the Department of Defence (DOD), told the news channel eNCA that his department had no knowledge of any private citizens being granted permission to use AFB Waterkloof.

'As you may very well know, it is indeed a military base and it is a strategic place for the government,' Dlamini told eNCA. 'As to whether they [the Guptas] have landed there or not I am not aware. All I'm aware of is we are in a position to indicate that authority to any private citizen has not been granted whatsoever. I am aware, however, that there is a plane that has landed there and I am still to verify who it belongs to.'[4]

The DOD's statement would be the first in a series of responses that day from various government departments, as well as the Gupta family itself, which at times would convey conflicting messages.

Clayson Monyela, spokesperson for the Department of International Relations and Cooperation (DIRCO), initially denied that his department was in any way involved in the landing.

'Whoever applied for permission to use the base did it with the SANDF [South African National Defence Force]; that had nothing to do with the department,' Monyela told reporters after the drama had morphed into the main news event of the day.[5]

The Guptas entered the fray when Haranath Ghosh, who had been appointed as the family's spokesperson and media liaison officer for the wedding, released a statement in which he claimed that the plane had indeed been officially cleared to land at the base.

Ghosh said that 'foreign dignitaries, including some [Indian] ministers', were among the passengers on the Jet Airways aircraft and that the flight had therefore been given full government permission to land at AFB Waterkloof.[6]

'Waterkloof was used as Lanseria Airport [Gauteng's second-largest commercial airport] could not accommodate the size of jet chartered by the family. The permissions were applied for and granted to the Indian High Commission and not the family,' Ghosh claimed.

He maintained that 'it is a conventional and common practice between countries in receiving officials from another state' and that 'these rights can be applied for by any foreign embassy'.

Nothing to see here, folks, the landing was perfectly normal, the statement seemed to suggest.

Ghosh's contribution put the DOD and DIRCO, which had both already claimed that they'd had no knowledge of the flight, on the back foot. But out of the two departments, it was DIRCO that had been forced onto the ropes by the Guptas' statement. Though Ghosh did not specifically point out which government departments or officials had been involved in the process, the claim that the aircraft had been given permission to land at the base on the grounds of it being a diplomatic flight inevitably implicated DIRCO. One of DIRCO's key functions, after all, is the administration of South Africa's diplomatic responsibilities, which includes the processing of requests for the reception of heads of state and other foreign dignitaries visiting the country.

DIRCO subsequently shook off the apparent bout of temporary amnesia it had suffered earlier that morning and in the afternoon indicated that the flight had indeed received official permission to land at the base.[7]

In an attempt to seek clarity on the situation, eNCA, which had been given what looked like an official media statement from the DOD admitting that government permission had been granted for the flight, went back to the department.

The DOD, however, insisted it was not the responsible department despite the fact that the above mentioned press release was apparently signed off by its own head of communications.

'The Department of Defence as well as the ministry of defence distances ourselves from a statement issued supposedly under the name of the Head of Communications in the department saying permission had been granted for an aircraft to land at Waterkloof airforce base. We wish to unequivocally reject this. Whoever gave such permission must take responsibility and own up to that,' the DOD told eNCA in a sharp blow apparently aimed at DIRCO.[8]

Or perhaps the DOD was admonishing an even more senior government official, someone whom it viewed as the ultimate source of the fiasco that was now playing out.

DIRCO, however, would have none of the DOD's denials and in an SMS to the television station's news team later that evening insisted that 'they [the DOD] granted approval. That's a fact.' The DOD and DIRCO had now become adversaries in a bizarre war of words.

The governing ANC, meanwhile, could not resist the temptation to voice its own opinion on developments and rather cynically joined the growing chorus of public disapproval. In a statement released by Jackson Mthembu, the ANC's spokesperson at the time, the party said:

'The African National Congress waited patiently for the South African National Defence Force (SANDF), the body delegated with authority over the Waterkloof Airforce Base, to explain to the nation how these private individuals managed to land aircraft at Waterkloof. Up until now, no explanation has been forthcoming. The African National Congress, driven by the concern for the safety and sovereignty of South Africa, shall never allow a situation where our ports of entry and National Key Points are penetrated with impunity.

'We demand that those who are responsible for granting access to land aircraft in our country also explain the basis upon which such permission was granted, particularly to land at Waterkloof Airforce Base. Those who cannot account must be brought to book. The African National Congress will never rest where there is any indication that all and sundry may be permitted to undermine the Republic, its citizens and its borders.'[9]

The fact that even the ruling party was willing to criticise those responsible for the debacle showed that the Guptas had gone too far with their latest stunt. However, as we will see in the first part of this book, the family started to 'undermine the Republic' long before the Waterkloof scandal put the Gupta name on the lips of just about every South African.

PART I

ORIGINS

1

Subcontinental drift

Saharanpur, a city with about 700 000 inhabitants, lies less than 200 kilometres to the north of India's capital, New Delhi. The city is situated in the northern state of Uttar Pradesh and its economy relies heavily on the agricultural, industrial and forestry sectors.[1]

It was here that Shiv Kumar Gupta established a collection of businesses that would later provide the capital for his sons Ajay, Atul and Rajesh's earliest business ventures abroad.

'My father was an industrialist dealing mainly in the manufacture of fertiliser and chemicals and also spices, clothing and accessories,' said Atul Gupta in an interview with the South African website *IT-Online* in 2007.[2]

Saharanpur locals knew the Gupta patriarch as Shiv Kumar depot-*waale* (Shiv Kumar, the depot owner) because he owned a ration depot at the city's marketplace.[3] According to a 2011 *Sunday Times* interview with Atul, his father ran so-called co-operative stores, where Saharanpur locals who had qualified for the government's ration-card system could buy foodstuffs such as cooking oil, rice and wheat flour.[4] Another of Shiv Kumar's businesses was SKG Marketing, which specialised in importing spices from Madagascar and Zanzibar.[5] Gupta and Company, a distributor of soapstone powder, was another business in his early Saharanpur empire.

Even though Shiv Kumar's businesses ensured that his children – oldest son Ajay, middle son Atul, youngest son Rajesh (also known as Tony), and a daughter, Achla – enjoyed a relatively comfortable life, the Guptas did not live in the lap of luxury. After having visited the family's old house in the Saharanpur neighbourhood of Rani Bazar in 2015, a journalist from the *Times of India* described the residence as 'dilapidated' and the streets that surrounded it as 'cramped'.[6]

'We are never shy of our background,' Atul told the *Sunday Times.*

'I am proud of it. We come from families that do not show or expose their business to others. It is considered showing off.'[7]

Pradip Agarwal, a cousin of the Gupta brothers who lived in the same house in Rani Bazar, told the *Times of India*: 'We grew up here together. We used to cycle through these bylanes to get to the government school we studied in.'[8] Another cousin, Sanjay Gupta, who still lives in Saharanpur, told the newspaper *India Samvad* that Ajay Gupta started working at the age of ten, when he was still attending school. Sanjay described his cousins as 'honest and hard-working'.[9]

The Guptas' day-to-day existence in India contrasted sharply with the lifestyle they would later adopt in South Africa, where, among other indulgences, chauffeurs drive their children to expensive private schools.

By the time the Gupta sons were teenagers in the late seventies and early eighties, however, the family had seemingly drifted from the innocent, carefree lifestyle they had led up until then. In the 2011 *Sunday Times* interview, Atul described how he and his brothers were accompanied to secondary school every day by an armed guard.

In an opinion piece in the *Daily Maverick* in 2013, South African businessman Kalim Rajab said of the Guptas: 'Before arriving in South Africa, they had been a middleweight family in the power stakes on the subcontinent ... Rumours, never proven ... swirled around of them providing money laundering facilities in Dubai.'[10] Evidently whispers of alleged dodgy dealings dogged the family even back then.

After high school, Ajay, Atul and Rajesh attended J.V. Jain College in Saharanpur. On its website, the college describes itself as one of Uttar Pradesh state's 'premier educational institutions' with 'a vast, beautiful and pollution-free campus'. Ajay Gupta obtained a Bachelor of Commerce degree, while younger siblings Atul and Rajesh later both completed Bachelor of Science degrees.[11] According to Oakbay Investments' website, Atul obtained his BSc from Meerut University, now known as Chaudhary Charan Singh University, in 1989. J.V. Jain College is an affiliate of Chaudhary Charan Singh.

After graduation, the Gupta trio became involved in the management of SKG Marketing, their father's spice venture. It meant that the brothers spent a lot of time in the bustling commercial hub of Delhi, where SKG Marketing was based at the time.[12] It was during these years that Atul took the first steps towards his future as a computer entrepreneur by doing courses on the assembly and repair of Apple products and taking a job as a computer supervisor at a printing business.[13]

The exact nature of the Gupta brothers' earliest activities as young businessmen is not clear. Apart from the scant information they have given in interviews, some of which appears contradictory, not much is known about what they got up to in the period between finishing college and eventually settling in South Africa.

At one point, the family sent Atul to China to explore business opportunities there, but it did not work out. 'Ajay wanted to … [but] we didn't have much option to invest in China because they only wanted us to buy between 5% and 12% [shares] in the factory, while Ajay wanted management control,' Atul told the *Sunday Times*.[14] Other media reports, however, claim that the Guptas went to Singapore, not China, in those early years. By all accounts, wherever they went during this time, it does not sound like the family enjoyed much overseas business success.

'When they were in Singapore, their business ran into some losses,' Pradip Agarwal told the *Times of India*. 'I do not know the details of their businesses, but I know the losses caused my uncle, their father, to have a heart attack.'[15]

A South African businessman who had dealings with the Guptas shortly after Atul arrived in South Africa in the early 1990s confirmed that the middle son told him that he had been in Singapore before coming to Africa. 'Atul actually said he was from Singapore. He initially didn't even mention that he'd grown up in India,' said the businessman.

Whatever the circumstances surrounding the Guptas' earlier forays into East Asia, it was eventually decided that Atul would be the family's pioneer into yet another unknown territory. This time, Shiv Kumar decided, his second eldest son would go to South Africa.

Atul was twenty-three years old when he arrived in South Africa in 1993. But the young businessman was not too keen on the idea of settling in the country. 'I had my heart set on going to Canada, but it was my father's wish to have his headquarters in South Africa and have me head it as a South African,' Atul told *IT-Online* in 2007.[16]

Atul's doubts about setting up a business in South Africa during that time are understandable. The country was in the midst of a transition to democracy that was marked by violence and uncertainty. In the year Atul arrived, 3 794 people were killed in politically motivated attacks, the highest number of fatalities in a single year in the decade between 1985 and 1995.[17] But such a drastic transferral of political power all but guarantees new business opportunities, something the shrewd Gupta patriarch must have known.

Shiv Kumar apparently had high hopes not only for South Africa's economic future, but for the whole continent's as well. 'Africa would become the America of the world,' he told his sons.[18]

Before pouring all of his energy into founding what would become the family's thriving information technology (IT) and computer empire, Atul first dabbled in selling shoes. Trading as Liberty Retail, he had a showroom at Johannesburg's Killarney Mall, but also sold shoes from a stall at the Bruma Lake flea market.[19] The plan had been to open twenty outlets of Liberty Retail, but the business never really took off and it was subsequently sold.[20]

Shiv Kumar passed away shortly after Atul arrived in South Africa. The Gupta patriarch's death apparently inspired his son to dump the idea of selling shoes and rather embrace the opportunities provided by South Africa's nascent IT and computer sector.

'In 1994, unfortunately, my father passed away and it was then that I decided I would make the best success I could of the IT business we had started ... that I'd be fully dedicated to it and establish the family headquarters in South Africa as was my father's wish,' Atul told *IT-Online*.[21]

Atul told the *Sunday Times* in 2011 that he opened Correct Marketing, the family's first IT business, in 1994. The company, which imported and sold computers and related products, was apparently established with seed funding of R1.2 million provided by the Guptas back home in India.[22] But according to company records at the Companies and Intellectual Property Commission (CIPC), Correct Marketing was only formally registered in July 1995. CIPC records also show that Atul registered a closed corporation called Correction Computers in the same period. These were the forebears of Sahara Computers, which would become one of the cornerstones of the Guptas' lucrative South African business empire.

The story Atul told *IT-Online* about these first businesses and the eventual formation of Sahara Computers contained details of his dramatic early successes in the local computer and IT industry. He also explained how the family chose the name Sahara for their new entity. Almost from the outset, the Guptas had had to defend themselves against accusations that they had deliberately copied the name of Sahara India Pariwar, India's largest conglomerate founded in 1978, and which now boasts a total group net worth of around R140 billion.[23] 'Those in the know,' wrote Kalim Rajab, 'used to scoff at them for having embellished their credentials through a clever sleight of hand, by naming their companies outside India "Sahara" – thereby trading off the powerful (and unconnected) brand name of the famous billionaire Subrata Roy's Sahara Group.'[24]

According to Atul, however, the name had been a way of paying homage to his family's hometown, Saharanpur. 'There's also the Sahara in Africa and we felt it would be appropriate with our involvement on the two continents,' he said.[25] But there was one problem. 'It is a hard fact that back then Ajay, our eldest brother, never wanted us to use the name. He said that he wanted us to target revenues of R100-million and then he would consider letting us adopt the Sahara name ... That only happened in 1997 when we reached, collectively, a turnover of R98-million,' Atul told *IT-Online*.[26]

In 1997, Atul finally registered Sahara Computers with the CIPC. His wife, Chetali, who had moved to South Africa with him, was also listed as a founding director. In 1998, the Sahara brand was formally launched at a local computer convention.[27] At first, business was conducted from a rented house in Bedfordview, but this modest set-up did not stop the Guptas from achieving an impressive turnover of R127 million by 1999.[28] According to Atul, the family eventually bought the Bedfordview property for R1.2 million. At this stage they were living in the neighbourhood, according to sources familiar with the family's dealings.

One source showed me where the Guptas stayed in those early days. The house is situated on a busy intersection, across the road from a petrol station. Though it is a far cry from the mansion the family would later occupy at their infamous Saxonwold estate, the property of just less than 1 700 square metres is not exactly modest. According to property records, the house still belongs to a company of which Atul Gupta is the sole director.

When Sahara's revenue exceeded R100 million, Ajay and younger brother Rajesh committed themselves to helping Atul with the booming enterprise. Rajesh had settled in the country in 1997, and Ajay, who had started visiting South Africa from as early as 1995, made it his permanent home in 2003.[29] Angoori Gupta, the family's matriarch and widow of the late Shiv Kumar, and her daughter, Achla, also settled in South Africa during this time, as did Shivani and Arti, married to Ajay and Rajesh respectively.

With the entire Gupta clan now united, the family could pour all their efforts into their South African business ventures.

2

Making friends

It was 1995 and South Africa appeared to have shaken off some of the early jitters of its transition to democracy. A wave of patriotism was now washing over the country, partly driven by the Springboks' fairy-tale victory over New Zealand in the Rugby World Cup final held in Johannesburg in June that year. Nelson Mandela's dream of a Rainbow Nation was within reach and the country's economy had absorbed some of the newfound optimism. Businesses, particularly those in the nascent IT sector, sought to exploit the opportunities that accompanied the new political dispensation.

It was within this context that John, a Johannesburg-based businessman, met Atul Gupta and his entourage for the first time.[1] John's business had a footprint in South Africa's young IT sector and Atul, who had been busy setting up Correction Computers and Correct Marketing, his two earliest IT ventures, needed help establishing a network of business contacts in his newly adopted city.

'I was at my business's premises when four guys pitched up there in a Toyota Camry, one of those with the little wing on the boot. One of the men introduced himself as Atul Gupta,' recalls John. The other men were introduced to him as Mr Roger, Ashu and Tony. Ashu would turn out to be Ashu Chawla, the Gupta associate who would later become the CEO of Sahara Computers. Tony may well have been Rajesh 'Tony' Gupta, the youngest of the Gupta brothers.

This first encounter was the start of a business relationship that would last for years, one that would give John a front-row seat to the rapid evolution of the Guptas' earliest ventures into a multibillion-rand business empire.

'Correction Computers was first operated from a house on Van Buuren Road in Bedfordview,' he recalls. 'It was one of those houses that had been converted into offices. At that stage they knew nobody in town. They were going around making contacts and finding people who could help them with various aspects concerning their new business.'

About two years after that first meeting, Atul told John that the family had decided to move their IT endeavours under the umbrella of a new brand and identity, namely Sahara Computers. This new venture, says John, originally operated from a small shop in a retail complex in Midrand. As the business grew, the Guptas opened a second store in Midrand. This would serve as an assembly facility for Sahara Computers.

'What they had was a [computer] box on which they put the Sahara logo. The motherboard came from whomever was making motherboards, the chip came from Intel, the hard drive came from another manufac-turer. They just put the computers together at the assembly facility in Midrand. But in those days that was how everyone did it, not just Sahara,' explains John.

Through his interaction with the Guptas, John witnessed some of Atul's less savoury business practices. 'He was very hard on his staff; he drove them like mad. It was like drawing blood from a rock. That was just how he operated.'

Atul apparently also had a way of getting, or at least trying to get, all manner of services for his businesses without having to pay for them. 'Even though we were in business, Atul always put pressure on me to do certain things for free,' recalls John. 'He actually wanted everything for free. It was a matter of putting one's foot down, otherwise you'd end up making a loss in your dealings with him.'

But when it came to getting paid himself, Atul made sure he was never short-changed. 'I once saw how one customer's cheque for a new computer bounced, and Atul would only finally be paid about a week later. He almost cried like a stuck pig over this one bounced cheque,' John remembers.

By 1998, about a year after Sahara Computers was established, Atul's Toyota Camry was replaced with a BMW M5. 'I remember how proud Atul was of his new car,' John recalls. 'He came to me just to show me his new set of wheels.' It would seem that by now Atul viewed John as a confidant, someone with whom he could share some of the more sensi-tive titbits about his business activities.

'It was around the time that Atul showed me his new car that he mentioned the name Jacob Zuma,' says John. 'It is actually crazy how frank he was about this, but he bragged about having an ANC guy in his pocket. Atul said that when this guy eventually becomes president, their [the Guptas'] ship was going to come in big time.'

Atul allegedly told John that he was paying school fees for some of Zuma's children.

'At the time I didn't really take it seriously,' says John. 'Zuma was a little-known guy with no hope of ever becoming president. I didn't think a Zulu would stand a chance in an ANC that was dominated by Xhosas.'[2]

Zuma had, in fact, been elected deputy president of the ANC in December 1997, with Thabo Mbeki as the party's president. At that stage Nelson Mandela was still president of the country. There was no guarantee that Zuma would become deputy president of South Africa after the next national elections in 1999, but he was certainly a rising star.

The Guptas themselves claim to have met Zuma in the early 2000s, when he was already deputy president of the country. Gary Naidoo, the family's long-standing spokesperson, once told the *Mail & Guardian* that Zuma met the Guptas in 2001.[3] Atul Gupta later told the *Sunday Times* that the family's first meeting with South Africa's then second-in-command took place 'around 2002, 2003', when Zuma attended an annual function hosted by Sahara Computers.[4]

But according to John, they met him earlier. And, considering the recent revelations about the Guptas' relationship with the Zuma-led government, John is convinced that what Atul allegedly told him all those years ago was true.

'Would the Guptas be as wealthy as they are without Zuma?' John asks. 'Not at all. They targeted him right from the start, and they chose to go into that type of business path way back then.'

These are all just allegations, of course. But John's knowledge of the Guptas' earliest business dealings in South Africa certainly suggests he was privy to information that could only have come from the family. This includes the name of the small insurance company which to this day insures the Guptas' businesses. A director at the insurer confirmed that his company is indeed a service provider to the Guptas. John also has a cellphone number for Atul that does indeed belong to the middle brother. In addition, John's claim that the Guptas met Zuma as early as the 1990s is backed up by a former Indian diplomat who was based in South Africa at the time.

In April 2016, after revelations came to light about the family's alleged job offers to top government officials, a former Indian high commissioner told the *Cape Times*: 'I remember them [the Guptas]. They were courteous but we were all familiar with their proximity with Zuma in the 1990s. It was understandable that they [would] prosper when he came to power.'[5]

John was also able to refer me to another of the Guptas' earliest business associates, a Gauteng-based businessman whom I will call Joe.[6]

Like John, Joe witnessed the rapid growth of the Guptas' computer and IT empire in its earliest days, from selling computers from a rented house in Bedfordview to the establishment of Sahara Computers and its subsidiaries.

Sometime during the mid- to late 1990s, Joe visited Atul Gupta at Sahara's first business premises in Midrand, Gauteng. Joe recalls how small the operation was at that stage: 'There was just Atul, the lady that was making the tea and a little Chinese guy called Evan Tak. It was just those three, and there were computer boxes lying everywhere.' (According to CIPC records, Tak became a director at Sahara in 2009.)

Soon thereafter, Sahara Computers moved to another office just around the corner from the first. It is the building that Sahara occupies to this day, while the former is now home to Annex Distribution, a Sahara-owned company that distributes Sahara's computer products.

'I remember how excited Atul had been about the new building,' remembers Joe. 'When they moved in it was in quite a bad state. The plugs were hanging from the wall and there were electrical wires coming out of the ceiling.'

He says it was 'incredible' that the Guptas were able to afford such large premises after launching their company just a few years earlier. And after the move, things 'just exploded' in terms of the business's success, he adds.

'I think they just really had a good business model at that stage, and their timing to enter the computer market was just perfect, seeing as everyone needed computers then,' Joe recalls. 'They were running specials for something like R2 000 or R3 000 for a whole computer set, which was significantly cheaper than most of their rivals in the industry.'

While he remembers Atul as a humble and friendly person, Joe, like

John, also experienced the Gupta brothers' more ruthless side. 'Whenever I did work for them, Atul would heckle over the bill I'd send him. He would always maintain that he could get the job done for much cheaper elsewhere, and then he'd end up paying me only half of what he owed me.'

Joe also witnessed first-hand the inner workings of the Gupta family structure. 'Ajay Gupta is definitely the main guy,' he says. 'When he walked into the office, everyone would stand up, and when he spoke, everyone would keep quiet to hear what the big boss had to say.'

Although the Guptas never discussed with him any details about their ties to government officials or politicians, Joe did pick up signs as far back as the early 2000s that Atul had a connection with Zuma. 'I do remember seeing a photo in Atul's office of him and Zuma at a school somewhere, with a whole bunch of computers,' remembers Joe. 'It was during the time when Zuma had still been deputy president, so it had to have been before 2005.'

While the context of the photograph is unclear, it is nevertheless interesting to note that one of the Guptas' first major government contracts was for the supply of computers to schools.

3

Mbeki's 'secret' council

Details about the Guptas' earliest inroads into South Africa's political establishment are scarce. The early to mid-1990s was a time of flux and uncertainty, but also one of hope and excitement. As the country came to terms with democracy, the Guptas settled into their new home without drawing too much attention.

Their most obvious and significant political friendship is with Jacob Zuma, whom they claim to have first met in the early 2000s, almost a decade after their arrival in South Africa, though others suggest they met him a few years earlier. Whatever the case, one is left wondering: did they have any friends in high places before him? There are indications that the Guptas started nurturing friendships with people in power long before they officially courted Zuma.

Essop Pahad, who served as minister in the Presidency during the Mbeki administration, is a former business partner of the Guptas who still views himself as a good friend of the family. According to Pahad, he was formally introduced to a young Atul Gupta during a visit to India with Mbeki in 1996, when Mbeki still shared the role of deputy president with former president F.W. de Klerk. It had been two years since South Africa's first democratic elections, and the purpose of Mbeki and Pahad's visit was partly to discuss investment and trade opportunities with India's business elite.

'There was a group of South African businesspeople who were part of the group, and then somebody came to me and said they wanted to introduce me to a family that has started businesses in South Africa. That was Atul,' Pahad told me in an interview in April 2016.

According to Pahad, the meeting was brief and he 'never really saw [Atul] again' until much later. Their second meeting, this time in South Africa, sparked a lasting friendship.

'He talked about his brother Ajay, and then I met with Ajay, and I later met the other brother, Tony [Rajesh], and then we became friends,' explained Pahad.

As the relationship between the minister and the Gupta brothers blossomed into friendship, Pahad grew to respect Ajay's uncanny talent for arithmetic. 'He is, in my view, one of the best number crunchers in South Africa,' Pahad told me. 'It is all in his head, he can make big calculations in his head.'

Later, in 2006, Ajay's 'good understanding of India, also China and other parts of Asia' prompted Pahad to nominate him for a position on the board of the International Marketing Council of South Africa (IMC), which had been established in 2000 by the Mbeki administration in order to 'create a positive, unified image of South Africa; one that builds pride, promotes investment and tourism, and helps new enterprises and job creation'.[1] It was later rebranded as Brand South Africa.

The IMC's first chairperson was then foreign affairs minister Nkosazana Dlamini-Zuma, and the organisation's founding board members included some of South Africa's foremost leaders from the private and public sectors, such as Naspers's then managing director Koos Bekker, film producer Anant Singh and Joel Netshitenzhe, the ANC intellectual who headed the GCIS.

While the Gupta-owned *The New Age* newspaper incorrectly reported that Ajay had been an IMC board member since the organisation's inception, he was in fact only appointed in 2006.[2] He has retained his position on the board, but does not appear to take his duties as a board member very seriously. According to the IMC's annual reports for the 2014–2015 and 2015–2016 financial years, he did not attend even one of the eight board meetings convened in that period.[3] One of the four former IMC board members I spoke to recalled that he had been surprised to learn that Pahad had put Ajay Gupta on the board in the first place: 'We were confused as to why an Indian citizen was put on the board of something that would be known as Brand South Africa. And it's not like Ajay was just a mere board member in the beginning. When he joined the IMC, he was put on the executive committee, meaning he was able to yield more influence within the organisation than an ordinary board member would have been able to.'

Despite this former board member's reservations regarding Ajay's appointment to the IMC board, there is no indication that it was done in an underhanded manner. His name, as well as his picture, appears in all of the organisation's annual reports after 2006, and these are publicly available documents.

But Ajay Gupta's inclusion during those years in an altogether different and largely unknown council is an entirely different matter.

In March and April 2016, as President Zuma was faced with the fallout from claims that the Guptas were meddling in government decisions, he and his allies thought it prudent to drag Mbeki into the matter, most likely in an attempt to redirect the negative Gupta-related attention onto the previous administration.

In March, as the ANC was bickering internally over the president's relationship with the Guptas, during two separate ANC meetings Zuma allegedly said that he had been introduced to the Guptas by Pahad and that Ajay Gupta had served on Mbeki's economic advisory council. According to the *Sowetan*, Zuma had even gone so far as to say that, unlike Mbeki, he had never appointed any members of the Gupta family to formal government positions.[4]

Amid the growing number of calls for Zuma to step down – driven to a large extent by the revelations about the Guptas – Mpho Masemola, deputy national secretary of the Ex-Political Prisoners Association, came out in strong defence of the president.

'The Gupta family has not come with Jacob Zuma. The Gupta family was introduced to Jacob Zuma by Thabo Mbeki and Essop Pahad,' Masemola claimed in an interview with eNCA. 'People are making noises now as if the President has been, you know, clinging to the Gupta family etc. It's not like that. Why Thabo Mbeki is keeping quiet? Why Essop Pahad is keeping quiet ...'[5]

These comments prompted the Thabo Mbeki Foundation to enter the fray on behalf of the former president. In a statement released to the media, the foundation strongly denied Masemola's claims, adding, apparently for purely academic reasons, that even if Mbeki had introduced the family to Zuma, such an introduction would not have been dubious: 'For the record, President Thabo Mbeki did not at any point introduce the Gupta family to President Zuma. Even if it were true that President Mbeki had introduced the Gupta family to President Zuma, unless it is alleged and proven that he did so with an improper motive, he would not be held responsible for whatever may or may not have transpired thereafter between President Zuma and the Gupta family.'[6]

The foundation also took exception to the suggestion that one of the Gupta brothers had served on any organisation associated with Mbeki's government other than the IMC: 'We have also noted reports which claim that a member of the Gupta family served as an economic advisor to President Mbeki. This too is false! No member of the Gupta family ever served in any economic advisory body during the time when President Mbeki served as Head of State. It is nevertheless true that Ajay Gupta served on the International Marketing Council board (now Brand South Africa). Mr. Ajay Gupta joined the board of the then IMC by agreement of the board on the recommendation of then Minister in The Presidency, Essop Pahad, who rightly or wrongly thought that he had the skills, knowledge and capacity to facilitate the work of the Council – not because of his alleged proximity to the President.'[7]

Ajay Gupta and one of his closest associates, however, recall a far more intimate relationship with Mbeki than the former president and his foundation care to admit.

When the press reported in April 2016 that the Guptas had fled South Africa, Nazeem Howa, then CEO of the Guptas' Oakbay Investments, told newspapers that Ajay Gupta had been friends with all three of President Nelson Mandela's successors, including Mbeki. Howa also alluded to Ajay's involvement in a government-linked body during the Mbeki era that had to have been something other than the IMC. 'The idea of *The New Age* had been born in discussions in Mbeki's advisory council of which … several of today's corporate and political leaders were also a part,' Howa told *City Press*.[8]

All of the former IMC board members I spoke to expressly denied that *The New Age* had ever been discussed at an IMC board meeting.

When Ajay Gupta later appeared on the SABC's *Morning Live* Business Briefing, a breakfast show sponsored by *The New Age*, he said in no uncertain terms that he had been part of some sort of advisory body that regularly met with Mbeki, but he seemed unable to remember what it was called.

'First time ever I sit [with members of cabinet] in maybe ten years before [i.e. circa 2006] when the previous president [Mbeki] put a one council [sic], it's called a president consultative council forum, or something, it was every first Sunday of the month we used to sit in the presidential guest house,' Ajay explained during the live televised event.[9]

He added that 'many cabinet ministers' attended these meetings and that billionaires Patrice Motsepe and Tokyo Sexwale were members too. According to Ajay, the group would 'all sit together and discuss the country and what best we can do for the country'.[10]

It appeared as if Ajay, in this unscripted account of his relationship with government, had inadvertently divulged information about an advisory body that Mbeki would rather have kept secret. In an attempt to learn more about this 'consultative council forum, or something', I requested clarification from the Thabo Mbeki Foundation and Mukoni Ratshitanga, Mbeki's spokesperson. Neither of them got back to me.

I was about to condemn the issue to the dusty vault of unsolvable Gupta mysteries when I stumbled on a *Mail & Guardian* article from 1996 that revealed details about an advisory body set up by Mbeki when he was still deputy president. This body, based on the newspaper's description, bore striking similarities to whatever it was that Ajay Gupta had spoken about at the Business Briefing: 'Deputy President Thabo Mbeki has set up a secretive, 24-strong think-tank called the Consultative Council to give him political advice,' wrote Marion Edmunds. The advisors included lawyers, businesspeople and select cabinet ministers, who would meet with Mbeki once a month at his official Pretoria residence. The article listed all twenty-four members – including Essop Pahad, who was identified as the group's convenor. However, Ajay Gupta's name was not among them.[11]

According to the newspaper, Pahad had 'reluctantly confirmed' the group's existence and did not seem to want his fellow council members to discuss the issue with the press. 'It is a set number of people and I don't think that they should speak to you about it,' he told the *Mail & Guardian*.

Seeing as Ajay Gupta had placed it on record that he had been part of a 'consultative forum' that sounded very much like the one Pahad had convened, I decided to go back and ask the former minister for clarity on the issue. He admitted that Ajay had indeed become a member of the Consultative Council at a later stage, most probably around 2005.

Pahad also confirmed that the group's existence was never meant to be public knowledge, although he does not like it being referred to as 'secret'. It seems that the original *Mail & Guardian* article caused some consternation within the group. Pahad blames a certain lawyer who had been a member of the council for leaking the information to the newspaper. 'We asked the lawyer, what are you doing? This was supposed to be a confidential group, [but] not a secret group, and people agreed to join because it was not going to go public,' Pahad told me.

There was no sinister motive behind the attempt to keep the Consultative Council's activities under wraps, Pahad insisted. According to him, the convenors wanted the group's members to be honest and frank in their monthly discussions. It was believed that in order to cultivate such an atmosphere of candour, the members would need assurance that the meetings would remain confidential.

'We didn't make anything public because we wanted people to speak freely, but it wasn't a secret organisation,' argued Pahad. 'I mean, we were meeting at the presidential guest house. I don't know how you can keep anything secret there because you have to give the security people the names of everyone going in there and your car's number plate is written down. It wasn't like we were meeting in the middle of the night surreptitiously.'

The Consultative Council was set up to allow Mbeki's government to source ideas and suggestions from people who were 'influential in their own areas of work', explained Pahad. Although there was no expectation that the issues raised at the meetings would affect official government policy- or decision-making, the group seemed to have at least some degree of influence.

'The council's members would raise certain issues, and if we [the cabinet members in the group] thought these issues were worth raising [in government], we would do so in the appropriate forums,' Pahad told me.

As with his role in the IMC, it was Ajay Gupta's knowledge of the East that secured him a seat on the Consultative Council. 'We needed to expand our horizons just a bit. We thought we'd bring in Ajay because he has a good understanding of India, and of how they do things in India and in other parts of Asia,' Pahad explained. '[We thought] he could give an opinion that could help us broaden our own understanding of what was happening in India and in other parts of the world.'

While Pahad told the *Mail & Guardian* in 1996 that it was Mbeki who convened the Consultative Council meetings, he now maintains that Mbeki never attended the actual meetings but instead only 'popped in' towards the end 'so that people could feel confident that what they had said was going to be said to him [and] also just to meet him'. Pahad was also dismissive – almost zealously so – of any suggestion that the Guptas, and Ajay in particular, had been close to Mbeki.

'It is not true that Mbeki had put Ajay Gupta on the IMC board or in the Consultative Council. That was me; it had nothing to do with Mbeki. Ajay Gupta never knew Mbeki. To the extent that he met Mbeki it would have been if and when Mbeki would sometimes come to our consultative meetings,' Pahad maintained during our discussion.

This was my second interview with Pahad. During the first, in April 2016, he curiously failed to mention Ajay's inclusion in the Consultative Council. In fact, he did not mention the council at all. At the time, Pahad insisted that Mbeki would only have met with the Guptas 'if there was a function and I had invited Ajay and then, like everybody else, they would go and shake hands with him, and take photos like everybody does at these things'.

But all indications are that the Guptas enjoyed a relationship with Mbeki that involved more than mere chit-chat at the odd public event.

Apart from Ajay's inclusion in Mbeki's Consultative Council, there is a final clue that suggests the Guptas were nearly as familiar with Mbeki as they later became with Zuma. In July 2008, the investigative magazine *Noseweek* ran an article on a failed attempt by the Guptas to become involved in an oil deal in Angola.[12]

According to the article, former Gupta associate Jagdish Parekh told one of the Guptas' would-be partners in the deal that Mbeki regularly had breakfast with the family at their home in Cape Town. The claim appears to have been an attempt to convince the Angolans of the Guptas' political connections back in South Africa.

One can only speculate as to why Mbeki and his friends seem so desperate to bury any notion that the former president was close to the Guptas. Perhaps the truth about the Consultative Council and those alleged meetings in Cape Town is simply too compromising for a former president known for his attempts to 'correct' the chapters in our history that cast him in a bad light.

PART II

MOVING UP

4

Gauteng offline

Ajay Gupta's inclusion in Thabo Mbeki's secretive advisory council suggests that the family had made considerable inroads into South Africa's political establishment several years before Jacob Zuma's rise to power at the ANC's 2007 elective conference in Polokwane.

But in the early 2000s, as the Guptas nurtured their ties with an Mbeki administration that was at the pinnacle of its power, they simultaneously made clear efforts to draw Zuma and his family into their fold.

The foundation for the friendship between Zuma and the Guptas in those early days seemed to be Sahara Holdings and its subsidiaries, including Sahara Computers and Sahara Systems (a provider of information and communications technology (ICT) services), which at that point represented the core of the family's business interests in South Africa. While there is some uncertainty over when exactly the Guptas met Zuma for the first time, the official account spun by them and by Zuma is that the first introduction occurred in 2002 or 2003 at a function hosted by Sahara. John, the businessman who worked with the Guptas and whom we met in Chapter 2, is adamant, however, that the Guptas met Zuma much earlier.

In a 2011 interview with *City Press*, Duduzane Zuma suggested that the relationship began earlier. 'I was introduced to the Gupta family by my father in late 2001, just like I met many people,' he told the newspaper.[1] It appears that in 2001 Jacob Zuma was already familiar enough with the Guptas to introduce them to his teenaged son.

In 2010, amid some of the earliest negative news reports on the links between the Guptas and the newly appointed president, Atul Gupta told the *Weekend Argus* that 'Duduzane Zuma started at Sahara Systems as a trainee manager about seven years ago'.[2] In other words, in around 2003 Jacob Zuma's son was officially absorbed into the Gupta business empire. Having been born in 1984, Duduzane would have been around nineteen when he joined Sahara.

'He's disciplined, systematic and organised and has become a fully fledged, matured businessman,' Atul told the *Weekend Argus* in 2010, dismissing accusations that the Guptas had appointed the president's son merely to score political points with his father. In any event, the decade saw few, if any, controversies surrounding the Guptas' appointment of Duduzane.

Instead, while the young Zuma was busy finding his feet at his new employer, the Guptas' Sahara Group focused on growing its revenues and expanding its footprint in the local computer and IT sector. This expansion saw the company land some relatively large government contracts, not all of which were concluded successfully.

A particularly ill-fated government project in which Sahara became involved at a relatively early stage was the Gauteng government's Gauteng Online Schools Project, better known as GautengOnline (GoL).

In 2001, the provincial government, under the leadership of then premier Mbhazima Samuel Shilowa, announced an ambitious plan to furnish each of the more than 2 400 schools in Gauteng with a computer laboratory. In his speech at the opening of the Gauteng provincial legislature in February 2001, Shilowa stated that the province had allocated some R500 million towards ensuring that each school would receive an average of twenty-five computers. The computers would be connected to the internet, Shilowa promised, which would 'help produce learners who are ready to take up employment in the new economy'.[3]

The idea was for the project to be allocated to six consortiums. Each of the consortiums would be led by a large computer hardware company, which would in turn team up with smaller software companies. These software companies would provide the e-learning programs and related software necessary for the project's success as an education initiative.

After a pilot project during which computer laboratories were set up at a small number of schools, it was announced in 2003 that the Sahara Consortium, led by Sahara Computers, was one of the six consortiums picked for the R500-million contract.[4] The other consortiums were led by larger, more established computer companies such as Dell, HP and Mecer.[5]

Instead of rolling out the initiative to all the schools in the province all at once, the Gauteng Department of Education (GDE) instead decided to target 500 schools in the project's first phase. The Sahara Consortium would install computers in 110 schools, Sahara Computers announced.[6] Apart from computers, Sahara would also install television sets, DVD players and printers at these schools.[7]

The contract was a noteworthy coup for Sahara. At that point the company was only six years old, yet it had managed to clinch the lion's share of GoL's first phase. The five rival consortiums, led by the well-known and established computer brands mentioned above, shared the remaining 390 schools.

Sahara was also fortunate enough to be singled out with a special blessing from a cabinet minister. 'We wish Sahara Computers everything of the best going forward and we look forward to providing greater accessibility and exposure to the benefits of communication technology, especially among rural communities,' then trade and industry minister Alec Erwin said at the start of the project.[8]

The company's access to top-level government officials seemed to have been guaranteed even at this early stage.

At the time, managing director Atul Gupta described Sahara's participation in GautengOnline in a manner that suggested the company had become involved in the project for charitable reasons. 'Accessibility and lower cost are key issues within the ICT industry and Sahara Computers is pleased to be at the forefront of this initiative,' he told the media. 'This represents a substantial investment in the education and training of our youth.'[9]

Previously Gupta had said, 'We believe that by educating the youth of our nation we are able to alter the status quo and impact communities at large.' He was, however, honest enough to suggest that Sahara's involvement in GoL was not just a grand act of kindness. 'Gupta does not shy away from the fact that this is also a good business opportunity for Sahara, citing it as yet another motivating factor that drives the company to deliver a sustainable, cost-effective and user-friendly solution to the Gauteng Department of Education,' read the promotional copy.[10]

Sahara was seemingly on a high. In December 2005, the new deputy president, Phumzile Mlambo-Ngcuka, opened the second annual Sahara Convention, an event that sought to bring together role-players in the IT industry.[11] It must have been a rather awkward affair for Mlambo-Ngcuka. She had replaced Jacob Zuma as deputy president only months before, after Mbeki had fired him over allegations of corruption. It is not clear whether the Guptas asked Mlambo-Ngcuka to appear at their event because their friend Zuma was no longer deputy president, or because they were close to her too. It is interesting to note that the new deputy president was married to Bulelani Ngcuka, the former National Director of Public Prosecutions (NDPP) whose investigation into Zuma's alleged corruption eventually led the National Prosecuting Authority (NPA) to charge him over his role in the controversial arms deal.

But despite the lofty ideals that accompanied the project's launch phase, GoL eventually came to be seen as one of the province's costliest failures. In fact, the project is now referred to as 'GautengOffline' by numerous role-players who were involved in its rollout, due to the fact that the computer labs never really became the fully connected e-learning centres they were intended to be.

By 2007, six years after Shilowa's announcement, GautengOnline was viewed as such a dismal failure that a new service provider was appointed to replace Sahara and the other consortiums, *The Star* reported in 2009. The GDE had already paid out about R1 billion for computer labs that were either mostly offline or plagued by technical problems.[12] The new service provider, which would eventually be paid about R2 billion, ended up doing no better than its predecessors.[13]

After speaking to three role-players in the IT sector who were involved in the initial bid to secure the Sahara Consortium its piece of the project, I believe that from the outset GautengOnline was viewed by the likes of Sahara as nothing more than an opportunity to supply government schools with computer hardware. All three sources independently told me a story that more or less goes as follows:

In early 2002, Sahara installed computer labs in five schools in Alexandra township and elsewhere in Gauteng. This was part of GoL's pilot phase, during which the provincial authorities would evaluate the offerings of the participating consortiums. As consortium partners to Sahara, several small to medium-sized software companies installed their software on the Sahara computers. Atul Gupta, over the course of several meetings with the owners of these companies, had made big promises about the huge amount of work that would come their way once the Sahara Consortium landed a slice of the GoL rollout.

'The software companies put in a lot of work, time and money install-ing software on those computers, without charging a cent for it,' one source told me. 'But we thought it would be worth it because the Guptas, who'd have meetings with us at Sahara's offices in Midrand, kept telling us we'd eventually get big software contracts.'

However, when the Gauteng government finally awarded the contracts to the six consortiums, those companies who had partnered with Sahara soon realised with great shock that they had been totally sidelined. 'When the tender was awarded, not a single cent came our way, despite the fact that we had to sponsor software in order for the consortium to be evalu-ated,' said a second source.

It appears that as soon as Sahara won the contract, they parted ways with their consortium partners and started pushing hundreds of computers and related hardware into the schools on their own, without the software that had helped Sahara land the contract in the first place. 'It became clear that the whole thing was just a big sham,' my third source told me. 'The idea was simply for the hardware guys, not just Sahara but also Mecer and the others, to just dump their hardware at these schools.'

A 2010–2011 audit of GautengOnline later revealed that, among other problems, most of the schools' computer laboratories had never gone online and that the service providers had not properly maintained the hardware.[14]

In 2013, after the Gauteng government had invested eleven years and R3 billion of taxpayers' money in an initiative that was supposed to bring much-needed opportunities to some of the province's poorest and most disenfranchised children, GautengOnline was scrapped.[15]

In December 2016, I set out to determine just how much money Sahara had made from GoL before it and the other five consortiums were booted off the project. Initially, the GDE told me it had paid Sahara R33 million for installing computer labs at 108 schools. But this was only for GoL's first phase. After reminding the department that Sahara had also been involved in further phases of the project, the GDE provided me with a new set of figures: Sahara's total payment for its role in GoL, which involved the installation of computer labs at 233 schools in phases one and two of the initiative, had been R67 million, the department stated.

The GDE's flip-flopping on its own figures makes me wonder whether there is more about Sahara's involvement in GoL that has yet to be uncovered. In any event, GautengOnline would not be Sahara's last troubled schools project.

In 2000, SchoolNet South Africa, a non-governmental organisation (NGO) active in the education sector, began rolling out two major projects for the supply of computers and related equipment to especially poor and rural schools.[16] One of these initiatives was the Thintana i-Learn Project. Thintana Communications, which at that stage was an equity partner to Telkom, South Africa's state-owned telecommunications company, had donated just over R21 million for the establishment of computer centres at 200 disadvantaged schools.[17]

As the project's implementing agent, SchoolNet was responsible for appointing third-party contractors for some of the work the NGO would not be able to do itself. One such contractor was SourceCom, a company that had been appointed by SchoolNet to perform the project's 'technical tasks'. SourceCom in turn subcontracted two companies, FreeCom and Memtek, which would respectively supply 2 000 refurbished computers and 800 new machines needed for the project. But according to a 2004 SchoolNet report, which assessed the Thintana i-Learn Project and some of the NGO's other schools initiatives, things took a turn for the worse when the Johannesburg Stock Exchange (JSE)-listed Siltek Group, which owned Memtek, went into liquidation. This occurred in October 2001, 'about halfway through the project and only four months after the commencement of the infrastructure rollout', according to the report. SourceCom then decided to contract Sahara Computers to provide the remaining new computers needed to complete the project.[18]

One would expect the refurbished computers, some of which had been donated to the project, to give at least some problems because they were not new. But SchoolNet seemed especially disappointed in the quality of the brand-new computers supplied by Sahara: 'Whilst the use of refurbished computers on the i-Learn Project did add to the set of problems experienced on this project, these computers were certainly not the root cause of all the problems incurred ... In fact, according to various reports, the new Sahara computers which replaced the Siltek-sourced computers gave as much if not more trouble than the refurbished computers.'[19]

The 2004 report specifically lists 'out of box failures with new computers sourced from Sahara' as one of the major issues the installation teams experienced with the project's rollout.

The headaches caused by Sahara's hardware in the Thintana i-Learn Project did not stop the company from becoming a preferred supplier of computers for similar schools projects, including some that were funded directly by government departments.

In 2006, Sahara Systems clinched another government tender from the Universal Service and Access Agency of South Africa (USAASA). The USAASA, a state-owned entity that reports to the Department of Tele-communications and Postal Services, appointed Sahara Systems 'to roll-out a number of telecentres and telecontainers in rural areas throughout South Africa'. Fitted with equipment such as computers, fax machines and telephones, these telecentres and telecontainers were supposed to 'facilitate education through IT courses, training and demonstration'.[20] It is not clear whether this project was successful or not, or what Sahara earned from its participation. The USAASA has failed to respond to any queries about Sahara Systems' role in the initiative.

In the mid- to late 2000s, Sahara Computers 'contributed significantly' to an initiative called the Free State Project, according to an article on *net.work*, a website that publishes news about the IT sector. The first phase of the project would see the installation of two Sahara computers and one printer at each of 300 schools in the province, while the company would deliver a laptop and a printer to each of another 152 schools during the second phase.[21]

The article also mentioned something called the Lejwelputswa Project, for which Sahara provided 'critical services in the form of installation and configuration of equipment' at new computer labs at twenty-five schools in the Free State.[22]

The Free State Department of Education became defensive when I queried Sahara's role in these projects. Howard Ndaba, the department's spokesperson, sounded irritated, if not angry, when I asked him about the two initiatives.

'Why do you want to know about this? It is just schools, standard schools computer projects,' he said when I spoke to him on the phone. He told me to send him an email detailing what I wanted to know about the Free State and Lejwelputswa projects and vowed to respond to my queries. I did so, but I never heard from him again.

Though the company seemed to be doing rather well as a result of these government projects, Sahara's board apparently resolved to cease doing business with the state in 2008.[23] It is not clear whether the GautengOnline disaster played a role in the board's supposed decision. It should be noted, however, that Sahara Systems quite openly did business with government well after 2008. There are also some indications that Sahara Computers itself continued to do so.

A case in point: As 2004 drew to a close, South Africa's entire IT business fraternity kept a close eye on what had been described as the South African government's 'most lucrative technology tender to date'.[24] The State Information Technology Agency (SITA) had issued a tender for the provision of an all-encompassing IT management service to government departments. Known as 'seat management' in the IT industry, the contract would include the supply and maintenance of both hardware and software. Basically, government wanted to outsource the entirety of its IT requirements. It would be a huge undertaking.

At the time, the contract was thought to be worth around R2.5 billion. The then chair of SITA's supplier selection authority described this amount as 'very conservative', which suggested that government was willing to fork out even more money for the rollout of the programme.[25]

After the awarding of the contract had been delayed several times over the course of the year, SITA made an announcement on the issue in November 2004. It had been decided that the contract would be split into three subcategories: an outright purchase option, a lease option and a provision of services option. SITA then gave the names of thirty-four companies and consortiums from which it would potentially procure IT equipment and services. Both Sahara Computers and Sahara Systems appeared on the list.[26]

After the anticipation and excitement that accompanied the bidding phase, the announcement was viewed by many role-players in the industry as a huge anti-climax.[27] Being on a list of preferred bidders did not guarantee any of the companies a contract. There was still no certainty with regard to which of the shortlisted bidders would actually secure supply contracts from SITA.

Mavuso Msimang, SITA's then CEO, said at the announcement of the shortlist that while none of the companies or consortiums would get 'a disproportionate amount of the business', each company's 'individual marketing efforts' would determine how big their 'slice of the pie' would be.[28]

It is not clear just how big a slice of this particular pie Sahara ended up getting. Even SITA, which oversaw the rollout, claims it does not know. The agency's spokesperson explained to me that it merely compiled the list of companies from which government departments would then directly procure their required IT products and services. 'SITA does not have a full view of how much, if any, orders were placed [by government departments] with Sahara Systems,' said the spokesperson.

A SITA spreadsheet compiled in June 2014 still listed Sahara Computers as a 'prime' supplier of IT products and services to government entities in that year. This and other documents related to the SITA contract cast doubt over Sahara's claim that it stopped doing business with government in 2008.

Then, in 2010, Sahara Systems found itself among twelve IT companies chosen as accredited suppliers of laptops to the Department of Basic Education's Teacher Laptop Initiative (TLI). The programme, which was supposed to have been managed by the Education and Labour Relations Council (ELRC), would have seen the government provide an allowance of R130 per month for five years to each of the country's 350 000 teachers in order to help them buy a laptop package from one of the accredited suppliers.[29]

The packages were to have cost between R250 and R390 and the teachers would have had to cover the shortfall from their own salaries. In other words, government intended to spend some R550 million a year on the programme. But the TLI never took off amid problems relating to obtaining credit approvals for some of the teachers.[30] After the education department wrested control of the project from the ELRC in 2013, the TLI was referred back to National Treasury for further deliberation on how it would be funded.[31] There is no indication of the TLI being any nearer to rolling out.

Next up, in April 2015, a government tender bulletin showed that Sahara Systems had been appointed by the Innovation Hub, a state-owned company belonging to the Gauteng provincial government, for the 'supply and configuration of ICT network equipment'. The contract was valued at R4.5 million.

* * *

When Oakbay Investments, the main holding company of the Guptas' business empire, released its 'maiden' annual results in September 2016, it did so on the back of a year that had been disastrous for the Guptas in terms of public relations.

Oakbay Investments, unlike its JSE-listed sister company Oakbay Resources & Energy, was under no obligation to release its results. But given the bad press the Guptas and their businesses had been receiving throughout 2016, the company decided to release its annual results – or at least a very condensed, terse version thereof – in order to 'dispel some of the myths that have been built up about our Group – especially the myth that we are heavily reliant on Government business, when nothing could be further from the truth', as Nazeem Howa said in his CEO's statement.[32]

It was in this results report that Oakbay claimed: 'Sahara [Computers] … does not have any government contracts, following a deliberate decision taken by its Board in 2008.' And further down: 'Sahara has undertaken no Government business since 2008.'[33]

No reference was made to Sahara Systems and its ongoing relationship with state entities and departments. Or the inclusion of Sahara Computers as a 'prime' supplier of computer products to government on a 2014 SITA document, which casts doubt over their claim.

Even if Sahara's board did genuinely decide to stop doing business with government in 2008, the company and its sister entities had already reaped heaps of government work before then. The value of those contracts, especially for a company that had been relatively new to the IT sector, cannot be underestimated. And while the Guptas undoubtedly benefited, some of the government projects with which their companies were involved brought nothing but disappointment and frustration to some of South Africa's poorest and most disenfranchised communities.

5

Capturing cricket

While Sahara Computers and its sister companies became increasingly involved in government-funded projects, the Guptas decided to take a swing at the local cricket establishment.

In April 2004, word got out that Sahara Computers had closed a deal with the United Cricket Board of South Africa (UCB), now called Cricket South Africa (CSA), for the naming rights of three of South Africa's most beloved cricket grounds.

A report by seasoned-cricket-journalist-turned-CSA-spin-doctor Michael Owen-Smith, published before the official announcement, set out some of the deal's details and captured the early disapproval of the cricketing establishment. Many cricket fans were beyond upset upon hearing that some of the country's most hallowed cricket grounds, including Cape Town's then 116-year-old Newlands stadium, would incorporate Sahara's name in their official titles.[1]

'You have ruined my evening. I nearly dropped the phone and now I want to throw something at the TV set,' an irked Hylton Ackerman, former Western Province captain and coach, told Owen-Smith after he had been informed that Newlands could be renamed Sahara Park Newlands.

Former South African cricket hero Garth le Roux thought the name change was a belated April Fools' joke.[2]

Two days later it was announced at an official ceremony at Newlands that Sahara had paid R25 million for the naming rights to Newlands, Port Elizabeth's St George's Park and Durban's Kingsmead Stadium.[3] St. George's Park, South Africa's oldest cricket ground, would be known as Sahara Oval St Georges, while Durban's famous ground was to be renamed Sahara Stadium Kingsmead. The contract was for a period of five years.

Apart from the anger in some quarters over the sudden changes, the deal also highlighted the confusion at that point over the relationship between the Guptas' Sahara Computers and Sahara India Pariwar, the much older and larger Indian conglomerate mentioned in Chapter 1, which was a sponsor of the Indian national cricket team. Almost all the cricket scribes writing about the deal incorrectly referred to the Guptas' company as an international company based in India.

'The deal has been struck with Sahara Computers, which is a subsidiary of Sahara Holdings, one of the largest industrial companies in India. They are the sponsors of the Indian cricket team,' wrote Owen-Smith in his original report, clearly confusing the two Saharas.

Altus Momberg, also a seasoned South African cricket writer, referred to Sahara as an 'Indian computer company ... which is also the main sponsor of the Indian national side'.[4]

The error was completely understandable. There had been widespread uncertainty within the South African IT industry about Sahara Computers' relationship with Sahara India Pariwar. Even today there is a widely held sentiment within the sector that the Guptas 'piggybacked' on the name of the better-established and better-known company. The Guptas have of course denied the accusation, but, for all their bluster about independence, Sahara Computers' decision to sponsor the UCB was a curious one, seeing that Sahara India Pariwar had become the main sponsor of the Indian cricket team in 2001.

Some of the most senior cricket officials involved in the deal also seemed to be confused about the identity of the company that had bought the naming rights to three of their stadiums. Defending the deal, Arnold Bloch, then president of the Western Province Cricket Association, insisted that 'we have taken a decision that takes our business interests into account ... This could lead to other international companies advertising at Newlands.'[5] He clearly thought the internationally renowned Sahara India Pariwar and Sahara Computers were one and the same.

To be fair, Atul Gupta did make an attempt to clear up the confusion. In a follow-up article by Owen-Smith, Gupta was quoted as saying that 'there is no financial connection at all' between his family's business and the Indian conglomerate.[6] The uncertainty over Sahara Computers' ownership, however, continued to linger.

As passionate cricket supporters struggled to come to terms with the name changes of their near-sacred cricket grounds, the Guptas decided to discharge a little PR magic to try to win the fans' hearts. To help them, they formed a somewhat unlikely alliance with Graeme Smith, at the time South Africa's national cricket captain.

At the official announcement of the deal, Sahara Computers introduced Smith as the company's new 'brand ambassador'.[7] His first task in his new role clearly involved convincing the cricketing public that the name changes would be good for the sport: 'The players realise how important money is to the game,' Smith told the media. 'Cricketers who were playing 20 years ago could not have dreamed that they would be playing 20 overs a side cricket today and, if the future of Newlands is at stake in 20 years' time, nobody is going to ask questions about where the money comes from.'[8]

Though details about the arrangement between Sahara and Smith were scant, the Proteas captain indicated that he would be required to represent the Guptas' computer firm at certain public events.[9] There were no details on how much money Smith stood to make from the deal.

Gary Naidoo, Sahara's marketing director, likened the cricket star, who was twenty-three at the time, to the Guptas' burgeoning computer firm: 'Like us, he is young, dynamic and growing.'[10]

The relationship between Sahara and Smith would last for the greater part of the Proteas captain's career. In 2009, Smith released his book, *A Captain's Diary*, at a function held at the Newlands cricket ground. According to a promotional board photographed at the event, Sahara was the 'official book sponsor'.

In a video from the event, a somewhat obsequious Smith, not known among the sporting press for his modesty, can be seen literally bowing his head to his paymasters at Sahara. 'You just heard that the relationship [between Smith and Sahara] has been going for five years and they've been an integral part of those five years. To Mr Gupta [bows head] and Gary [Naidoo], thank you very much,' says Smith, standing in front of a Sahara placard.[11]

There is a brief moment of awkwardness when Smith refers to his home ground but forgets to mention Sahara's name: 'To Western Province Cricket, who've obviously played a massive role in my life since I arrived here at Newlands as a young eighteen-year-old trying to—'

'Sahara Park Newlands,' interrupts an unknown audience member, out of shot.

But Smith would have plenty more opportunities to get the stadium's name right. Naidoo, speaking before Smith, announced that Sahara had secured another five-year naming-rights agreement for Newlands. He also used the opportunity to announce that Smith's contract as Sahara brand ambassador had been extended.

Smith was not the only Proteas star roped in by the Guptas for marketing purposes. In December 2004, teammates Shaun Pollock, Jacques Kallis, Makhaya Ntini, Boeta Dippenaar, Jacques Rudolph, Martin van Jaarsveld and Neil McKenzie all signed on to become 'brand representatives' of Sahara.[12]

By the end of 2005, the Guptas' grip on the Proteas and CSA was so firmly established that the family managed to make significant alterations to the team's schedule for a tour to India in November of that year.

Smith and his team played and won convincingly the first of their five One Day International matches against India in Hyderabad on Wednesday 16 November.[13] The next morning, the South Africans were put on two chartered planes and flown to Saharanpur, some 1 400 kilometres north of Hyderabad. A former member of the Proteas squad says the detour was inconvenient. 'It was between matches, so it was a bit irritating,' he told me.

The trip turned into a bit of circus once they reached the Guptas' hometown. A video of the visit, which I obtained from one of the South Africans, shows the Proteas being paraded through the streets of Saharanpur on horse-drawn carriages. According to a report by the Press Trust of India, a newswire service, coach Mickey Arthur and the likes of Jacques Kallis, Ashwell Prince and Justin Kemp 'were overwhelmed by the grand reception offered to them … by the star-starved public'. At a 'grand gathering' at Saharanpur's B.R. Ambedkar Stadium, the South Africans, 'donning tikas and traditional turbans, swung to the tunes "Mere Desh ki Dharti" [a song from a classic 1960s Bollywood film] and "Vande Mataram" [an Indian folk song]'.[14] The video shows the Proteas wearing bright orange turbans, but none of them look particularly pleased about it. In fact, wicketkeeper Mark Boucher can be heard uttering a string of profanities because of the outfit he had been made to wear.

The Proteas' next match against India was in the southern city of Bangalore. The aerial distance between Saharanpur and Bangalore is just under 1900 kilometres. After having travelled at least 3300 kilometres in about two days for the sole purpose of pleasing the Guptas, the Proteas played against the Indian national team on Saturday 19 November. The South Africans batted first and this time only managed to scrape together a paltry 169 runs. India won the match after easing past the low target in just 35 overs.[15] The Proteas – who thankfully had no further Gupta-related obligations for the rest of the tour – did, however, end up winning the series.

The sponsorship agreements between Sahara and some of the Proteas' biggest stars would provide for some awkward – if not downright cringe-worthy – moments. A Sahara TV commercial uploaded onto YouTube in 2011 serves as a case in point. Apparently made for Indian television, it is unlikely that many South Africans would have seen the production.

The advert features Smith, Ntini and fellow Proteas cricketer A.B. de Villiers on a game drive through what is supposedly the Indian jungle, although the landscape looks remarkably similar to the South African bushveld. Smith, seated in the front passenger seat and looking like a sullen teenager on a family road trip, can be seen playing a cricket computer game with bad graphics on a Sahara notebook.

Suddenly, one of the female passengers in the back of the roofless safari vehicle spots an animal and tells Ntini, who is doing the driving, to stop. De Villiers, also seated in the back, starts bouncing a cricket ball on a bat, as one does on a game drive.

'Hey Makhaya, catch it!' shouts De Villiers as he whacks the ball into the bush. Except it is not De Villiers's voice. All the 'actors' have been dubbed over. Makhaya lunges for the ball but misses.

'Go get it, Makhaya,' Smith tells Ntini with a patronising shake of the head.

'I won't go. What if there is a lion?' Ntini simpers.

And so it is up to Smith, who now gets out of the vehicle, to retrieve the ball and educate his hapless teammate.

'No lions in India, mate,' smirks Smith as he runs into the bush.

As the Proteas captain enters a patch of long grass, the soundtrack becomes ominous. Suddenly, Smith comes face to face with a Bengal tiger. They square off in a brief staring contest. There is a roar. The camera shakes. And then the animal backs down and dashes off. Smith has saved the day. The next shot is of a Sahara computer set-up, accompanied by a voice artist saying: 'Sahara Computers – the South African legend, now in India'.[16]

It is unlikely that the advert would have been considered for India's equivalent of the South African Loerie Awards.

You may by now have begun to wonder what the Guptas stood to benefit from their association with CSA and the Proteas. Initially, Sahara Computers made their relationship with the sport's administrative body sound like it was informed by charitable considerations, much like they had done at the start of the various government schools projects in which they had become involved.

In December 2004, about eight months after Sahara and the UCB announced the naming-rights deal for the three South African cricket grounds, Sahara released an advertorial which explained how the company's technology had 'played a crucial role in helping SA's new cricket coach Ray Jennings strategise during the Protea's current tour in India'. According to Atul Gupta, who was quoted in the piece, 'Sahara Computers is proud to offer its key expertise and help coach Ray Jennings with technology to instantly capture and analyse match and player statistics'.[17]

Ever the socially conscious company, Sahara teamed up in June 2005 with the UCB and Gauteng's Eastern Cricket Union (now known simply as Eastern Cricket) to host a coaching clinic for 724 young cricket players in the province's East Rand area. Smith, by then more than a year into his tenure as Sahara's brand ambassador, put the youngsters 'through their paces' and helped them refine their 'batting, bowling and fielding' skills. Marketing director Gary Naidoo said of the event: 'Sahara Computers is passionate about South African cricket and we are equally as passionate about helping to develop resources … We are very excited about the advent of coaching clinics – a tried and tested method of ensuring skills development at an early age. It bodes well for the sport and for SA.'[18]

Viewed in isolation, the initiative looked like an admirable example of corporate social responsibility. But with the Guptas, charity appears to be nothing more than the first step in a journey towards eventual profit.

Just four months later, in October 2005, Sahara Computers announced that it had 'secured a four-year contract with the United Cricket Board (UCB), incorporating its commercial arm Cricket South Africa, and the

South African national cricket team (the Proteas), to supply a range of hardware and software products'. The Guptas' computer firm would become 'the exclusive IT hardware supplier' to the sport's administrative body and its member provinces. There was no mention of exactly how much the contract was worth, beyond the fact that 'all cricket provincial unions stand to benefit from the multimillion-rand deal by improving their IT infrastructure, thereby enabling them to be more efficient in their administration and ticketing, among others'. As before, the Guptas spoke about the contract as if it was some kind of benevolent act, not an opportunity to make money. 'This opportunity adds depth to our existing involvement in provincial and national cricket and we look forward to many years of contribution towards the development of players, resources and the sport in general,' said Atul Gupta of the deal.[19]

Four months later, in February 2006, Sahara Computers announced that it had scored a similar long-term contract with the South African Rugby Union. 'As official IT supplier the company has committed to a three-year contract with the sports administration and regulation body to supply hardware and software designed to support the union's existing technical infrastructure and enhance its digital resources,' said Sahara after clinching the contract.[20]

Then, in 2008, Gary Naidoo was appointed to the CSA board as an independent non-executive director.[21] The fact that there was no outcry over this development, especially in light of Sahara's ongoing business dealings with CSA, is indicative of how well the Guptas and their associates managed to fly under the radar in those days.

There would be a slight slip-up the following year, however, when a nasty incident during the 2009 Indian Premier League (IPL) T20 tournament in South Africa would see the family receive a fair amount of up-until-then rare negative publicity.

IPL founder and chairman Lalit Modi had decided to move the 2009 edition of the famous tournament to South Africa after the 2008 terrorist attacks in Mumbai. It is widely believed that the Guptas, who have close ties with Modi, played a key role in convincing the Indian cricket boss to bring the tournament to South Africa.[22] (The IPL would eventually be the downfall of Cricket South Africa CEO Gerald Majola, the man under whose watch the Guptas came to be so influential in the sport. In May 2012,

Majola was suspended as CSA CEO after he was found guilty of negotiating and accepting illicit bonuses relating to the IPL and abusing his travel allowance, among other transgressions. He was fired a few months later, in October.[23])

During the inaugural tournament in South Africa, at a match between the Punjab XI and the Deccan Chargers in Johannesburg, an incident occurred involving the Guptas that drew the attention of the Indian press. According to the *Times of India*, the Guptas were enjoying the match in a VIP box along with co-owners of the Punjab XI, the powerful Indian businessmen Ness Wadia and Mohit Burman, when an intoxicated Burman began prodding a female spectator with the flagpole of a Punjab XI pennant because she was blocking his view. It turned out that the spectator was the daughter-in-law of Ajay Gupta, whom the newspaper described as the 'owner of one of South Africa's biggest conglomerates, the Sahara Group, and a friend of the new South African President Jacob Zuma'. In response, she summoned her security guards, who charged into the box and started assaulting Burman and Wadia. Some South African police officers allegedly also joined in the fray. In the midst of the ruckus, a furious Ajay threatened to have Wadia and Burman deported. Eventually Modi had to intervene in order to save the tournament from an international scandal. At Modi's insistence, Burman and Wadia later went to the Guptas' Saxonwold estate where, like two misbehaved schoolboys, they apologised to the Guptas.[24]

While fists flew at the cricket stadium, the affairs of CSA and Sahara became further entangled. CSA's annual reports shed light on significant cash flows between Gupta-owned ventures and the sporting body. In the 2010–2011 financial year, *The New Age* newspaper, launched by the Guptas in September 2010, provided 'sponsorship' to CSA amounting to R2.8 million.[25] In the following year, it pumped in a further R3.8 million.[26]

By 2012, the Guptas' influence within Cricket South Africa was strong enough for them to force their very own cricket team into the country's top T20 cricket tournament. Enter the short-lived and spectacularly disastrous experiment called The New Age Impi.

In February 2012, CSA announced that a new team would compete in that year's MiWay T20 Challenge, a competition that normally features South Africa's top six cricket franchises and which is now known as the RAM Slam T20 Challenge.

Speaking at the launch event for the new team, Majola heaped praise on the Guptas' *The New Age*: 'We are most grateful to *The New Age* for the support they have shown for this new venture and I am sure their confidence will be rewarded as the tournament unfolds. The launch of this new franchise is a very important moment for our domestic cricket as it will give more opportunities for players to perform at the highest domestic level and push for inclusion in the Proteas' squad ... I would also like to thank *The New Age* for what they have done to make it possible for us to recruit four high quality overseas players.'[27]

The international players referred to included former England captain Paul Collingwood and Dutch batting star Ryan ten Doeschate.

Nazeem Howa, as CEO of TNA Media, *The New Age*'s holding company, said that 'when the opportunity to own the seventh team came we had no hesitation in making an offer'.[28] An opportunity, of course, concocted by a CSA board that included Gary Naidoo, Howa's fellow Gupta associate.

The New Age Impi were based at Benoni's Willowmoore Park, which by then had been renamed Sahara Park Willowmoore. By the time the tournament's group phase had come to an end, the Impi had lost ten of their twelve matches. They would probably have lost all twelve of their games had it not been for Gauteng's famously tempestuous weather – two of their home fixtures had to be abandoned due to heavy rain.[29] It would be The New Age Impi's first and final flirtation with professional cricket.

In May, it was announced that the Impi were being booted from the T20 Challenge. Jacques Faul, who had taken over as acting CSA CEO after Majola's suspension less than two weeks earlier, tried to be diplomatic in his assessment of the Impi saga. 'It was a good idea but not all good ideas pan out to be that successful,' he said at a press briefing after a CSA meeting.[30]

The sporting press were not as kind.

It was only due to 'rules having been bent and precedents set to smuggle them in' that the Impi were allowed to compete in the MiWay T20 Challenge, wrote sports journalist Luke Alfred in the *Sunday Times*, before calling the team's campaign 'an unmitigated disaster'.[31]

As cricket writer Stuart Hess saw it, the assembly of the Guptas' team appeared to have been an eleventh-hour rush job. 'Though the idea for a seventh team was mooted last year [2011], the logistics thereof – team selection, kit, sponsorship – were only handled days before the tournament kicked off,' he wrote in *The Star*.[32]

The team's outfit turned out to be something of a billboard for the Guptas' business ventures. Though the Impi were sponsored by *The New Age*, Sahara's branding was also slapped onto the team shirts. The Impi may not have won any silverware for the Guptas' trophy cabinet at Saxonwold, but the marketing the family's businesses scored from the team's televised matches surely made up for that.

In its 2011–2012 annual report, CSA did manage to find the silver lining in the Impi's embarrassing run: 'They had predictably little success as a team but the very fact that one of their number, Khaya Zondo, scored the competition's only century justified their participation on its own.'[33]

The T20 Challenge was not the only marketing opportunity that came the Guptas' way in 2012 courtesy of CSA. At the end of March that year, the South African national team played India in a T20 match at the Wanderers cricket stadium in Johannesburg. The Guptas' newspaper had clinched the naming rights to the match, which had been dubbed The New Age Friendship T20 Cup. According to one source, CSA had even initially agreed to place R500 000 worth of advertising for the fixture in *The New Age*, 'to the exclusion of advertising elsewhere'. CSA, however, ultimately decided against providing the Guptas with such an obvious boon.[34]

But the match did ensure that *The New Age*'s logo would again enjoy some prime television airtime. The Guptas apparently also felt it necessary to parade their dearest and most valued friend at the event – President Jacob Zuma and first wife Nompumelelo Ntuli-Zuma enjoyed the match in a VIP area with the Gupta clan. A photo taken at the event showing Atul Gupta and Zuma seated next to one another would later become one of the most widely used images of the two men together. In the picture, Zuma appears engrossed in the action on the field. Gupta is leaning in to his neighbour, his hand raised and his mouth ajar, perhaps schooling his friend in the finer intricacies of the game the Guptas hold so dear. Or perhaps the two men are discussing more pressing issues.

In a video uploaded onto YouTube by the Presidency, Zuma is seen thanking the organisers of the event and claiming in his somewhat awkward speech that it had been *his* idea to host another friendly T20 match between the two countries after he had attended a similar game in Durban the previous year. 'When we had this first tournament in Durban it was so wonderful, so nice, that you have this short version of cricket that brings everybody together,' Zuma said. 'And I could see the excitement in both the cricketers from India and from South Africa and the fans. And I was told this was just once off, and I made a proposal, why don't we have this annually so that we could have cricket fans happy, to look forward to this on an annual basis.'[35]

The match was interrupted by a thunderstorm and South Africa was declared the winner based on the Duckworth–Lewis method. Zuma, Atul Gupta and Howa handed medals and a trophy to the South African team afterwards. Even Angoori, the Gupta matriarch, got in on the action, handing Proteas star Jacques Kallis a cheque made out to his charitable foundation.

In the week before the match, the Guptas had hosted both the Proteas and the Indian team at their estate in Saxonwold, according to a former CSA employee who attended the function. '*That* is power!' said the source. 'Being able to just summon two national cricket teams to your house.'

Another former South African cricket administrator said it was not uncommon for the Proteas and even CSA board members to be entertained at Saxonwold in those days. According to this source, some of the board members would sometimes meet at the Guptas' estate on the eve of CSA board meetings in Johannesburg.

In any event, 2012 was somewhat of a high-water mark for the Guptas in terms of their involvement with CSA, at least with regard to their visible proximity to the sporting body. The New Age Friendship T20 Cup was not held again, despite Zuma's wish for it to take place annually. 'It was just a very bad deal for CSA,' a former CSA employee told me. '*The New Age* only paid a few hundred thousand rand for the naming rights, and the match probably cost us more than we made from it.'

As if to confirm the Guptas' exit from cricket's governing body, Naidoo, their man on the inside, resigned as an independent non-executive director of CSA in February 2013.[36]

It is not clear whether the Guptas were forced out of cricket or chose to back off from the game of their own accord. What is clear, though, is that they had become involved in lucrative mining deals by the time their influence at CSA started to wane. Perhaps the family simply did not deem the gentleman's game to be profitable enough to be worth any more of their time and effort.

6

Zuma's rise to power

South Africa is the land of the 'grand conspiracy'. Our political narrative has become infused with so many secret plots and schemes, whether plausibly true or obviously concocted, that it would be foolhardy to try to unravel them all.

The bitter rivalry between different factions within the ANC – most prominently those aligned to Thabo Mbeki and to Jacob Zuma – was speeding towards a dramatic culmination in 2007 as the ruling party readied itself for its national conference in Polokwane in December. It was within the context of this leadership feud that some of the country's most enduring conspiracy theories came into being.

Back in 2001, business barons and long-standing ANC members Tokyo Sexwale, Mathews Phosa and Cyril Ramaphosa were implicated by then safety and security minister Steve Tshwete in a plot to undermine, maybe even overthrow, the Mbeki administration.[1] There was even talk of their alleged intention to physically harm the president in order to achieve their objective.[2] Though all three strongly denied the allegations, Mbeki deemed the matter serious enough to discuss it on national television.

'It's a conspiratorial thing,' he told e.tv. 'I know you have business people who say, "We will set up a fund to promote our particular candidate and we will then try to influence particular journalists".'[3] He called for those with more information to come forward and assist in the official government investigation that had been launched to probe the matter.

But the story eventually fizzled out amid whispers that the Mbeki camp had deliberately spread the rumours about the alleged coup in order to strengthen his position ahead of the ANC's 2002 elective conference.

Fast-forward to 2006 and it was Zuma and his supporters' turn to claim that they were the victims of a conspiracy. It had been a particularly unpleasant time for Zuma. Less than a year earlier, Mbeki had fired him as deputy president when he became implicated in alleged corrupt dealings related to the now-infamous arms deal and involving Schabir Shaik, his former financial advisor. Then, in December 2005, he was charged with raping an HIV-positive woman. His supporters immediately jumped to his defence, claiming that the rape charges and the allegations of corruption were part of a plot to sabotage Zuma's chances of successfully challenging Mbeki at the national conference in Polokwane in 2007. Despite his camp's enthusiasm, things did not look good for the former deputy president.

But come May 2006, Zuma stood victorious outside the High Court in Johannesburg, having been cleared of the rape charges. Emboldened by the outcome, Team Zuma repeated their earlier claim that the charges were part of a grand conspiracy.[4] They carried such talk right to the doorstep of the Polokwane conference. In November 2007, mere weeks before the start of the gathering, then defence minister, ANC chairperson and staunch Mbeki ally Mosiuoa Lekota accused Zuma of being 'divisive'. Zuma hit back by saying that Lekota was part of the 'political conspiracy' against him.[5]

Mbeki was standing for a third term as ANC president, but would be unable to serve a third term as president of the country. It was believed that one of his allies would become national president, and that Mbeki would run the show from behind the scenes.

The conference itself was an all-out slugfest, with the two main opposing groups accusing one another of vote rigging, among other things.[6] When some of the Mbekites arrived at the venue on the first day, they were loudly booed by the 4 000 delegates who would soon vote for the party's top six leaders, as well as for the remaining positions on the National Executive Committee (NEC), the party's highest decision-making body.[7] Things were looking very bad for Mbeki and his allies.

In the end, the booing was backed up by actual votes – on the third day of the conference, the delegates were informed that Zuma had defeated Mbeki by 2 329 votes to 1 505.[8] Apart from his pending corruption trial, Zuma's ascent to the Union Buildings seemed all but guaranteed.

The topic of Mbeki's defeat at Polokwane has been discussed at length over the years, analysed to its core by dozens of political commentators, journalists and authors. Many reasons have been proffered for Mbeki's demise: his infamous aloofness; the alienation of the ANC's leftist alliance partners, driven by the enrichment of a small group of black economic empowerment (BEE) barons at the expense of the majority, thanks to the administration's narrow implementation of its economic empowerment policy; the controversies around Mbeki's handling of HIV/AIDS; and so on.

Now, with the benefit of hindsight, it is tempting to reassess Zuma's rise to power through the lens of a bit of Gupta-theory. It is not as far-fetched as you might imagine. There are multiple sets of Gupta fingerprints that suggest the family played a bigger role in Zuma's good fortune than anyone now seems to remember, or cares to admit.

Sexwale, one of the alleged co-conspirators in the rumoured anti-Mbeki plot of 2001, is Exhibit A. Two unrelated events on two consecutive days in September 2006 serve as a good starting point for my theory.

On 20 September 2006, Jacob Zuma's political life was suddenly and unexpectedly revived when Pietermaritzburg High Court judge Herbert Msimang struck the former deputy president's corruption charges from the roll, citing the NPA's poor preparation for the case as the reason for his decision. While Msimang's ruling did not completely shut the door on future efforts by the NPA to charge Zuma with the same arms deal–related counts of corruption, fraud and racketeering, the development was seen as a major boost for Zuma's bid to oust Mbeki.[9]

The previous day, 19 September, the Guptas' Sahara Holdings had made a big announcement about significant changes to the group's shareholding structure. Sexwale's Mvelaphanda Holdings, which had been active mainly in the mining sector, and Lazarus Zim's Afripalm Consortium would each acquire a 12 per cent stake in Sahara Holdings.[10]

It was a particularly sweet deal for Sexwale and Zim. Sahara had decided to sell the stake for R173 million, a figure that reflected a 33 per cent 'BEE discount' which the Guptas had granted their new partners.[11] As if the discount was not enough of a sweetener, Sexwale and Zim were only required to advance altogether R15 million of their own money. A large chunk of the purchase price of R173 million was covered by the Guptas themselves, who had extended 'vendor finance' to their new partners worth R73 million. One of South Africa's major banks contributed a further R85 million worth of financing to the purchase price.[12]

At the time, Zim spoke to *Finweek* about the origins of the deal: 'Both Tokyo and I have been friends of the Gupta family for some time and eventually it got to the point where we said it was high time we got into business together.'[13]

It was apparent throughout 2007 that Sexwale, a prominent ANC member, intended to make himself available for the party's top spot at the upcoming December conference. Although the ANC's aversion to overt campaigning barred him from formally announcing his plans, there were clear indications that Sexwale had his sights set on becoming the ANC's next president. In August, the *Mail & Guardian* reported that his campaign was 'gathering momentum'. An Mbeki supporter from within the intelligence community told the newspaper that Sexwale's bid would boost Mbeki's chances of re-election, seeing as the business tycoon would draw votes from people who would otherwise have voted for Zuma if it had been a two-horse race.[14]

But a few days before the conference was set to begin, Sexwale pulled out of the contest and instead threw his weight behind Zuma.[15] Appearing alongside Zuma at a gathering of ANC members in the Eastern Cape, Sexwale said that no ANC leader 'should be there forever', an obvious reference to Mbeki. 'Cadres, when you go to Limpopo you must be wary of people offering you money to buy away your vote. You should not be sell-outs,' he told the audience.[16] (In light of the 2006 Sahara deal and his subsequent about-turn in the leadership contest, Sexwale's words now seem deeply ironic.) The sudden move must have stunned Mbeki and his supporters, who were left to face the 'Zunami' on their own.

In an assessment of the 2007 Polokwane conference, seasoned political journalist Jan-Jan Joubert described Sexwale's role in Mbeki's demise as 'pivotal'.[17] Given what has since transpired in terms of the Guptas' influence over senior ANC figures, I am left wondering whether Sexwale's earlier BEE deal with Sahara and his subsequent political ambush of Mbeki are more than mere coincidence. It raises questions as to whether Sexwale ever had any serious intention of becoming ANC president. I sent him a detailed set of questions about his relationship with the Guptas, and explicitly asked him whether the family had in any way influenced his decision to abandon his own campaign in favour of Zuma. Sexwale never responded to my queries.

An interesting titbit concerning Sexwale's Sahara deal is the involvement of Vusi Mavimbela, a former director general of the National Intelligence

Agency (NIA) during the Mbeki administration who would eventually be appointed director general in the Presidency under Zuma.

Mavimbela was one of the ANC's Russian-trained spooks. He served as Mbeki's intelligence and security advisor during the latter's term as deputy president, and then in 1999 was appointed director general of the NIA. In 2004, he left the civil service for the private sector, eventually joining Sexwale's Mvelaphanda Holdings in 2005.[18] As group executive director of business strategy at Mvelaphanda, Mavimbela was quoted in news reports about the 2006 Sahara deal. 'Mvelaphanda Holdings has selected Sahara and Afripalm Consortium as strategic broad-based black economic empowerment partners based on the credentials of these established organizations,' he said at the time.[19]

In 2009, somewhat surprisingly, Mavimbela returned to the public sector when Zuma appointed him as director general in the Presidency. He was one of the few officials who had served under Mbeki to be appointed to the new administration. But more significantly, there was now a Gupta business associate in Zuma's office. A year later, however, Mavimbela was replaced as director general amid speculation that he had had a falling-out with Zuma.[20]

Exhibit B takes the form of two short news articles pulled from the online vaults of websites dedicated to South Africa's IT sector.

On Wednesday 19 December 2007, the day after Zuma so convincingly booted Mbeki off of his ANC throne, *IT-Online* ran an article that highlighted the successful running of an internet café at the Polokwane conference.[21] The internet café, it turned out, was sponsored by none other than the Guptas' Sahara Computers.

According to the article, the event organisers had identified 'internet connectivity and digital resources ... as a priority', after which Sahara 'agreed to set up and fully equip an onsite Internet cafe'. Sahara's offering had included a free WiFi service, 'access points with full connectivity', internet and email. Gary Naidoo, Sahara's then managing director, was quoted: 'Technology can play a very important role in conferences of this magnitude, taking place at this level. Connectivity is imperative to facilitate realtime communication, which can make a meaningful difference.'[22]

Several weeks later, Sahara 'confirmed' in an article on *ITWeb* that it had 'sponsored infrastructure to ensure reliable connectivity for an Internet

Café to be used by delegates at the 52nd ANC Conference'.[23] This time Naidoo described Sahara as a 'recognised supplier to government, a key focus area for the company'. The fact that Sahara felt it needed to 'confirm' its sponsorship of the internet café suggests that there may have been questions about it, although there appear to be no media articles or any other reports on the matter dating from that time.

Sahara's, and by extension the Guptas', presence at Polokwane is note-worthy. Running the internet café could have put them in a powerful position during the all-important conference. It would not have been dif-ficult for Sahara's technical staff to keep tabs on who the delegates were in contact with after they had logged onto the Sahara computers. Their control over the digital information flow before the vote for the ANC's top positions could have provided the Guptas with an opportunity to deter-mine which way the wind was blowing in terms of the leadership battle.

Nic Wolpe, the son of anti-apartheid activists Harold and AnnMarie Wolpe and the person responsible for managing the networking tent at Polokwane, says the internet café provided by Sahara represented only a small benefit-in-kind contribution to the event. 'It was minimal compared to what others gave and provided,' he recalls. As had been the case with all the other benefactors, Wolpe had had to 'work to secure their support', he says. 'It wasn't like I sat back in my office and they came to me and said what can they do to assist.'

According to Wolpe, the idea to approach Sahara had come from Mendi Msimang, the ANC's then treasurer general. Msimang, whose ten-ure as treasurer general included an array of financial scandals involving the ANC, did not respond to queries about how or why he picked Sahara Computers to supply the internet café.

Exhibit C provides compelling evidence that the Guptas were directly involved in Zuma's electioneering efforts in the period between the Polo-kwane conference in 2007 and the 2009 general elections.

After Zuma was sworn in as South Africa's new president, journalists Carol Paton and Thebe Mabanga co-wrote an article in which they pon-dered which individuals from the business world would be allowed into the inner circle of the country's newly elected president.[24]

After naming the familiar businesspeople with whom Zuma was asso-ciated, including Vivian Reddy, Sandile Zungu and Robert Gumede, Paton and Mabanga introduced Atul Gupta as a Zuma-linked businessman who had been 'flying a little lower under the radar' but who had started to become 'a more visible ANC and Zuma supporter' in recent months. What is most interesting about this article, however, is a brief reference to Zuma's travel arrangements during the 2009 election campaign. 'Gupta and Tokyo Sexwale, who own private jets and helicopters, have seen to Zuma's transport needs during the election campaign,' wrote the journalists.[25] If true, this revelation supports the notion that the Guptas and Sexwale pursued the same political objective after they became business partners in 2006 – namely, the eventual election of Zuma as South Africa's president.

An article in the July 2008 edition of the investigative magazine *Noseweek* had also mentioned 'talk' by the Guptas themselves that they had been 'regularly flying Jacob Zuma in their private jet to his campaign engagements'.[26]

And then there's the matter of Exhibit D: Zuma's offspring. As the newly elected ANC president was preparing for the 2009 general elections, Duduzane Zuma and his twin sister, Duduzile, were appointed directors in a string of companies in which one or more of the Gupta brothers were also directors.

In July 2008, Duduzane, who had been working for the Guptas since at least 2003, became a director of Mabengela Investments alongside Rajesh Gupta. Mabengela would later serve as Duduzane's doorway into the lucrative Tegeta coal-supply deal. Two months later, in September 2008, he was made a director of Westdawn Investments, where Rajesh and several other Gupta associates were also directors. In less than two and a half years after he assumed his first directorship within the Gupta business empire, Duduzane had become a director in a further eleven Gupta-linked companies, according to CIPC records.[27]

Duduzile Zuma, meanwhile, had been appointed as a director of Sahara Computers in June 2008. She also became a director of Sahara Systems and Sahara Consumables in October of that year, according to CIPC records.

The fact that the Guptas gave Zuma's children multiple business opportunities suggests a deep investment in the fortunes of Zuma and his family. It was in their interests not only to see Zuma succeed, but also to court him in order to ensure a future return on investment. To this end they mingled socially with Zuma during this time. Several sources who have done work for Sahara Computers say that Zuma attended functions and parties hosted by the Guptas in 2007 and 2008. One such function was a year-end party held at a house in Killarney, Johannesburg, where part of the Gupta clan lived. Zuma also made an appearance at a Sahara year-end function held at Gallagher Estate, according to sources.

It is worth reviewing the string of events connecting the Guptas to Zuma in the years leading up to the latter's dramatic rise to power.

Circa 1998, Atul Gupta allegedly tells John, the businessman from Chapter 2, that the family had become acquainted with an ANC politician named Jacob Zuma. As an unverified claim from a single source, this does not constitute a very strong piece of evidence, but viewed within the context of what then transpired, it is certainly worth mentioning.

In around 2001, Zuma introduces his son Duduzane to the Guptas,[28] after which Duduzane is employed by Sahara Computers in 2003.[29]

In 2006, the Guptas make an unbelievably generous offer to ANC-big-wig-cum-businessman Tokyo Sexwale to become a shareholder of Sahara. Subsequently, in a move that stuns many, Sexwale in 2007 abolishes his plans to contest the position for ANC president and instead throws his support behind Zuma at Polokwane, a development viewed as one of the major contributing factors to Zuma's victory. The equipment used by the delegates at said conference to communicate with the outside world happens to be supplied by the Guptas' Sahara Computers.

Almost directly after the conference, two of Zuma's children are made directors of several Gupta companies, and Zuma himself socialises with the family during this time.

Finally, the Guptas and Sexwale make their various private jets and helicopters available to Zuma during his campaign for the 2009 general elections.

While none of this constitutes proof that the Guptas were involved in a plot to ensure Zuma's rise to power, these developments do raise questions about the family's role in their friend's political coup. And subsequent events certainly add fuel to this grand-conspiracy theory's fire.

7

The Sishen saga

It is 11 February 2010. The buzz around the Parliament buildings in Cape Town has mostly fizzled out as members of Parliament, dignitaries and other guests listen to President Jacob Zuma's second annual State of the Nation Address.

About three-quarters into his speech, Zuma makes what would become a customary reference to his administration's supposed attempts to curtail corruption.

'We continue our efforts to eradicate corruption and fraud in procurement and tender processes,' Zuma tells the country.[1] There is no heckling from the opposition. The Economic Freedom Fighters have not been formed yet, so the anarchy that they fuel in the National Assembly is a few years away. The Democratic Alliance (DA) is not yet as vocally cynical as it will later become during Zuma's tenure.

'Our Inter-Ministerial Committee on Corruption is looking at ways to decisively defeat corruption,' Zuma promises the nation.

But even as he supposedly commits himself to this earnest undertaking, the Guptas and Zuma's own family are well under way with some pretty dubious business deals. One such deal involves Duduzane Zuma and a company called Imperial Crown Trading (ICT), and is set to become the first large-scale scandal following the young Zuma's absorption into the Gupta business empire, namely the Sishen iron ore saga.

The deal's genesis, coincidentally, can be traced back to 30 April 2009, nine days before Jacob Zuma was sworn in as South Africa's new president. Since 2001, Africa's largest steel manufacturer, ArcelorMittal South Africa, had held a 21.4 per cent stake in the Sishen mine, one of the largest iron ore reserves in the world. The other 78.6 per cent was held by the Sishen Iron Ore Company, a subsidiary of Kumba Iron Ore, the majority shareholder of which is the international mining conglomerate Anglo

American plc. Situated near the town of Kathu in the Northern Cape, the Sishen mine was Sishen Iron Ore's most prized asset.

ArcelorMittal's old-order mining rights to the Sishen mine were set to expire on 30 April 2009 in accordance with the Mineral and Petroleum Resources Development Act of 2002. In order to maintain their stake in the mine, ArcelorMittal had to apply for new-order mining rights from the Department of Mineral Resources (DMR), but the company mysteriously failed to do so, allowing its rights to expire. When it became apparent that ArcelorMittal's old-order rights would cease to exist, Kumba/Sishen Iron Ore decided to apply for the minority rights.[2]

But they were not the only ones. On 4 May, the DMR supposedly received two applications to secure the rights previously held by Arcelor-Mittal: one from the Sishen Iron Ore Company and another from Imperial Crown Trading 289 (Pty) Ltd. The fact that it seemed as if both companies had applied for the mineral rights on the same day is important, because the Mineral and Petroleum Resources Development Act allows rights to be administered on a 'first-in, first-assessed' basis. In November, the DMR awarded ICT a prospecting right in relation to the residual undivided 21.4 per cent of the Sishen mine 'because they had better BEE policies than Kumba's Sishen Iron Ore Company'. Because both applications were allegedly received at the same time, the department was in its right to take into account factors such as empowerment policies when assessing the competing applications.[3]

The unknown shelf company, which had been registered just seven months before it applied for the stake in the Sishen mine, had no apparent footprint in the mining industry and there were questions from the outset over whether political connections had helped ICT in its bid to secure a slice of the lucrative mine. Prudence 'Gugu' Mtshali, the long-term romantic partner of former president Kgalema Mothlante, was a director and shareholder of ICT.[4]

Fearing that the prospecting rights awarded to ICT would later be converted to fully fledged mining rights, on 1 March 2010 Sishen lodged an appeal against the DMR's granting of a prospecting right to ICT.[5]

Enter the Guptas. On 12 March 2010, a month after Zuma's State of the Nation Address, a company called Pragat Investments secured 50 per cent of ICT's shares. Pragat's sole shareholder was none other than Gupta associate and business partner Jagdish Parekh, then CEO and a share-holder of JIC Mining Services, a company controlled by the Gupta brothers and Duduzane Zuma.[6] There were suggestions in the media at the time that Parekh's Pragat Investments was actually controlling the stake in ICT on behalf of JIC. According to Jan de Lange of *Fin24*, 'it's highly unlikely that [Parekh] owns this stake in his personal capacity – that would make him one of the richest people in the country overnight. He probably represents JIC as the actual shareholder.'[7]

In an interview with the *Mail & Guardian* on 21 May, however, Ajay Gupta distanced his family from ICT, saying that Parekh's 50 per cent stake in the company that had been awarded Sishen prospecting rights had nothing to do with them.[8]

Meanwhile, coincidentally on the same day in May, Sishen instituted review proceedings against ICT and the DMR in the North Gauteng High Court, Pretoria, essentially seeking to overturn the DMR's decision. The legal battle would last for more than three years and would go all the way to South Africa's highest court.

Then, in August 2010, Kumba opened up a case of corruption with the police's Directorate for Priority Crime Investigation (DPCI), commonly known as the Hawks, when it emerged that ICT may have obtained the prospecting rights in a fraudulent manner.[9] This included allegedly copying necessary supporting documents from Sishen's own application, which it could only have done with the help of DMR officials;[10] and forging signatures from a drilling company and fabricating geologist reports.[11]

It also transpired that while ICT's application was stamped by the DMR as received on 4 May 2009, the signature on the application form was clearly marked 5 May and key accompanying documents attached to the application were dated 8 and 9 May.[12] In other words, it appeared that ICT had not actually submitted a complete application on 4 May. As mining and prospecting rights are supposed to be handled by the DMR on a first-come, first-serve basis, and as Kumba had submitted its complete application by 4 May, ICT's should not even have been considered.

But the DMR and ICT both insisted that the application had been submitted in time. In other court action, they even alleged that Kumba had failed to 'play by the book when submitting their application' by actually handing in their mining rights application prematurely, on Friday 30 April, the day that ArcelorMittal's rights were set to expire. It appears that Sishen made arrangements with officials to stamp their application as received on 1 May, a public holiday. Sishen's application fee was then only receipted on 4 May. ICT and the DMR 'were not happy with the premature lodging of … Sishen's application on April 30'.[13]

While Kumba and Sishen were battling the DMR and ICT, Arcelor-Mittal and Kumba were engaged in a skirmish of their own. ArcelorMittal's failure to renew its mining rights' stake in the Sishen mine allowed Kumba 'to find a legal loophole to wrangle its way out of a nine-year agreement to supply Arcelor Mittal with iron ore, at preferential prices'.[14] Arcelor-Mittal, however, insisted the favourable pricing deal still stood, with the result that the two companies became locked in arbitration proceedings.[15]

But ArcelorMittal was clearly not prepared to take any chances with its future supply of cheap iron ore. Instead of sitting back and waiting for the arbitration with Kumba to come to an end, the steel giant announced on 10 August 2010 that it would buy ICT for a staggering R800 million, conditional on ICT being awarded the Sishen mining rights. In addition, shareholders in ICT would be included in ArcelorMittal's R9.1-billion BEE deal.[16]

This is where it gets interesting: ArcelorMittal's proposed BEE transaction would see it 'sell' 21 per cent of its shares to the Ayigobi Consortium,[17] 'a BEE special purpose vehicle that provided for the economic empowerment of women, youth and other strategic groups'.[18] The Ayigobi Consortium included, maybe unsurprisingly at this point, the Guptas' Oakbay Investments, Duduzane Zuma and Rajesh Gupta's Mabengela Investments and Jagdish Parekh's Pragat Investments. The Guptas and their associates were now poised to benefit greatly from the Sishen saga and could no longer deny their involvement.

Almost immediately after the ArcelorMittal deal was announced, questions were asked as to how an Indian-born family who had emigrated from India in 1993 could be cut into a BEE transaction, in seeming contravention of South Africa's empowerment legislation. When questioned about the matter, Sandile Zungu, the head of the Ayigobi Consortium, told *City Press*: 'The Guptas brokered the deal and brought ICT and ArcelorMittal together. How else should they have been rewarded?'[19] ArcelorMittal itself admitted that the Guptas had played a central role in the huge transaction.

The company's CEO, Nonkululeko Nyembezi-Heita, told *Moneyweb* that the Guptas were 'major facilitators' of the deal. 'We've only ever dealt with those two individuals or entities … By the time we did start engaging with ICT, we were engaging with the Guptas and Parekh,' she said. Furthermore, Nyembezi-Heita revealed that talks had begun in about March or April 2010, meaning that when Ajay Gupta was distancing his family from ICT and from rumours that were circulating about a possible deal with ArcelorMittal, they were already involved in negotiations.[20]

Whatever the validity of the Guptas' involvement, the multibillion-rand marriage between ArcelorMittal and the Ayigobi Consortium, along with ArcelorMittal's purchase of ICT, was not a done deal. ICT still needed to properly secure the prospecting rights, and eventually the mining rights, of the 21.4 per cent slice of the Sishen mine.

A week after ArcelorMittal announced its intention to buy ICT and do a BEE deal with the Ayigobi Consortium, mining minister Susan Shabangu dismissed the Sishen Iron Ore Company's appeal. At a press conference she said that her department had 'sent a letter to Kumba informing them that the decision of the DMR to grant a prospecting right to ICT will be upheld', adding that 'the law is clear when it comes to applying for prospecting rights, it's based on a first come–first served basis, and when two companies apply for the same right, the company with a stronger BEE status is given first preference'.[21] She made no reference to the fact that there were troubling questions over the actual date of submission of ICT's complete application and alleged fraud relating to some of its supporting documents.

The South African government had clearly decided to side with ICT in the ongoing battle over the Sishen mining rights. With the benefit of hindsight, it now seems overwhelmingly obvious that the Guptas probably lobbied Shabangu and government during the early days of the Sishen saga.

A few days after Shabangu's announcement, *Business Day* reported on a state visit to the UK that Jacob Zuma had undertaken in March. He had been accompanied by a business delegation of over a hundred South African businesspeople, including Nyembezi-Heita, Ajay Gupta, Parekh and Kumba chairman Lazarus Zim. According to a senior source at Kumba, Gupta, Zuma and Nyembezi-Heita had 'informal conversations' during the trip with Cynthia Carroll and Chris Griffith, the then CEOs of Anglo

American and Kumba respectively. The main theme of these talks appeared to be Kumba's cancellation of its favourable iron ore–supply agreement with ArcelorMittal. According to the source, 'Zuma wanted to know how is it possible for everyone to win'. Carroll, for her part, denied that any such meetings took place.[22]

During my own research, I spoke to sources familiar with the Sishen saga who corroborated that these conversations did indeed take place. They claimed that the purpose of the meetings had been to either strong-arm or coax Anglo into convincing its subsidiary Kumba to cease fighting for the stake in the Sishen mine. Given later revelations about current mining minister Mosebenzi Zwane's 2015 trip to Switzerland to assist the Guptas in their negotiations with Glencore, the claims about what transpired in the UK are not far-fetched. Whatever the truth, it is interesting to note that Parekh became a 50 per cent shareholder in ICT within a month after the UK visit.

Something that is not in dispute is Shabangu's personal friendship with the Guptas. In March 2011, Ajay Gupta admitted in an interview with *City Press* that Shabangu was among a group of top-level government leaders who regularly visited them at their home in Saxonwold.[23] Shabangu would also later be one of the many VIP guests at Vega Gupta's controversial wedding at Sun City in 2013.[24] And it seems unlikely that their relationship was purely social in nature.

One source, a former senior government official, recalled attending a government lekgotla at the Bryntirion Estate in Pretoria in 2010. At lunchtime, Shabangu and the DMR's then director general, Sandile Nogxina, indicated that they had to leave to attend a meeting with Ajay Gupta and President Zuma. The meeting was supposed to have taken place at the nearby Sheraton Hotel, said the source, but then Shabangu received a phone call from Ajay Gupta. 'He told her that the meeting would take place at Mahlamba Ndlopfu [the official presidential residence located in the Bryntirion Estate].' Shabangu apparently seemed a bit unsure about the change of location, so she approached Zuma, who was also at the lekgotla, to ask him if he knew about it. According to my source, Zuma confirmed that the meeting would take place at his official residence.

Another source, a former Gupta employee who worked in Ajay and Atul Gupta's office at Sahara Computers in Midrand, Johannesburg, recalled that there were meetings scheduled between Shabangu and the Gupta brothers in 2011 – in other words, while the Sishen saga was playing out. 'I remember one specific time when Ajay's bodyguards had to drive out to Centurion, because they had to go and secure a location where Ajay and Atul were due to meet with Susan Shabangu,' said the former employee.

In January 2011, news broke that ICT had applied to the DMR for a bona fide mining right to the 21.4 per cent stake of the Sishen mine on 9 December 2010. The application was accepted by the DMR on 23 December. Seeing as ICT's prospecting right was still being challenged in court, the Sishen Iron Ore Company said it did not 'believe that it was lawful for the Department of Mineral Resources to have accepted ICT's application, pending the high court review initiated in May 2010'.[25]

As if to confirm that it had chosen to side with ICT in the ongoing dispute, the DMR sent a letter to Sishen at the end of January 2011 informing the company that its application for the 21.4 per cent stake of the mine had been rejected. The letter, signed by Nogxina, stated that Sishen's 'application was submitted prematurely and in an irregular, misleading and fraudulent manner'.[26] Again, the department seemed completely dismissive of any allegations that it had been ICT who had committed fraud.

The SAPS, however, were not so trusting. Thanks to the criminal charges brought by Kumba against ICT and the DMR in August 2010, an investigation got under way and in July 2011 the Hawks raided two of ICT's business premises along with two offices of the DMR. 'Our operation resulted in the seizure of documents which the Hawks need for further investigations. We are busy investigating charges of forgery, uttering, corruption and fraud,' said Hawks spokesperson McIntosh Polela in a statement.[27]

At one point, it even seemed likely that the matter would lead to criminal prosecution. But Glynnis Breytenbach, the fierce state prosecutor leading the case, was forced to withdraw from the matter after ICT's lawyer, Ronnie Mendelow, lodged a complaint against her with the NDPP. On 31 October 2011, Mendelow accused Breytenbach of having an improperly close relationship with Mike Hellens, Sishen's legal counsel, and of allowing Hellens to dictate the terms of the NPA's Sishen probe. The accusation, which was never proved, would later form a key part of a disciplinary hearing against Breytenbach, in which the NPA ultimately suffered a decisive defeat. Nevertheless, Breytenbach withdrew from the ICT case just shy of a month after being told that a complaint had been laid against her. Her departure apparently signalled the death of the ICT probe.[28]

Meanwhile, at the end of May 2011, ArcelorMittal stunned everyone when it announced that it would join the Sishen Iron Ore Company in its court bid against ICT and the DMR. In its supporting affidavit, Arcelor-Mittal now argued that the Sishen Iron Ore Company should have been given 100 per cent of the mining rights at the Sishen mine when their old-order rights were converted to new-order rights in 2008.[29]

The development did not bode well for Duduzane Zuma, the Guptas and the other members of the Ayigobi Consortium. It was viewed as an early indication that the massive R9-billion empowerment deal between the steel giant and the consortium of well-connected businesspeople, as well as ArcelorMittal's purchase of ICT, would not go ahead. There was quite a bit of speculation over ArcelorMittal's sudden U-turn, but the company probably simply realised that it would save R800 million if the court ruled in its favour and it did not have to buy ICT in order to maintain its supply of cheap iron ore. All indications were that ArcelorMittal and Kumba would instead try to negotiate a new supply agreement. In addition, for months leading up to the decision, ArcelorMittal had been under tremendous pressure from many of its shareholders over the dubious nature of the pending BEE transaction with the politically connected Ayigobi Consortium.[30] Apart from saving tons of money, the company probably realised that it would also save face if the deal with the Guptas and their partners did not go ahead.

In September 2011, ArcelorMittal finally announced that the deal with the Ayigobi Consortium was off the table, saying that the time frame within which the deal had to be concluded had lapsed.[31] But there were strong indications that the company had canned the transaction after a due diligence found it would have been in breach of local and international anti-corruption legislation.[32] ArcelorMittal's backtracking meant that the Guptas and Duduzane Zuma had to watch as earmarked shares worth more than R1.5 billion slipped through their fingers.[33]

Parekh and ICT ultimately fared no better in their court battle against the Sishen Iron Ore Company. In December 2011, Judge Raymond Zondo of the North Gauteng High Court found that when Sishen converted its mining right in 2008, it had been awarded 100 per cent of the mining right and was thus the sole holder of the mining rights over Sishen. The DMR therefore had no right to grant a right to a third party, as it had done when it awarded a prospecting right to ICT in 2010.[34]

ICT and the DMR challenged Zondo's decision, but in March 2013 the Supreme Court of Appeal dismissed their appeal.[35] The matter then went to the Constitutional Court, where Justice Chris Jafta in December 2013 concluded 'that Sishen is the only party competent to apply for and be granted the mining right'.[36]

8

Nuclear family

The Guptas' mining ambitions were not limited to iron. In December 2008, they had begun negotiations to get their hands on one of South Africa's largest uranium deposits.[1] The Dominion uranium mine, located outside Klerksdorp in the North West province, was owned by Canadian mining company Uranium One when the family began to show interest in buying it. At the time, the mine's operations were on hold after Uranium One had placed Dominion 'on care and maintenance' in October 2008 due to a 'significant deterioration in the Project's economics' associated with a worldwide decline in uranium prices.[2] Nevertheless, the Guptas were keen to take ownership of the asset.[3] The family's Oakbay Resources & Energy concluded a sale agreement with Uranium One in May 2009, and on 14 April 2010 Oakbay obtained a 74 per cent interest in Uranium One Africa, a subsidiary of Uranium One whose main asset was the Dominion mine, and renamed it Shiva Uranium.[4] At the beginning of May 2010, Uranium One announced that it had sold Dominion for $37.3 million (about R270 million at the time) in cash.[5]

It was apparent from the outset that President Zuma's son Duduzane was involved. Just four days after Uranium One's announcement, investigative journalists from amaBhungane reported that 'company registration documents show that Atul Gupta and Duduzane Zuma took over as directors of the Dominion holding company [Shiva Uranium] on April 14, the day the sale was finalised'.[6] On the same day, *Mining Weekly* reported that 'Duduzane Zuma would be on the Shiva board, which will be chaired by Atul Gupta'.[7] Incidentally, Jagdish Parekh, he of the Sishen saga, who had been made CEO of Shiva Uranium, said in a statement that a consortium of black investors had acquired 26 per cent of Shiva from Oakbay 'through a vendor-funded transaction'.[8] At the time it was reported that the consortium included Islandsite Investments 255, the MK Military Veterans

Association and its women's group, a local community trust and an employee trust. It did not take long for amaBhungane to uncover that Islandsite's majority shareholder was Mabengela Investments, of which Duduzane Zuma and Rajesh Gupta were both directors. Islandsite was essentially 'controlled by Duduzane Zuma and Rajesh, the youngest of three Gupta brothers'.[9]

But Duduzane's involvement apparently did not end there. In the same *Mail & Guardian* article, amaBhungane revealed that the Guptas were seeking state-sector investment in the mine, specifically from the Public Investment Corporation (PIC), a government-owned investment entity that manages government investments worth more than R1.8 trillion.[10] When the sale was announced, Oakbay Resources & Energy said it had secured part of the funding for the Dominion transaction from the state-owned Industrial Development Corporation (IDC). But now there was talk of the PIC investing too. It appeared as if the transaction would be made possible thanks to a fair amount of dubious-looking manoeuvring behind the scenes by Duduzane's father and president of the republic, Jacob Zuma, and the PIC's then CEO Brian Molefe. Molefe's tenure as PIC boss had been due to come to an end on 12 April 2010, two days before the Dominion mine deal was finalised, when his contract was suddenly and inexplicably extended for three months. According to a *Sunday Times* report at the time, 'following intense lobbying by Molefe's supporters and well-known businessmen', President Zuma had 'personally intervened' to ensure that Molefe was retained. 'Zuma is understood to have phoned a senior official in the finance ministry to ask that Molefe remain in the job,' the newspaper alleged.[11] A source quoted in the amaBhungane report said that Zuma had in fact called then deputy minister of finance Nhlanhla Nene, who was also PIC chairperson at the time, a week before Molefe's contract was due to expire to request that he be kept on. The source added that it was the Guptas who had lobbied Zuma to ensure Molefe stayed on, as they were expecting the latter to green-light PIC funding for the purchase of Dominion.[12]

Molefe would later be excoriated in the public protector's 2016 'State of Capture' report for his close relationship with the Guptas during his tenure as CEO of Eskom. Many commentators have traced his capture by the infamous family to his time at the PIC. An Mbekite despised by the Zuma coterie, Molefe found himself out of favour, vulnerable and alone after Polokwane. It was in his hour of need, or so people surmise, that the Guptas approached him, ensnared him and 'facilitated a rapprochement' with Zuma. By the time Molefe moved on to his next position, as CEO of Transnet in 2011, 'there were murmurs in ANC and government circles that this was a Gupta appointment'.[13]

In the end, the PIC investment did not materialise. Perhaps Zuma, Molefe and the Guptas were a little rattled by the media attention that the would-be loan had attracted. AmaBhungane had summed it up well: 'Duduzane's participation [in Shiva Uranium] leaves the president exposed to the accusation that his reported intervention last month to extend the tenure of controversial Public Investment Corporation (PIC) boss Brian Molefe was designed to smooth negotiations towards a large PIC investment in the project.'[14] Perhaps the whole affair had just become too compromising for the president.

When Oakbay Resources & Energy listed on the JSE at the end of 2014, the public saw for the first time just how much money the IDC had poured into the Shiva transaction. According to the company's mandatory pre-listing statement, the state-owned investment entity had loaned Oakbay R250 million of the R270 million it needed to buy Dominion.[15] But that was not the most controversial aspect of the revelation. After carefully analysing Oakbay's financials, amaBhungane reported that the company was supposed to have repaid its IDC loan by April 2013, but it had been unable to do so because it had not generated enough profit from Shiva Uranium. By February 2014, Oakbay had only managed to repay R20 million. By then, the company's obligation to the IDC, which included interest on the original loan, had swelled to R399 million.[16]

It seemed the Guptas were in trouble, until once again a government entity proved more than willing to help them out. According to Oakbay's pre-listing statement, the IDC had agreed to restructure the loan agreement in June 2014. 'In terms of the IDC Loan Restructuring Agreement, the outstanding interest portion of the IDC Loan as at 31 May 2014 will be converted into equity in Oakbay,' read the statement. 'The total outstanding balance of the IDC Loan, being capital and interest as at 28 February 2014 was R398 909 000. Of this amount, R256 757 826, being outstanding interest, will be converted into equity on the Listing Date.' In lieu of repaying the almost R257 million worth of accrued interest, representing almost

65 per cent of the total debt, the IDC had agreed to take a measly roughly 3.6 per cent stake in Oakbay. Furthermore, the interest rate on the loan had been altered in favour of Oakbay; instead of having to pay the Johannesburg Interbank Agreed Rate plus 8 per cent per annum, as dictated by the original loan agreement, Oakbay now only had to pay interest at prime plus 2 per cent. On top of that, the repayment date for the remainder of the loan had been extended to 31 October 2018.[17]

The important question was whether the 28.5 million of Oakbay's 800 million issued shares which it gave to the IDC in lieu of the interest on the loan were really worth R257 million. Had the Guptas short-changed the IDC? There were strong indications that the shares were indeed worth much less. When Oakbay listed on the JSE in December 2014, its 800 million issued shares – at R10 a share – gave the company a value of R8 billion. In accordance with the restructured loan agreement, the IDC was given a 10 per cent discount and therefore 'paid' R9 per share.[18] But even this discounted price, according to amaBhungane, appeared overinflated. Oakbay's own interim financial results released at the end of August 2014 gave the company a net asset value of R4.6 billion, which translated into about R5.74 a share. Even worse, the valuer appointed as part of the JSE listing process valued the shares at just R4.84 each. Compare this to the R10 share price that Oakbay had listed when the IDC got its stake in the company, and the Guptas apparently received a discount of between R93 million and R119 million on the interest they owed.[19]

An interesting aspect of the Guptas' acquisition of the Dominion uranium mine is the tangential involvement of Russian state-owned nuclear energy corporation Rosatom in Uranium One. Rosatom has become inextricably linked to fears that South Africa's pending nuclear power plant expansion programme is drenched in large-scale corruption.

In June 2009, as the Guptas' Oakbay Resources & Energy was wrapping up its purchase agreement with Uranium One to buy the Dominion mine, Rosatom mining subsidiary AtomRedMetZoloto (ARMZ Uranium Holding Co.) obtained 16.6 per cent of Uranium One.[20] The transaction would be the start of ARMZ's wholesale takeover of the company. In 2010, ARMZ became the majority shareholder in Uranium One, before buying all of the Canadian company's remaining shares in 2013.[21]

In other words, the Guptas' purchase of the Dominion mine from Uranium One coincided with Rosatom's drive to become the sole shareholder of Uranium One. What this means is that Rosatom and the Guptas, in all likelihood, became acquainted with one another sometime during 2009, which happened to be President Jacob Zuma's first year in office. And as we all know, under Zuma's rule the South African government reignited its plans for investing in new nuclear power plants.

At the 2009 UN Climate Change Conference in Copenhagen, Zuma told delegates: 'With financial and technical support from developed countries, South Africa ... will be able to reduce [carbon] emissions by 34% below "business as usual" levels by 2020 and by 42% by 2025.'[22] According to the *Rand Daily Mail*, 'his announcement took both local and international commentators by surprise, but it revealed Zuma's nuclear ambitions'.[23] His ambitions were confirmed in 2011 when then energy minister Dipuo Peters announced that government planned to issue a tender for the construction of six new nuclear power plants.[24] It was subsequently widely reported that the programme could cost the country as much as R1 trillion, leading critics to ask how South Africa would afford it.

Zuma's government did not seem to share concerns over the affordability of the new nuclear power plants. In September 2014, Rosatom announced that it had signed a 'strategic partnership' agreement with the South African government that ensured the country would use Russian reactors in the upcoming build programme.[25] Seeing as government had been nowhere near to starting a competitive bid process for the nuclear contract, as is required by the South African constitution, Rosatom's announcement shocked and angered the nation. The outrage was so immense that both Rosatom and the South African government later backtracked on the announcement, claiming that government would sign similar agreements with other potential bidders. But the damage had been done. Today, many South Africans remain highly suspicious of government's plans to build the nuclear plants, especially when it comes to Rosatom's possible participation in the programme.

However, if the deal does finally go ahead, the demand for uranium in South Africa will certainly climb to unprecedented heights. The Guptas' Shiva Uranium – in which Duduzane Zuma has a sizeable stake – will be perfectly positioned to supply government with uranium for the new power plants.

Critics of the pending nuclear power programme have openly asked whether the Zuma administration's enthusiasm for nuclear power is not perhaps rooted in the fact that the president's son and the Guptas stand to benefit from it.

Veteran journalist Allister Sparks was but one of many who believe the Guptas are behind Zuma's nuclear ambitions. 'Nuclear power stations require enriched uranium to operate and, with advance knowledge of the president's intentions (Duduzane surely told his partners what daddy was up to), the Guptas stood to make a killing,' Sparks wrote in *Business Day* in 2016.[26]

As long as the Gupta–Zuma network remains intact, the potential disaster of a financially crippling nuclear deal remains on the horizon.

9

Spooked

Almost two years before the Hawks and the NPA started looking into the Sishen matter, several sets of eyes representing far more powerful interests were drawn to the Guptas for an entirely different reason.

At some point in 2009, the Central Intelligence Agency (CIA) and the Secret Intelligence Service (commonly known as MI6), the foreign intelligence services of the US and the UK respectively, got wind of the fact that one of South Africa's largest uranium deposits was about to change ownership. Given the potential for disaster if enriched uranium were to fall into the wrong hands, it should come as no surprise that the world's foremost intelligence services keep a very close eye on uranium mining and processing operations all over the world.

In the words of one former South African intelligence officer familiar with developments, America and Britain were 'not comfortable' when they learnt that the Guptas would be the Dominion mine's new owners.[1] Towards the end of 2009, the CIA and MI6 approached South Africa's newly formed State Security Agency (SSA), created in October 2009 to incorporate the formerly separate National Intelligence Agency, South African Secret Service and other local intelligence outfits.

'The Yanks and the Brits basically told us that they were concerned about a certain Gupta family taking control of the Dominion mine,' the former intelligence officer told me. 'The Guptas weren't very well known at that stage, so the CIA and MI6 asked us to help them keep an eye on the development and find out a little bit more about the family.' According to this source, the CIA and MI6 feared that the Guptas might sell uranium to a country like Pakistan. Although both India and Pakistan have nuclear arsenals, it is Pakistan's possession of such weapons that is most concerning for Western powers.

Unbeknown to the foreign intelligence agencies, the SSA was already well aware of the Guptas by this time. 'We knew they were close to [President] Zuma and that they were boasting about their close ties with several cabinet ministers,' another former role-player within South Africa's intelligence structures told me. Nevertheless, the request from overseas did prompt the SSA to put the Guptas on a formal list of issues to monitor.

'In early 2010, at our annual planning and strategy meeting, it was decided that the Guptas would formally become the target of an ongoing SSA probe,' said this second source. But instead of focusing on the potential export of weapons-grade uranium to countries such as Pakistan, the SSA decided to deal with the family as an 'economic intelligence threat', explained the former intelligence operative.

It would not take long for the SSA's Gupta file to become rather bulky. The agency gathered information on how the family did business with government departments and state-owned companies, and how the brothers Ajay, Atul and Rajesh were mingling socially with some of the country's most senior government officials. 'We became aware of social gatherings at the Guptas' estate in Saxonwold that were attended by ministers in Zuma's cabinet,' recounted the first source. 'This included an annual Diwali gathering they hosted at their house.'

The SSA started to compile a list of government ministers who appeared to be suspiciously close to the Guptas. It included then public enterprises minister Malusi Gigaba; then home affairs minister Nkosazana Dlamini-Zuma; then human settlements minister and Gupta business partner Tokyo Sexwale; then mining minister Susan Shabangu; and then minister of social development Edna Molewa.

The SSA was especially concerned about the Guptas' apparent influence over President Zuma. According to my second source, 'it is like they built a wall around the president. They controlled who had access to him.'

This became particularly evident during Zuma's first state visit to India in June 2010. The president was accompanied by a delegation of 200 South African businesspeople. The purpose of the trip was to foster business relations between India and South Africa, but it appeared to the SSA as if the Guptas had taken complete control of Zuma's itinerary. And they were not the only ones to notice.

Less than two months after Zuma's return to South Africa, the *Mail & Guardian* reported that there had been great unease among members of both the South African and the Indian delegation as a result of the Guptas' conduct. 'It was clear that they had organised things beforehand and took charge of at least some parts of his [Zuma's] diary,' a member of the South African delegation told the newspaper. Some South African government officials were apparently probed by their Indian counterparts as to why the Guptas enjoyed such a close relationship with Zuma. 'They were asked why the president is hanging around with these guys; they don't have a great reputation in India,' said a government source.[2] One businessman who was part of the delegation told me that the seating arrangements at some of the social events said everything about the relationship between the president and the Guptas: 'The Guptas sat at the main table with Zuma and his people. I am aware that this also happened on a number of other state visits after the India trip.'

Meanwhile, the SSA also learnt that the Guptas were putting undue pressure on the premiers of some of South Africa's nine provinces in the lead-up to the launch of their newspaper, *The New Age*, in December 2010. The Guptas allegedly wanted provincial governments to subscribe to the paper. Some of the premiers showed them the door, while others allegedly complied.

Around mid-2010, word about the SSA's monitoring of the Guptas reached Zuma. It would set off a chain of events that would culminate in the biggest crisis within the South African intelligence community since the restructuring of the intelligence services in 2009.

According to my sources, then state security minister Siyabonga Cwele summoned the country's top spy bosses to a meeting in Cape Town. Among those called to the meeting were SSA director general Jeff Maqetuka, head of foreign intelligence Moe Shaik and head of domestic intelligence Gibson Njenje. Cwele apparently told them in no uncertain terms that the SSA's probe into the Guptas was problematic. Both sources I spoke to said it was very clear to them that Cwele was under tremendous pressure to halt the investigation, and that such pressure had to have emanated from Zuma's office. But the trio of intelligence heads refused to back down. They remained adamant that the Guptas posed a security threat to South Africa and therefore needed to be kept under the magnifying glass.

Even more troubling than Zuma's alleged instruction to Cwele was the fact that the state security minister had also seemingly come under the influence of the Guptas. 'Cwele wanted the SSA to do business with the Guptas,' said my second source. And it is clear from at least one media report that the Guptas wanted to do business with the SSA. In 2013, two senior intelligence sources told the *Mail & Guardian* that the Guptas had approached Cwele in 2011 to try to sell interception and surveillance software to the country's intelligence services, but there were concerns within the agency about its potential for abuse. At the time, Cwele and the Guptas refused to comment on the matter.[3]

By mid-2011, the relationship between the minister and his three most senior intelligence bosses had deteriorated beyond the point of any possible reconciliation. According to my sources, Cwele kept on insisting that the SSA back off from their Gupta probe, but Njenje, Maqetuka and Shaik refused to budge. Something was bound to give.

Towards the end of 2011, Cwele made his move. In September, *City Press* reported that the minister had asked the three intelligence chiefs to quit the SSA.[4] Njenje was the first to resign. By the end of 2011, Maqetuka and Shaik had also left the agency. The trio's departure sent shock waves through the local intelligence community.

At the time, none of the media outlets reporting on the resignations picked up on the Guptas' role in the drama. *City Press* reported that a spat between the minister and his top intelligence officers over his drug-dealing wife was at the centre of their axing. Sheryl Cwele had been convicted in May 2011 for trafficking cocaine. According to *City Press*, Njenje, Maqetuka and Shaik had been deeply unhappy with the minister's alleged decision to provide his wife with SSA protection during her trial.[5]

When it became clear that Njenje would be the first of the three to leave the SSA, the *Sunday Independent* reported that his pending departure was linked to his unhappiness over the alleged abuse of the country's intelligence resources. According to the paper, Njenje was opposed to what he deemed to be politically motivated intelligence operations that were being carried out in the run-up to the ANC's 2012 elective conference.[6]

Njenje, Shaik and Maqetuka all kept their silence, and the SSA and Cwele succeeded in keeping any hint of an intelligence probe into the Guptas under wraps for more than a year. But the Waterkloof fiasco of 2013 would finally bring the issue to the surface. As government and the rest of the country were coming to terms with the Guptas' audacious stunt at the air force base, the *Daily Maverick* revealed for the first time that the SSA had been thoroughly aware of the Guptas' influence as early as 2011. The news site also reported that Njenje, Shaik and Maqetuka were all involved in an SSA probe into the family and that this had been the main reason for Cwele's decision to force them out of the agency.[7]

The ghost of the SSA's Gupta probe had come back to haunt Cwele, who now had to field some very uncomfortable questions over the real reason for the departure of his top officials in 2011. The DA vowed to grill Cwele over the issue in Parliament. 'If it is true that the Minister intervened [in the Gupta probe], then it would be very difficult to conclude that he intervened for any other reason than to protect President Jacob Zuma,' said David Maynier, the party's then spokesperson on defence and military veterans.[8]

Speaking at a press conference in Cape Town a week after the *Daily Maverick* report, Cwele's comments on the issue were defensive and contradictory: 'Did I stop the Gupta influence (on) government investigation? I can say categorically, "No". I'm not aware of such an investigation. But, as the minister responsible, what I also stop is the abuse of our intelligence capacity because we're supposed to control it.' He added that his department would not allow the use of intelligence 'platforms and capabilities to fight personal and individual battles, particularly business battles'.[9]

Cwele was denying that he had been aware of an SSA probe into the Guptas, but, at the same time, seemed to be intimating that Njenje, Shaik and Maqetuka had conducted a rogue operation driven by personal interests. If Cwele was referring to anything other than the Gupta probe, he did not provide further details as to the nature of the trio's supposedly rogue project.

The minister's comments prompted Njenje to break his silence. In an interview with the *Mail & Guardian* a few days later, he accused Cwele of lying when he said he was not aware of the SSA's monitoring of the Guptas. 'Why say there is no investigation and in the same breath say I was involved in an irregular investigation?' asked a livid Njenje. The former spy boss then indicated that he wanted the ruling party to take up the matter. 'I'm going to talk to the ANC about this. It has the potential to unravel a lot of things in the country ... There is a lot of information we picked up from intelligence [about the Guptas],' he told the newspaper.[10]

Despite Njenje's anger, the matter faded into the background as the public's outrage over the Waterkloof debacle eventually died down. But it floated to the surface once more after Mcebisi Jonas's dramatic claims in March 2016 about having been offered a ministerial post by the Guptas.

This time around, Njenje, Shaik and Maqetuka seemed more adamant than ever to see to it that the SSA's earlier discoveries about the Guptas be aired on the right platform. The three former intelligence bosses were among twenty-five former Umkhonto we Sizwe (MK) operatives who penned a memorandum harshly criticising the Zuma-led government over the latest allegations about the Guptas and state capture.[11] It also seemed likely that the three would assist the ANC in its internal state capture probe, which was to be led by ANC secretary general Gwede Mantashe.[12] In addition, Shaik spoke out on the issue for the first time, telling the *Mail & Guardian*, 'If I look at myself in the mirror and ask if I did the right thing as a government official to say the [SSA] investigation is necessary, yes I did. If I'm doing the right thing now to bring it under the attention of the ANC leadership, yes I am.'[13]

Little did Shaik and his former colleagues know that any attempt to assist Mantashe and the ANC would be in vain. Barely two months after the party launched its state capture probe, Mantashe announced that he was pulling the plug because not enough people were willing to cooperate.[14]

But it seemed that Mantashe had been very selective in what he chose to include in the scope of the investigation. After his announcement that the probe would be canned, the *Sunday Times* reported that Mantashe had apparently ignored the advice of former senior intelligence officers who said 'he should request an intelligence report on the Gupta family's state influence from the inspector-general of intelligence'. The report, allegedly compiled in 2010, was 'said to detail how the Guptas influenced the appointment of ministers and the awarding of government tenders'. 'At least one representative of the heads of intelligence did meet with Mantashe. But the dilemma was that you can't give an intelligence documentation to the ANC: you will be charged with revealing state secrets,' an 'intelligence insider' told the weekend paper. 'We advised as to how that process can be achieved by just approaching the inspector-general. We don't know if that advice was followed up at all.'[15]

What the *Sunday Times* failed to point out, however, was that there was no inspector general of intelligence to approach at that juncture. The important position had been vacant since the term of the previous inspector general, Faith Radebe, had come to an end in March 2015. Only in November 2016 did Parliament's joint standing committee on intelligence finally nominate a new candidate to fill the post.[16]

That being said, it seems unlikely that Mantashe would have gone out of his way to get hold of the documents the former spooks advised him about, even if there had been an inspector general in place. Even some of the ANC's alliance partners thought the failed state capture probe had been nothing but a cover-up.[17] Ultimately, three of South Africa's foremost intelligence officers lost their jobs because they wanted to protect the country from the Guptas. The saga illustrated once more how frighteningly powerful the family appeared to have become.

PART III

MEDIA MOGULS

10

The dawn of a New Age

It is no secret that newspaper sales around the world have been in heavy decline since about 2007.[1] South Africa's newspaper industry has not been immune to the trend. The annual figures released by the Audit Bureau of Circulation (ABC), an independent entity that monitors the distribution and readership numbers of printed publications in South Africa, usually make for pretty grim reading. The ABC statistics released in 2010 showed that the circulation figures for weekly newspapers had dropped by 15 per cent over the preceding three years.[2] But these findings did not discourage the Guptas, who were getting ready to launch their own newspaper. Their friendship with government's top leaders, after all, pretty much guaranteed the paper's success.

Given the new publication's title, the Guptas should not have been surprised when, from the outset, critics called their latest venture a 'mouthpiece' for the ANC-led government. In the 1950s and early 1960s, an ANC-aligned newspaper called *New Age* was widely distributed throughout South Africa. The publication ran into financial trouble and eventually ceased production after it was banned by the National Party government in 1962.[3]

Essop Pahad, the minister in the Presidency under Thabo Mbeki who later became a business partner of the Guptas, says it was his idea that the family use the name of the struggle-era publication for their newspaper. As a member of the ANC-aligned Transvaal Indian Youth Congress, Pahad had sold copies of the *New Age* in and around Ferreirasdorp, the Johannesburg neighbourhood where he lived as a student.

'If you call your newspaper *New Age*, you will have a very important name, seeing as it was a very important paper, at least in the history of our movement,' Pahad recalls telling the Guptas. They agreed, adding only *The* to the historical publication's title. Pahad was appointed as a director and senior advisor of TNA Media, the holding company established by the Guptas in June 2010 and that owns *The New Age* newspaper.

According to Pahad, it was always his and the Guptas' intention to launch a publication that would be 'broadly sympathetic to the ANC and to the government', but he insists that this did not mean it would be a government or ANC mouthpiece. 'It would be wrong if you became the voice of either of these; they would destroy you,' says Pahad. At the time of *The New Age*'s launch in July 2010, though, the Guptas were having a tough time convincing people that broadly sympathetic and pro-government were indeed two different concepts.

'People are not stupid,' said political commentator Justice Malala at the time. 'When they're being fed propaganda they will see through it and won't buy the paper. The Guptas are embroiled in several serious scandals including the Sishen iron ore mining dispute with a Zuma relative. How would the newspaper report on this, if at all?'[4]

In the midst of the Sishen saga, amaBhungane reported that President Zuma and chief operating officer in the Presidency Jessie Duarte had attended a meeting at the Guptas' Saxonwold estate in February 2010 to discuss the Guptas' plans to establish a newspaper. According to a source, 'a lawyer was also present to give advice on possible legal obstacles to providing government advertising to support the publication'. Duarte and the Guptas at the time denied that there had been any such meeting with Zuma.[5]

But Pahad, who was a director of TNA Media until July 2011,[6] makes no secret of the fact that he and the Guptas discussed the newspaper with the ANC's most senior leaders before its launch. '[We decided] the best thing is also to brief the leadership of the ANC, as well as the leadership of COSATU [Congress of South African Trade Unions], which we did ... We talked to the [ANC's] top six,' says Pahad. It was during one of these meeting that Pahad gave the ruling party the undertaking that *The New Age* would be 'broadly sympathetic to the ANC', he recalls.

At the newspaper's launch event at a posh conference venue in Johannesburg in July 2010, where scantily clad women holding up mock front pages of *The New Age* stole the show, Atul Gupta described how he envisioned the paper's coverage of matters relating to government by saying that everyone at *The New Age* would be required to see 'the glass half full and not just half empty'.[7] In other words, the newspaper's reporting on government affairs would be coated in a layer of positivity.

'The media is damaging South Africa by deterring investment and making people depressed with critical stories that are at times without credible sources,' Gupta told the *Daily Maverick* in an attempt to explain the rationale behind the paper's editorial policy.[8]

A week after *The New Age*'s launch event, the ANC released a discussion document prepared for the party's upcoming National General Council (NGC) meeting to be held in Durban in September. Apart from proposing the establishment of a media tribunal to regulate the media, an idea that has since been widely condemned, the party's harsh criticism of the media was eerily similar to the views expressed by Atul Gupta at his newspaper's launch: 'The ANC is of the view that the media needs to contribute towards the building of a new society and be accountable for its actions'; '[A] cursory scan on the print media reveals an astonishing degree of dishonesty, lack of professional integrity and lack of independence'; 'Media cannot demand respect if it fails to assume its responsibility as a public utility in the popular search for a better life'. These are just some of the gems from the discussion document.[9]

At the NGC meeting, party delegates were given the very first copies of *The New Age*.[10] It was a special edition compiled specifically for the event, which did not exactly help disprove the widely held view that the newspaper would be aligned to the ruling party. The front-page lead story detailed how Zuma's patience with ANC 'dissidents' had supposedly run out. 'Zuma tightens his grip,' declared the headline.[11] 'The Guptas tighten their grip' would have been equally fitting. If the special edition was anything to go by, the newspaper's critics were right when they predicted that government adspend would help *The New Age* to stay afloat. The special edition was awash with government advertisements, including half- and full-page advertorials by the Free State and Gauteng provincial governments and various national departments.[12]

Although it evidently had the backing of the ruling party, *The New Age* experienced serious problems from the start. The paper was supposed to go on sale to the general public in the same month as the ANC NGC meeting, but the launch had been postponed to 20 October. 'It has proved harder to put the systems and people in place to deliver on provincial coverage than we originally anticipated,' Vuyo Mvoko, the newspaper's first editor, was quoted as saying in a statement released by TNA Media on 14 September.[13] Then disaster struck. The day before the new launch date, Mvoko and four other senior staff members resigned.[14] TNA Media's statement on the development was a masterclass in passive-aggressive finger-wagging. 'It was with regret that we received the resignations of five senior members of our editorial team, at 3pm today, the day before we were due to publish our newspaper,' read the statement.[15] There had obviously been some seriously bad vibes behind the scenes, but the five departing staffers remained mum on their reasons for leaving. 'Collectively, we have taken the decision that it would be neither proper nor professionally acceptable for us to speak publicly about the reason for our decision,' they said in a joint statement.[16]

Mvoko was replaced by Henry Jeffreys, a former editor of the Afrikaans daily *Die Burger*, and the first edition of *The New Age* finally went on sale on 6 December 2010. In a front-page editor's note headlined 'Dawn of The New Age', Jeffreys denied suggestions that the newspaper would be a propaganda tool for the ruling party. 'Despite what has been said about us, we hold no brief for any political party or formation,' he wrote. 'There is no hotline between my office in Midrand and Luthuli House in Sauer Street.'[17] Given the increasingly cosy relationship between the Guptas and Zuma's administration, however, Jeffrey's promises sounded hollow.

About a month after *The New Age* hit the streets, Zuma and several of his cabinet members flew from Polokwane – where the ANC had celebrated its ninety-ninth anniversary – to Durban, where they attended a gala dinner hosted by *The New Age*. Zuma was accompanied by then rural development minister Tokyo Sexwale, then transport minister Sbu Ndebele and then defence minister Lindiwe Sisulu, among other high-profile politicians. Zuma used his speech at the event to heap praise on the Guptas' new publication. It was good to hear that *The New Age* intended to 'report [with] balance and fairness', said the president. 'We appreciate this and believe that it's a new breath of fresh air in terms of the media because of the number of debates we have had on the way the media should report.' Echoing Atul Gupta, Zuma said, 'There are many good things that happen in this country that are not reported on.'[18]

The 'unfair' segment of the media, in the meantime, continued to question *The New Age*'s ability to report on government-related matters without fear or favour. This prompted Jeffreys to strongly defend the Guptas in another opinion piece in *The New Age*. He took exception to a column by the editor of another newspaper, in which it was 'strongly intimated that *The New Age* was the family's gift to President Jacob Zuma, ostensibly in return for certain unspecified favours – which of course it is not'. And he bemoaned the fact that the Guptas' 'detractors' labelled the family as 'suspect', seeing as he was 'certain they are not'.[19] Ultimately, Jeffreys's stint with the Guptas would be seen as a low point in the once-respected journalist's career. In May 2011, he resigned after only five months as editor of *The New Age*. Nazeem Howa, CEO of TNA Media, assured the media that 'we always knew it was not going to be a long-term arrangement'.[20]

By the time *The New Age* had appointed its fourth editor in August 2012 (Jeffrey's replacement, Ryland Fisher, resigned after seventeen months[21]), TNA Media was facing growing criticism over the fact that it refused to have the newspaper's circulation figures audited by the ABC.

'Without an ABC certificate, there is no transparency, because nobody knows what you are doing. Honestly, there is no justification why any publication should not have an Audit Bureau of Circulation certificate. For me it screams some sort of deception,' said Gordon Patterson, the ABC's then vice president, at the time.[22]

A document setting out the newspaper's advertising rates for 2010 details just how hopelessly naive the Guptas had been when they launched *The New Age*. According to *The New Age* rate card, TNA Media envisioned a circulation figure of 170 000 copies per day, which would have ensured a total readership figure of 850 000 per day (readership figures are generally three to five times higher than circulation figures, based on the assumption that between three and five people share each newspaper sold).[23] While *The New Age* would not submit itself to an ABC audit, figures contained in the South African Audience Research Foundation's All Media and Products Survey suggested the newspaper's daily readership throughout 2011 was closer to 39 000 per day, giving *The New Age* a circulation figure between 7 800 and 13 000 copies per day, a small fraction of the 170 000 TNA Media had promised potential advertisers.[24]

In January 2013 Nazeem Howa hit back, saying that *The New Age* was selling 50 000 copies a day and distributing a further 25 000 for free.[25] When the *Mail & Guardian* asked Howa how much of the 50 000 'sold-for copies' were bought in bulk by government departments and state-owned companies, he failed to provide an answer.[26]

Despite the opacity surrounding the newspaper's circulation figures, government departments and state-owned companies kept forking out millions to advertise in *The New Age*. A Nielsen advertising expenditure (AdEx) report that covered the period December 2011 to November 2012 indicated that almost R69 million of the newspaper's R108 million in advertising revenue came from national and provincial government departments and state-owned entities, *City Press* reported. Telkom and Transnet, which at that stage was led by CEO Brian Molefe, counted among *The New Age*'s biggest advertising clients.[27] The newspaper also targeted South African Airways (SAA). A report by amaBhungane revealed that the famously troubled state-owned airline had signed a contract to buy 3 000 copies of the newspaper per day.[28] In October 2015, finance minister Nhlanhla Nene revealed in Parliament that SAA had spent more than R9 million on almost six million copies of *The New Age*.[29] Other notable government clients of *The New Age* have included the departments of energy, higher education, and trade and industry.[30]

The newspaper's launch spawned another big money-spinner for the Guptas: the now infamous *The New Age* Business Briefings, which were broadcast on the South African Broadcasting Corporation (SABC) *Morning Live* show. In October 2012, the *Sunday Times* revealed that the SABC was broadcasting the Guptas' forty-five-minute breakfast show for free. Normally, according to the report, advertisers would be required to pay R18 000 per thirty seconds of airtime just to profile their logo in this spot. The newspaper also revealed that Hlaudi Motsoeneng, the SABC's soon-to-be-disgraced chief operating officer, had closed a deal with Howa that saw the public broadcaster buy 1 800 copies of *The New Age* each day.[31] In January 2013, *City Press* revealed that Transnet and fellow parastatal Eskom had paid *The New Age* nearly R25 million to 'sponsor' twenty-four *The New Age* Business Briefings. An earlier report had revealed that state-owned telecoms giant Telkom had forked out R12 million for twelve such events.[32] As time wore on, *The New Age* somehow convinced the bosses of the country's biggest state-owned companies to commit ever-increasing slices of their advertising budgets to the newspaper's breakfast events. In 2014, Eskom signed a contract worth R43 million to sponsor the *The New Age* Business Briefings for a period of three years, amaBhungane revealed. Collin Matjila, Eskom's then CEO, had previously had business dealings with Gupta associate Salim Essa. Matjila had signed the contract with *The New Age* despite explicit objections from Eskom's audit and risk committee, the report indicated.[33]

Further details about how the SABC's resources were abused to benefit *The New Age* surfaced at a parliamentary inquiry into the mess at the public broadcaster at the end of 2016. Vuyo Mvoko, who had joined the SABC after quitting as *The New Age*'s first editor, testified that '*Morning Live* resources get diverted to pay for the production costs of those TNA [*The New Age*] breakfasts that you see'. According to Mvoko, the SABC spent between R200 000 and R500 000 for each *The New Age* Business Briefing. 'We pay for the production costs, we pay for the presenters to be there, for all those people, that whole tribe that has to travel to Bloemfontein or to the Northern Cape to do those broadcasts. The owners of TNA don't pay any of that money,' Mvoko alleged.[34]

Essop Pahad says it should come as no surprise that the majority of *The New Age*'s advertising revenue comes from government. He says the premiers of South Africa's provinces were 'briefed' before the newspaper was launched. 'We said to them we would appreciate it if you advertised in *The New Age*,' recalls Pahad. The fact that the newspaper relied on government advertising 'is not hidden', he insists. 'You can see who is advertising regularly in the newspaper.'

What was less visible, however, was the apparently underhanded manner in which *The New Age* secured its revenue from government. In 2013, amaBhungane revealed how decision-makers at key state-owned entities and government departments were 'bullied' into supporting the newspaper. A former employee of *The New Age* described how the family dealt with difficult officials: 'In some cases, more junior media practitioners in government would also be cautious of advertising in the paper because they could not justify the spending. A simple phone call from one of the Guptas to a minister and the junior official would phone back, asking why the *New Age* had tried to make him look stupid by going above his head and calling his superior. After that, he would agree to advertise.'[35]

11

Gupta TV

Despite growing criticism over the fact that a significant amount of tax-payers' money was being channelled to *The New Age*, the Guptas pressed ahead with the expansion of their burgeoning media empire. In February 2013, TNA Media CEO Nazeem Howa announced plans for the launch of a new twenty-four-hour news channel. Howa revealed that the new television channel would be owned by Infinity Media Networks, a joint venture between the Guptas' Oakbay Investments and Essel Media, a company based in India. A yet-to-be-named 'broad-based black economic empowerment structure' would also receive shares in Infinity Media Networks, Howa stated.[1] A few weeks before the channel was due to go on air, the Guptas released a statement disclosing that Duduzane Zuma, through his stake in BEE company Mabengela Investments, 'would be a shareholder in the venture'.[2] By then it was common knowledge that the news channel would be called Africa News Network 7, or ANN7. The channel promised to focus on 'constructive, nation-building stories in the interests of building a culture of unity and pride in SA'.[3] In other words, like *The New Age*, ANN7 was mandated to put a positive spin on its news coverage, including its coverage of government affairs.

Duduzane was not the only member of the Zuma family to take an interest in the channel. On the day of the channel's launch, 21 August 2013, *The Star* revealed that President Jacob Zuma had 'secretly' visited the ANN7 studios in Midrand two days earlier. Mac Maharaj, Zuma's spokesperson at the time, tried to downplay the visit, saying it was merely part of an attempt by Zuma to 'promote relations and understanding' with media outlets.[4]

But the president's visit would soon be forgotten amid the channel's absolute disaster of a launch. If the Guptas thought that getting *The New Age* up and running had been a challenge, ANN7's first few weeks on air would be nothing short of a nightmare.

On the evening of ANN7's maiden broadcast, the Guptas hosted a flashy gala dinner at the Sandton Convention Centre. The requisite top-level government touch was provided by then communications minister Yunus Carrim, who delivered the keynote address and helped Moegsien Williams, editor of *The New Age* and ANN7's new editor-in-chief, push a red button symbolically putting the channel live on air.[5] Things got pretty awkward later in the evening, however, when some of the guests saw on their phones that the channel's hopelessly inept presenters and news anchors were being torn apart on social media.[6]

In the days following the launch, ANN7 probably drew far more viewers than it would have under normal circumstances, as thousands of South Africans tuned in to see what cringeworthy gaffes the channel's presenters and technical staff would make next. Some of the most note-worthy blunders included news anchors completely mispronouncing the names of political parties, presenters freezing mid-sentence after they had apparently outrun the teleprompter, and technical staff who could be heard talking in the background. The *Daily Maverick*'s Rebecca Davis wrote that it was difficult to keep track of all the blunders: 'There's the one where the news anchor repeats exactly the same piece of news, word for word, twice in quick succession. There's the one where the news anchor announces that racing driver "Louise" Hamilton has won the "Grand Pricks". There's the one where the weather girl moves on to "the mother city, Johannesburg".'[7]

It turned out that instead of recruiting experienced television journalists and presenters, ANN7 had appointed a cast of models and wannabes to read the news, the *Sunday Times* reported after the station's disastrous first week on air. The channel's executives 'believe that men will enjoy watching the news when they see pretty girls', one ANN7 insider told the newspaper. The station's staff was also not properly trained to use the advanced broadcasting equipment, according to the report.[8]

Little more than a week after ANN7 went live, the Guptas' channel received even worse publicity. Rajesh Sundaram, a television editor from India who had moved to South Africa to work at ANN7, started spilling the beans on some of the goings-on at the channel. Sundaram had resigned after only three months at ANN7, citing interference in the channel's editorial policy and poor working conditions as his main reasons for leaving.[9]

His dramatic departure shed new light on the way in which the Guptas apparently treated their employees. Sundaram told *City Press* that when he tendered his resignation, he insisted on being paid for the overtime he had put in at the channel. After he refused to sign the severance package the Guptas offered him, which did not take into account any of the overtime, and feeling threatened, Sundaram fled the channel's offices in Midrand with one of the Guptas' armed bodyguards allegedly chasing after him.[10] Sundaram eventually made his way back to India, from where he told the *Mail & Guardian* that he still feared for his life.[11]

Sundaram claimed that during his time at ANN7 he witnessed the close ties between the Guptas and President Zuma, and it made him very uncomfortable. 'There was a lot of interference on an editorial level by Mr Atul Gupta,' he told *City Press*. 'The policy was to support the ANC and President Zuma ... I was taken to see President Zuma thrice, where he was given assurances by the Guptas that this channel was going to be pro-ANC.' Sundaram was able to give specific details about these meetings, which he said took place at Mahlamba Ndlopfu, the president's official residence in Pretoria. 'We were taken to a room to the right of the main entrance. There was Ajay and Atul Gupta, Howa and Moegsien Williams on a couple of occasions,' Sundaram told the paper. Apparently, at one such meeting, a proposal was made that an ANN7 crew be made available to follow Zuma around. The president was also shown a recording of a practice news bulletin made in preparation for the channel's launch, which he apparently enjoyed very much. Mac Maharaj, who did not deny the meetings, stated that 'President Zuma always makes time to meet management of news houses that ask to see him, who wish to get the government perspective on the country and to share what they intend to do'.[12]

Sundaram also alleged that many of the channel's Indian employees did not have South African work permits and were therefore working at ANN7 illegally. An investigation by *Eyewitness News* later showed that at least seven of the channel's foreign employees had indeed travelled to South Africa on normal visitor visas, which barred them from working in the country.[13] The Department of Home Affairs subsequently probed the matter, but apart from ordering some of the affected Indian employees to leave the country, the channel has to date faced no serious censure from government over this blatant abuse of South Africa's immigration laws.

Sundaram later signed a publishing deal for a tell-all book in which he promised to reveal even more details of his stint with the Guptas. According to promotional material for *Indentured: Behind the Scenes at Gupta TV*, which was to be published by Jacana Media, Sundaram planned to lift the lid on ANN7's 'capricious, micro-managing owners'.[14] But in June 2014, Jacana told television journalist Thinus Ferreira that they would no longer publish the book. According to Ferreira, 'there were apparently some legal reservations'.[15] *Indentured* has yet to be published.

In 2014, the dismissal of ANN7 reporter Asanda Magaqa also made headlines. Magaqa, who was escorted from the channel's premises by security guards, was fired for alleged insubordination. At the time, further indications of substandard working conditions at the station surfaced. According to a list of grievances submitted to ANN7's managers by the Communication Workers Union (CWU), of which Magaqa was a member, staff had complained that they were forced to work overtime without extra pay and were generally underpaid.[16] One year later, the Commission for Conciliation, Mediation and Arbitration (CCMA) found that Magaqa's dismissal had been 'procedurally and substantially unfair' and ordered ANN7 to pay her R500 000 in backdated salaries.[17] It would not be the CWU's last encounter with the news channel's bosses.

In April 2016, after South Africa's major banks decided to close the accounts of all Gupta-owned companies, an open letter claiming to represent Oakbay Investments' 7 500 employees started doing the rounds. The letter, which was signed by two Oakbay staffers, was an appeal to the banks to reopen the Guptas' accounts, seeing as thousands of their employees supposedly now risked losing their jobs. 'We are not politically connected. We have not captured the state. We do not know if any of the allegations against the Gupta family or Oakbay's management are true. We do not care. All we care about is providing for our families,' read the letter.[18]

Instead of thanking the letter's two authors for ostensibly fighting their cause, many Oakbay staff members were furious that they were being spoken for without first being consulted. 'The first time we saw the letter was when *Fin24* reported on it,' says a former ANN7 staffer. A group of angry employees at the news station decided to confront Phuti Mosomane, *The New Age* and ANN7's online manager and one of the letter's signatories.

Robbie Russo, the general manager at Sahara Computers, was Mosomane's co-signatory.

'We made it very clear we couldn't have our names attached to something that impacted on our integrity as journalists,' recalls my source. 'We demanded a retraction of that letter before the end of the day.' But instead of acceding to their demands, Mosomane laid charges of intimidation, victimisation and harassment against everyone who had confronted him.

Mere hours after the contents of the letter were made public, Oakbay employees were treated to a special visit by ANC Youth League leader Collen Maine, one of the Guptas' dearest friends. Maine would later claim that employees at Oakbay and ANN7 had invited him to their offices in Midrand to listen to their grievances about the banks closing the Gupta-owned companies' accounts.[19] But the chubby politician, whose pro-Gupta stance had once prompted deputy EFF leader Floyd Shivambu to call him a 'Gupta-controlled Oros [man]' on Twitter, had completely misread the situation.

The former ANN7 employee I spoke to remembers the day's events as follows: Soon after Mosomane was given a tongue-lashing by his ANN7 colleagues, Oakbay sent out an email to its employees to notify them of a press conference that was due to take place at a warehouse on ANN7's premises. After the ANN7 staffers were joined by their colleagues from Sahara Computers, whose offices are across the road from the television station, Maine arrived at the warehouse in a car. At this point, the ANN7 staff, who were already livid about the letter sent out on their behalf, realised what was happening.

'Maine said he was there on invitation from the staff,' says my source, 'but it is impossible to get onto ANN7's premises if you're not invited [by the company itself] and security doesn't know about it. This only let us know that management had orchestrated the whole thing.'

Although there were as yet no hostilities, Maine was made to understand that he was not welcome at ANN7. 'This was an employee issue; it was massively inappropriate for a politician to get involved,' explains the source. Maine then rather awkwardly got back in his car and drove up to Sahara's offices. A few of the ANN7 staffers followed on foot, and this is where things got really heated. 'Some of the ANN7 guys started to shout "*Voetsek*, Collen!" They told him that he doesn't really give a shit about the employees' well-being,' says the former ANN7 insider. 'Why are you fighting for Guptas?' an angry employee can be heard asking Maine on a video filmed by *News24* as the group gathered outside Sahara's offices chant 'Maine must fall! Maine must fall!' Defeated, the youth leader climbs in the back of a shiny BMW and leaves the premises.[20]

Less than two weeks after the fiasco, the public were shown just how deep in the Guptas' pockets Maine appeared to be. According to an exposé by amaBhungane, all indications were that the Guptas had helped Maine buy a R5.4-million house six weeks after he was elected Youth League president in 2015.[21]

Meanwhile, the events outside Sahara's offices evidently scratched open some wounds that had been left to fester for far too long. Two ANN7 employees told *News24* that they were 'oppressed' by Oakbay's management and would never back their bosses in a letter like the one signed by Mosomane and Russo. 'They treat us like dogs and then they expect us to speak on their behalf. That is nonsense,' one of them told the news site.[22]

Two weeks after the Maine debacle, the group of about thirty ANN7 employees who had originally confronted Mosomane about the letter were issued with summonses to appear in disciplinary hearings. They were being charged with an array of alleged offences, including harassing and intimidating Mosomane and abandoning their posts when they left ANN7's premises to listen to Maine. The station ultimately fired eight of them in June. The rest were served with warnings.[23]

After the dismissals, the CWU and the Right2Know Campaign organised a small lunchtime demonstration outside ANN7's offices. According to the former ANN7 staffer, the channel's managers told employees that anyone caught joining the protest would be summarily fired. But despite the threat, a small group of journalists and cameramen did join the proceedings. When the demonstration kicked off, ANN7 managers came out and filmed the event in order to later identify the 'offenders', a tactic often used by anti-riot police. Ever the philanthropist, Ajay Gupta also went outside and handed the protestors bottles of water. They told him they did not want his water and some threw the bottles away. A few days later, five more journalists were fired from ANN7. According to an *Eyewitness News* report, among other offences, the journalists who took part in the demonstration 'were accused of misusing water bottles or stealing water bottles'.[24] My inside source says two employees were fired simply because they were caught on the managers' camera walking to their cars after their shifts had ended.

The first group of dismissed employees had in the meantime taken ANN7 to the CCMA. They were assisted by the Broadcasting, Electronic, Media and Allied Workers Union. In September 2016, they reached a settlement with the channel. As none of them wanted to be reinstated, their employer was ordered to pay them an undisclosed amount of money.[25] With the help of the CWU, the second group of fired employees eventually reached an agreement with ANN7 to return to work. However, they had to sign a letter of apology for bringing the company into disrepute, says the ANN7 insider.

Meanwhile, the cosy relations between the channel and the broader pro-Zuma faction appeared to be unaffected by the problems at ANN7. Even the Guptas' and Duduzane Zuma's resignations as directors of Oakbay in April 2016 in the wake of the banking drama did not seem to change the status quo.[26] In December 2016, Des van Rooyen, South Africa's 'weekend special' former finance minister, said he wanted to propose a resolution that the country's military veterans read *The New Age* and watch ANN7.[27] Van Rooyen was speaking in his capacity as treasurer general of the MK Military Veterans Association, an organisation that has in the past proudly admitted its business ties with the Guptas.[28]

In the build-up to the ANC's 105th anniversary in January 2017, ANN7 gave ample airtime to senior party members who were known Zuma allies. 'It is not the last dance because President Zuma will continue and take this national executive committee to the national elective conference ... Many of us appreciate his leadership,' said water and sanitation minister Nomvula Mokonyane, before thanking the president on air for his 'groundbreaking interventions' and 'wisdom' in leading the party.[29]

But the Guptas' most prominent role as newsmakers lay not in their ownership of newspapers or news channels, but in their appearance as subjects in controversial news stories. The next of these stories, and the biggest so far, involved the landing of a private aeroplane filled with wedding guests at Air Force Base Waterkloof in April 2013.

PART IV

WATERKLOOFGATE

12

The R75-million wedding splurge

Tuesday 30 April – Friday 3 May 2013
The use of an air force base for the landing of Jet Airways flight JAI 9900 at AFB Waterkloof quickly snowballed into a public scandal that would become known as 'Waterkloofgate' and 'Guptagate'. As the media and government departments pointed fingers at one another, the guests for Vega Gupta and Aakash Jahajgarhia's wedding began to arrive in Sun City.

Marida Fitzpatrick, who had been accredited to cover the wedding for the magazines *Huisgenoot* and *You*, took a moment to photograph the arch of fresh flowers through which the guests had to pass in order to get to the first of the wedding's many ceremonies that would be held over four days.

The elevated floral arrangement probably cost more than her entire wedding, the journalist mused as she made her way across yet another red carpet before finally entering the paved area around the huge azure swimming pool at Sun City's Palace hotel.

Now surveying her surroundings, she felt silly for having deemed the floral arch worthy of a picture, for the circumference of the giant pool was decorated with thousands of flower bouquets. The colourful arrangements of fresh chrysanthemums, carnations and other bright flowers, tucked into beds of leatherleaf fern and aspidistra leaves, must have required a significant chunk of South Africa's entire supply of fresh flowers, she thought.

She was absolutely right. A role-player in the local wedding industry, who had been privy to information about the planning for the wedding, would later confirm that the more than 30 000 bouquets and stems ordered for the entire event had literally gobbled up most of South Africa's available floral products. For particular kinds of flowers, especially pink and white roses, the demand exceeded supply to such an extent that the prices for these items shot through the roof across the country. Meanwhile, other brides throughout South Africa had to make do without these varieties of roses because practically every single bloom available at that stage had been bought for the Gupta wedding. According to the source, the florists' bill alone had been in the region of R5 million. The price tag for the entire wedding, according to the industry insider, had been a jaw-dropping R75 million.

As Fitzpatrick continued to explore the area around the pool, she almost winced at the sheer and blatant excess with which the space had been transformed into a wedding wonderland. It was obvious that no expense had been spared to convert Sun City into Gupta City for the duration of the four-day-long wedding festival.

But the day's first event was merely the start of a bizarre experience that Fitzpatrick would later liken to a prolonged psychedelic voyage into a fantasy realm that was, at least to her, at once spectacular and horrific.

Fitzpatrick had not been thrilled when she heard she would be covering the event. Her previous job as a news reporter at the Afrikaans daily newspaper *Beeld* had given her more than enough exposure to the growing controversy surrounding the Gupta brothers.

Her lack of enthusiasm for the wedding only increased when she scrolled through her Twitter feed moments after arriving at Sun City and saw that while she had been on the road a storm had erupted on social media around her hosts' choice of airport for the arrival of their guests from India.

Looking around her, Fitzpatrick assumed the news either had not reached her fellow wedding attendees or they simply didn't care about it. Some of the guests were seated in lavishly decorated lounges set up under gazebos, while others stood in small circles near the pool, chatting and laughing and ostensibly ignoring the decadence around them in a show of practised aloofness that only the really wealthy are able to pull off with conviction. The Guptas' most prized guests had access to personal servants who would be on call to attend to their needs for the duration of the drawn-out wedding.

Fitzpatrick strolled over to a Willy Wonka-esque stall where a dedicated team of servants were handing out limitless scoops of Häagen-Dazs ice cream.

'I'd better get me some of this before Khulubuse Zuma gets here,' Fitzpatrick thought as she pictured President Jacob Zuma's famously corpulent nephew rushing over to get his share of the expensive dairy treats.

She spied Atul Gupta standing among some of the guests, so she walked over to him and introduced herself.

He seemed at once jovial and friendly, but also somewhat anxious. Could it be that he was worried the guests wouldn't enjoy the wedding, despite the astonishing level of excess with which the event had been executed?

Before she could ponder further, it was time for the first of seven traditional Hindu wedding ceremonies to start. Vega and Aakash appeared on a dome-like stage that had been decked out in white satin. Strings of mother-of-pearl butterflies hung off the structure's roof, while two harp players, seated on a bench behind the couple, coaxed sweet, airy melodies from their instruments.

The bride and groom were clad in traditional attire in matching colours of gold and silver. Vega, whose outfit was a display of fantastically intricate patterns and shiny jewellery, wore a demure expression on her face. Tradition dictates that the bride at a Hindu wedding is not supposed to radiate joy and excitement, but must instead maintain an air of subservience and modesty. Fitzpatrick thought Vega's eyes perhaps reflected a certain sadness that went beyond the feigned meekness the ceremony required her to exhibit. This was, after all, an arranged marriage.

Or was the apparent lack of any chemistry between Vega and Aakash merely the result of the overwhelming amount of attention the couple had to endure, Fitzpatrick wondered as a group of at least ten photographers clicked and flashed away around the couple. ·

After the ceremony had ended and everyone had been treated to a feast of traditional Indian food at brightly decorated tables set up under white tents, the guests left the pool area. Some returned to their hotels, of which the largest and most expensive were booked out for the exclusive use of the Gupta wedding party.

Later, at the wedding's first evening function, Fitzpatrick witnessed the Guptas' apparent propensity for brash ostentation. The Palace hotel's courtyard had been transformed into something that at once resembled a Bollywood fantasy land and an outdoor trance party. Neon lights cast a mesmerising blue and purple glow on the hotel's outer walls. Even the trees were adorned with strange and colourful decorations. Amid all of this, the hotel's life-size elephant statue towered over the festivities. The animal's body is sculpted in a manner that seems to imitate the gestures of an elephant in distress. Its left front foot is lifted off the ground while its big head tilts to the right, leaving its left ear dramatically suspended in the air. It gave Fitzpatrick the impression that it too was recoiling in horror from the onslaught of sensory stimuli that had erupted around it.

'The real LSD explosion of flames, crystal, colours and deafening sound only began that night,' the journalist later wrote in an article for *Netwerk24*.[1]

In the piece, Fitzpatrick likens the wedding to a so-called LSD tunnel: a simulator that supposedly mimicked the effects of hallucinatory substances and which was used by the South African Police in the 1990s in order to deter teenagers from using such drugs.

'The tunnel had an unsteady floor and it rotated, deafening noises played [from loudspeakers] and lights blinded you in all manner of migraine colours and by the time you exited at the other side you were dizzy, drunk, nauseous … That is the nearest, actually the only thing with which I can compare my four days with the Guptas,' Fitzpatrick wrote.

Things only got more surreal and extravagant as the wedding progressed.

On the Wednesday morning Fitzpatrick found herself at the Valley of the Waves, a huge water park consisting of a wave pool, a man-made beach and a variety of slides and entertainment. It is one of Sun City's biggest tourist attractions. But on that day there would be no normal visitors allowed near it, for the Guptas had booked the entire water park for their exclusive use.

Again, the scale of the preparations was astonishing. Scores of large gazebos decorated in a variety of brightly coloured drapes stood next to one another on the famous fake beach. Between the tents and the edge of the wave pool, large ornamental sea stars and shells lay strewn across the sand, accentuating the day's maritime theme.

To Fitzpatrick the scene had an oddly infantile feel to it. It was as if someone had asked the twenty-three-year-old Vega what her childhood fantasy had been and then, on hearing that it was something along the lines of *The Little Mermaid*, had proceeded to throw mountains of money at turning a little girl's dream into reality.

A large stage, fully kitted out with the type of speakers and other sound equipment one would expect to find at a professional music concert, had been set up at the shallow end of the wave pool. The day's highlights included performances by large groups of dancers and drummers, singers and other entertainers.

Later, the traditional Sagai ceremony saw Aakash and Vega exchange engagement rings, which were dramatically brought to them by two 'armed knights' who would have looked more at home in medieval England than at a Bollywood beach wedding.[2]

While the ceremonies and entertainment continued, scores of Indian chefs, who had been flown into South Africa especially for the occasion, served up rotis, naan and other traditional Indian foods.

The wedding's food logistics, however, left Fitzpatrick a little uneasy. The Indian chefs had apparently brought their own cooking equipment to South Africa, which involved the use of open flames and gas bottles. Sometime on day one or two, one of these gas bottles exploded, and this would not be a one-off occurrence.

It seemed to Fitzpatrick as if the Guptas' temporary capture of Sun City had been accompanied by a complete and total abandonment of all the rules, regulations and safety provisions that would normally apply to a gathering of this magnitude.

'By the time Vega and Aakash were finally married, after what felt like about 85 ceremonies and never-ending sensory explosions, I felt like an overstimulated baby. I wanted to lie in the foetal position and rock [myself] and cry,' she reflected in her article.

The final and grandest of the wedding parties occurred on the Thursday night at Sun City's Superbowl, a large indoor arena known for hosting big local and international musicians and entertainers.

The evening's entertainment included a concert featuring Bollywood stars and other Indian celebrities. And, as always, the occasion was marked by an overload of sights and sounds. By then, Fitzpatrick felt close to going insane, she later only half-jokingly recalled in her article: 'At 02:00 that morning I didn't know if it was real or if I was hallucinating, whether I was at a wedding or inside the LSD tunnel, whether – due to the pure trauma – I'd finally lost my mind and had become psychotic. Because somewhere in the early hours of the morning a gas bottle exploded and a chef caught fire, as in literally went up in flames. The guests were shocked for a moment and nearly became upset, but then somebody quickly took the burning chef to the back, the music started playing again and the party went on!'

I have not been able to establish what became of the poor man.

Fitzpatrick was only too happy when the last day of the wedding dawned on Gupta City.

'I couldn't believe what happened at Sun City that week,' she wrote later. 'I couldn't believe one family could take over a whole holiday resort for practically an entire week. Little did I know that Sun City was but a microcosm of what was happening in the country. On day four I drove back to Johannesburg with my broken body and overloaded senses. And all I wanted to do for the rest of my life was to remain in a quiet, dark room.'

13

Zwane's guest

Friday 3 May 2013

The auditorium on the first floor of the Government Communication and Information System's head office in central Pretoria was stuffy and cramped as the all-star cast of five cabinet ministers sat facing the large pack of journalists, photographers and television cameramen.

Jeff Radebe, who was justice minister at the time, was addressing the media on the 'unauthorised' landing of the Guptas' chartered plane at AFB Waterkloof earlier that week.

'Government has investigated this security breach,' he read from his written statement. 'Government is gravely concerned at this violation of the security protocol and total disregard of established practice for clearing the landing of aircraft in a military facility that is of strategic importance to the country.'[1]

International relations minister Maite Nkoana-Mashabane, then home affairs minister Naledi Pandor, defence minister Nosiviwe Mapisa-Nqakula and then minister in the Presidency Collins Chabane sat in a row next to Radebe. One could only speculate as to whether the stern-faced Pandor, with her characteristic demeanour of a benevolent yet strict high-school principal, had been purposely placed between Nkoana-Mashabane and Mapisa-Nqakula. The latter ministers' departments were still locked in a war of words over the landing. Perhaps Pandor had been instructed to sit between them, like a parent between two bickering children right before a church service.

'Our particular concern is that the aircraft was carrying international passengers who do not fit the category of government officials or VIPs on official duty,' Radebe continued, effectively rubbishing the Gupta spokesperson's claim from three days earlier that 'foreign dignitaries' and 'some ministers' had been on board the flight.

Radebe then announced that a team of directors general from various state departments had been appointed to do an in-depth investigation into the matter. They would have to report back with their findings within seven days, he said.

In the meantime, five government, military and police officials who were found to have been 'involved in coordinating the landing of the aircraft, without the requisite executive authority', would be placed on immediate compulsory leave, the minister explained.

These officials were Ambassador Vusi Bruce Koloane, DIRCO's chief of state protocol; Brigadier General Leslie Lombard, the commanding officer at the Air Force Command Post (AFCP), which is where all flights to and from military bases are cleared; Brigadier General Tebogo Samuel Madumane, AFB Waterkloof's commanding officer; Lieutenant Colonel Christine Anderson, the base's movement control officer; and Major General Phumza Gela from the SAPS Operational Response Services in Gauteng.

The naming of these officials planted the first seeds of doubt among some of the journalists as to the government's commitment to determine who had really been responsible for the fiasco. Some of them wondered whether they were witnessing the start of a grand cover-up that would involve blaming lower-ranked government and military officials in order to save their bosses from a massive political scandal.

The journalists also noted that the Guptas themselves were seemingly not in any trouble for their role in the saga.

Apparently anticipating his audience's scepticism, Radebe made the following promise: 'The government would like to assure the South African public that no stone will be left unturned to ensure that we get to the bottom of this matter, and hold all those responsible for bringing our country into disrepute, whoever they are and whatever position they hold.'

When the briefing was eventually opened up to the floor, one of the journalists asked the ministers whether any of them had been invited to the wedding and whether they had actually attended it.

Pandor admitted that she had been to Sun City for the wedding. Mapisa-Nqakula said that all of them had been invited, but that she chose not to go. Radebe also stated that he didn't go.

Mapisa-Nqakula added that there was nothing wrong with any of their cabinet colleagues attending the event.

'Maybe some of them are still there,' she told the media contingency.

There was no need for Chabane to state whether or not he had attended the wedding. The previous day, during a press briefing on the outcome of an earlier cabinet meeting, the minister had stated that both he and Zuma had been invited but that neither would attend.

While the government investigation into the landing continued, the *Mail & Guardian* revealed that an invitation from the Free State provincial government may have played a key role in helping the Guptas secure a landing clearance at Waterkloof for their chartered plane.[2]

The newspaper report detailed how one Shivpal Yadav, a minister from the state of Uttar Pradesh in India, had received an invitation from the Free State's Department of Agriculture and Rural Development to visit the province.

The invitation, which was extended to Yadav towards the end of March 2013, was signed by Mosebenzi Zwane, the Free State's member of the executive council (MEC) for agriculture and rural development at the time. Zwane would eventually become South Africa's national minister of mineral resources. The role Zwane would later play in a controversial mining deal involving the Guptas and his support for the family after they had been dropped by South Africa's major banks is explored in a later chapter.

The *Mail & Guardian* report included an excerpt from Zwane's letter to Yadav: 'I would like to cordially invite you to visit South Africa to explore potential areas of mutual co-operation in the areas of irrigation and public works.'

As the newspaper pointed out, the timing of Zwane's invitation to his Indian counterpart was suspicious. Zwane's sudden desire to host a foreign regional government official with whom he had presumably never had contact before just didn't add up. Furthermore, it seemed Zwane's invitation to Yadav had been preceded by a failed attempt by Atul Gupta and one of his associates to secure permission for the landing at AFB Waterkloof from defence minister Nosiviwe Mapisa-Nqakula. All indications were that Zwane's office decided to extend its invitation to Yadav only *after* the Guptas were turned down by the defence minister.

The government's investigative team released its report just shy of two weeks after the *Mail & Guardian* article. Titled 'Landing of a Chartered Commercial Aircraft at Air Force Base Waterkloof', the report shed further light on how Atul Gupta and an associate had unsuccessfully approached various government entities and officials in February, before Zwane's letter.

Was it fair, therefore, for the public to infer that Zwane had somehow been roped in by the Guptas to invite Yadav to the Free State in order to have the Jet Airways flight cleared for landing at Waterkloof?

The authors of the government's report on the matter thought not: 'The reference to an invitation from the Free State Provincial Government was opaque, as no member of this party travelled to the Free State for any such meeting. However, an Indian State Minister was received by the Free State MEC for Agriculture three days prior to the arrival of the Gupta wedding party; this Indian Minister therefore arrived and departed from South Africa completely separate from the Gupta wedding party, despite attending the wedding at Sun City.'[3]

The details of official government-to-government visits, whether on a regional or national level, for the purpose of something as seemingly above board as issues around 'irrigation and public works' could hardly be deemed classified. Yet, apart from this vague reference, the government report did not provide any further details as to the identity of the visiting Indian official.

Given Zwane's letter, it would be fair to assume that the state minister mentioned in the report was indeed Yadav. And if this was the case, information later unearthed during an official SANDF board of inquiry into the involvement of certain military personnel in the saga serves as shocking proof that the South African government, alongside Radebe who had repeated the report's findings in Parliament, blatantly lied about the Yadav angle.

The SANDF board of inquiry report, a once secret document which has since been declassified, includes a complete list of passengers who were on board Jet Airways flight JAI 9900 when it landed at AFB Waterkloof on 30 April 2013. Seated next to Sarla Devi Yadav, wife of the infamous Uttar Pradesh politician, was none other than 'Shivpal Singh', the given names of Minister Yadav.[4] This small yet significant detail casts serious doubt over the government's claims that Zwane hosted his Indian counterpart 'three days prior to the arrival of the Gupta wedding party'. Instead, it appears as if the invitation to Yadav from Zwane's office had indeed been nothing but a cynical ploy to help get the Jet Airways flight cleared for landing at AFB Waterkloof on the grounds that it would be carrying an Indian government official.

In the course of writing this book, I invited Zwane to provide details to prove that Yadav had indeed travelled to the Free State to meet with officials from the province's agriculture department. But the minister failed to do so.

'In his role as MEC, Minister Zwane never dealt with issues of protocol in any capacity or jurisdiction' was all his spokesperson at the Department of Mineral Resources was willing to say on the matter.

I even lodged a Promotion of Access to Information Act (PAIA) request at the Free State Department of Agriculture and Rural Development to obtain the documentation on the mysterious Indian dignitary's visit to the province.

To date, the department has failed to comply with the request.

14

Clusterfuck

It took the Justice, Crime Prevention and Security (JCPS) cluster – a collection of government departments and agencies that cooperate on issues relating to national security, intelligence and crime – just fifteen days to complete its report on the landing of the Guptas' wedding jet. The JCPS finished its work on Friday 17 May 2013 and released its report, 'Landing of a Chartered Commercial Aircraft at Air Force Base Waterkloof', the following week.

The cluster's investigation was led by four senior government officials from the State Security Agency, the Department of Justice and Constitutional Development, the National Intelligence Coordinating Committee (NICOC) and the Department of Correctional Services. Interestingly, the latter was represented by Tom Moyane, the department's then national commissioner. Moyane would later be appointed commissioner of the South African Revenue Service (SARS) and become a key figure in the widely publicised saga around the establishment and subsequent disbanding of the so-called rogue unit operating within the tax-collecting agency. Moyane is seen by many as a staunch ally of Jacob Zuma, their relationship apparently stretching back to the era of the ANC's struggle against apartheid. As head of the party's intelligence wing, Zuma spent long stretches of time in the ANC's military camps in countries such as Zambia and Angola. On these occasions, Moyane would care for Zuma's children at home in South Africa.[1]

When the JCPS cluster report was released to the public, it quickly became evident that Moyane and his colleagues had applied a rather selective methodology in researching the landing and the events preceding it. Curiously, and perhaps most importantly, they had not deemed it necessary to interview the key military officials who were fingered in the report as being the main culprits – namely, Lieutenant Colonel Anderson, who had already been mentioned by Radebe at the media briefing on 3 May, and Sergeant Major Thabo Ntshisi and Lieutenant Colonel Stephan van Zyl, both from the AFCP in Pretoria.

Pikkie Greeff, a feisty advocate who has been assisting military personnel with all manner of disciplinary and legal procedures for almost twenty years, first as the legal advisor to the South African National Defence Union and later as the union's national secretary, remains convinced that the JCPS report was nothing more than a whitewash meant to cover up the role played by Zuma and other senior officials in the saga.

At the time, Greeff bemoaned the fact that the JCPS investigation had raced towards its questionable conclusion without allowing for any meaningful consultation with the officials who would be blamed as the supposedly lone-wolf offenders.

The JCPS report determined that the events leading up to the Gupta landing at AFB Waterkloof and the subsequent fallout played out in more or less the following way:

On an unspecified day in February 2013, one Tony Gupta (this can only be Rajesh, the youngest of the Gupta brothers) approached Airports Company South Africa (ACSA) to determine whether a private aeroplane carrying 'at least five heads of state, ministers and senior Indian Government officials' might be allowed to land at Johannesburg's O.R. Tambo International Airport. The purpose of the visit, Tony explained to the ACSA personnel, was for a four-day wedding festival at Sun City.[2]

In an ensuing meeting attended by Tony Gupta, DIRCO chief of state protocol Bruce Koloane, ACSA acting CEO Bongani Maseko and national transport minister Ben Martins, the attending parties concluded that it would not be possible to accommodate the chartered plane at O.R. Tambo. The main reason for this refusal was the Guptas' intention to welcome their wedding guests with 'an elaborate welcoming ceremony'. Maseko and the other officials apparently told Tony Gupta that such a ceremony would interfere with the Department of Home Affairs' passport-checking activities at South Africa's largest airport.

It should be noted that the JCPS report's mention of a meeting between a member of the Gupta family and such senior government officials as Martins and Maseko did not trigger the sheer avalanche of public outrage that such a revelation would undoubtedly engender had it been made known today. The reason for this is that the Guptas' apparent ease of access to top-level government officials, as evidenced by the countless meetings and approaches that only surfaced in the public domain in the first half of 2016, was largely unknown in 2013.

Rajesh Gupta would not be deterred, and he again approached ACSA, this time asking the state-owned entity whether the wedding plane could perhaps land at either Lanseria, Gauteng's second-largest commercial airport, or at the Pilanesberg airport, which is conveniently close to Sun City.

But Rajesh was once again rebuffed. Lanseria was a no-go because its runway was in the process of being upgraded, and Pilanesberg's apron was deemed by ACSA to be incompatible with the Airbus A330-200 that the Guptas intended to use.

The JCPS report's findings suggest that the Guptas may have decided a tactical change was necessary at this juncture. 'In early March 2013,' reads the report, 'the Minister of Defence and Military Veterans [Mapisa-Nqakula] was approached by Mr Atul Gupta. The Minister's Political Advisor, Mr Michael Ramagoma, was also approached by Mr Ashu Chawla on behalf of the Gupta family.'[3]

At that stage, Chawla, a long-time associate and business partner of the Guptas, was the CEO of Sahara Computers, one of the family's main business ventures in South Africa.

The revised strategy of simultaneously approaching two high-ranking government officials, along with the replacement of Rajesh Gupta by the older and perhaps more influential Atul, suggests that the Guptas had by then become somewhat agitated given the fast-approaching wedding date.

At this point, Ramagoma asked Lieutenant General Fabian Msimang, chief of the South African Air Force (SAAF), what military regulations governed the landing and taking off of civilian aircraft at AFB Waterkloof.

'The Chief of the Air Force informed the Political Advisor that it would be irregular for an aircraft carrying Indian wedding guests to land at the base,' states the JCPS report. Msimang also told Ramagoma that 'the matter should not be entertained any further'.[4]

It is at this juncture that DIRCO's Koloane again entered the negotiations.

'On 2 April 2013 the Chief of State Protocol contacted the Political Advisor to the Minister of Defence and Military Veterans to enquire as to progress with the request.' Koloane reportedly told Ramagoma that he was 'under pressure from Number 1' to ensure that the Guptas' chartered plane found a place to land.[5]

Nowhere in the JCPS report is this shadowy and influential 'Number 1' explicitly unmasked as President Zuma, but the reader is left to draw his or her own conclusions when, further down the page, Koloane is quoted as saying to Sergeant Major Ntshisi of the AFCP that transport minister Martins had been instructed 'by the President to assist the Gupta family'.

This conversation between Koloane and Ntshisi occurred on 9 April and had been preceded by yet another patch of turbulence as far as the Guptas' landing plans were concerned. On 3 April, according to the JCPS report, Ramagoma met with Chawla to inform him that defence minister Mapisa-Nqakula had denied the family's request to have a chartered plane land at AFB Waterkloof.

This, incredibly, did not deter the indefatigable Guptas. According to the report, the equally resolute Chawla had by now established a line of contact with the Indian High Commission in Pretoria in order to have the latter lobby appropriate officials within the South African government to have the flight cleared on the pretext that it would be transporting high-ranking Indian government delegates.

The Guptas clearly did not encounter much resistance in terms of getting the Indian embassy to join them in their efforts to get the flight approved. On 4 April – the day after Mapisa-Nqakula's advisor poured cold water over the Guptas' request – a letter was faxed by an unnamed official at the Indian High Commission to the AFCP. The letter and accompanying document, titled 'Request for Diplomatic Overflight and Landing Clearance: South Africa', indicate that at least one official at the Indian diplomatic mission had by then become a willing partner in the Guptas' ruse to have the wedding party's flight cleared under the pretence that it was an official state visit.

On Tuesday 9 April, five days after the request was sent to the AFCP by the Indian High Commission, Koloane had his conversation with Sergeant Major Ntshisi.

Ntshisi, the report suggests, was not comfortable with the way things were developing. He reportedly told Koloane that AFB Waterkloof could only be utilised for flights transporting heads of state and their deputies.

Koloane, like Atul and Rajesh Gupta before him, refused to let an obstacle as petty as fixed protocol discourage him. He told Ntshisi that the chartered flight would indeed be carrying 'four to five Ministers'. He added that Mapisa-Nqakula, who had refused Chawla's request only five days prior, had 'no objection'. In an effort to assuage the young officer's fears, Koloane said that 'this was a unique case'.[6]

But Ntshisi apparently needed more convincing. He asked Koloane to put the request in 'a note or a letter', to which Koloane responded that 'the challenge was that this could not be put in writing'. Koloane was in all likelihood unwilling to put his name on a document that essentially would be requesting clearance for a bogus diplomatic flight.

Koloane went on to assure Ntshisi that he had been in contact with Lieutenant Colonel Anderson, AFB Waterkloof's movement control officer, the previous week and that Anderson had shown him around the base. He implored Ntshisi to contact Anderson for confirmation.

When Anderson and Ntshisi eventually spoke a little while later, at least according to the report, Anderson basically told Ntshisi that he had no right to query Koloane's request. Ntishisi stated that he had merely sought written confirmation from the chief of state protocol. Anderson then explained to Ntshisi why Koloane's request could not be put in writing: 'in confidentiality, I must be very careful now, our Number 1 knows about this. It is political. Allow them. I'll phone the Ambassador [Koloane] back to find out who's the senior minister'.[7]

The 'minister' she was referring to would have been whichever high-ranking Indian government official supposedly intended to travel with the wedding guests.

At this stage the Guptas' desire to have the plane land at the base finally seemed like it could become a reality.

Koloane again phoned Ntshisi to confirm whether the latter had spoken to Anderson. Ntshisi replied in the affirmative and told Koloane that he would immediately start the process of clearing the flight for landing at AFB Waterkloof.

Ntshisi asked Koloane whether it was necessary to fax a copy of the clearance to William Matjila, an official at DIRCO's directorate of state visits. Koloane told him to rather send copies to his (Koloane's) private and work email addresses.

Koloane then got hold of Matjila himself in order to instruct him 'to assist with the clearance of the Indian delegation'.[8]

In response to Ntshisi's earlier request to see some sort of written confirmation from Koloane that the planned flight was above board, Matjila forwarded an email sent to him by Marilyn Morris, Koloane's secretary, which apparently sought to convince Matjila and other DIRCO officials that the flight was indeed for an official Indian state delegation.

'As per your discussion with Ambassador Koloane with regards to the request for flight clearances and landing at Waterkloof AFB for the Indian Delegation, kindly note that Amb Koloane telephonically approved the request,' the email sent on 9 April stated. Besides Ntshisi, Matjila also forwarded this email to several other DIRCO officials 'for your urgent assistance and information'.[9]

Later that day, Captain Shaji Kutty, a defence attaché at the Indian High Commission, faxed a letter to the AFCP's air command unit requesting forty tonnes of fuel for 'refueling of the VVIP chartered aircraft' that was earmarked to land at the base.[10]

According to the JCPS report, the official clearance for the flight was finally given on that Tuesday, exactly three weeks before the plane was scheduled to arrive in Pretoria: 'On 9 April 2013 Lieutenant-Colonel S.J. van Zyl, who has the authority to clear flights at the Air Force Command Post, signed RSA05 External Clearance on the strength of the documentation received [from the Indian High Commission] and conversations conducted that morning [between Ntshisi and Koloane, among others].'[11]

With the clearance having been processed, the finer details and planning for the so-called delegation's arrival could now be addressed by the base's own officials.

Someone from the Indian High Commission contacted Koloane on 24 April to request his 'assistance with arranging the reception and logistics at the base', states the JCPS report. Later that day, Koloane met with Lieutenant Colonel Anderson and 'an individual in the Indian High Commission' at AFB Waterkloof 'to discuss arrangements'.[12]

On 25 April the AFCP again received a letter from the Indian High Commission, this time requesting further flight clearances for private helicopters and chartered flights to land at the base. According to the report,

'The request stated that the aircraft would be required to ferry the delegation from the base to Sun City on 30 April 2013, and back again on 3 May 2013. Tail and registration numbers for the seven helicopters and two fixed-wing aircraft were provided.'[13] The AFCP eventually cleared these domestic flights on 29 April.

On 26 April, Anderson briefed AFB Waterkloof's loadmasters, the personnel tasked with handling cargo and baggage for all arriving and departing flights, on the pending arrival of the 'VIP flight from India'. The base's mission board, a constantly updated list of future flights and other events, at that point reflected the flight as being a 'Delegation Visit', again pointing to the fact that as far as the official military communication channels and administrative procedures were concerned, the flight was warranted to land at AFB Waterkloof given its official status.[14]

The final preparations were concluded when 'an unvetted private company' was allowed to enter the base on 29 April to decorate the lounges where the Guptas intended to welcome their guests.[15]

Jet Airways flight JAI 9900 may have managed to secure the necessary clearance from the AFCP to set down at AFB Waterkloof, but the highly irregular nature of the flight was manifest in the events that unfolded right after the Airbus came to a halt outside the base's terminal buildings.

The landing itself occurred without significant hiccups. Johannesburg Area Control, the communications nerve centre from where all flights in the region are managed from the ground, established radio communications with the plane at 06:00 on the morning of 30 April. Because of the gloomy weather conditions that day, Johannesburg Area Control made some routing adjustments to the aircraft's flight plan. After having started their descent, the flight crew informed flight controllers on the ground that the pilots 'did not have Waterkloof in sight due to the cloud cover'.[16]

The plane then repositioned itself for another attempt to land, and at 06:53 the flight crew told the controllers at Johannesburg radar that they could now see AFB Waterkloof. The Airbus finally landed at the base just before 07:00.

The JCPS report describes the disorganised and unusual scenes that played out at the base after the plane landed.

'The passengers started to disembark and were well behaved,' reads the report. 'The situation was, however, somewhat confused with some passengers walking to the lounges and others being ferried there by white Range Rovers. A reception had been arranged at the entrance to the lounges consisting of music and dancing.'[17]

Guests could then enjoy some refreshments in the lounges served by the private catering company identified earlier in the JCPS report as having somehow sidestepped the necessary vetting process needed to legally enter the base.

The fact that AFB Waterkloof, the SAAF and the country had just been taken for one hell of a ride courtesy of the Guptas was starting to dawn on the officials witnessing the fiasco.

'Colonel Visser [Waterkloof's base logistics coordinator] was on duty to receive VIP's,' the report continues. 'Two red carpets were laid out at the entrances to the lounges. No VIP's were identified. He ended up greeting everybody who greeted him.'[18]

Koloane only arrived at the base after an unnamed individual in the Indian High Commission phoned him at 07:10 to tell him that the flight had arrived. Koloane later told the JCPS investigators that he 'found in excess of 50 vehicles there to transport the guests' and 'noted that there were no familiar VIP protectors in the cars'.[19]

Anderson informed Koloane that the arrival and processing of the group had gone 'smoothly'. Somewhat alarmingly, 'No DIRCO protocol officers were present'.[20]

The JCPS report not only examined the military's role in granting flight JAI 9900 permission to land at AFB Waterkloof, but also the use of SAPS and Tshwane Metro Police Department vehicles and officers to accompany the Gupta entourage from the base to Sun City.

According to the report, the SAPS North West provincial commissioner, Lieutenant General Zukiswa Mbombo, received a letter from Ronica Ragavan, another representative of the Gupta family, on 19 April 'requesting protection for the convoys that would be travelling from the base to Sun City'.[21]

The Guptas again had to push hard for this request to be granted.

On 22 April, Sun City's security department submitted an application to the SAPS for an 'Event Risk Categorisation'. This was to ensure that any police protection and assistance given at the wedding itself would have official approval. However, 'On hearing about the nature of the visit, the Provincial Commissioner [Mbombo] turned down the request, and also declined to attend the wedding as a guest.'[22]

The JCPS report failed to mention the hilarious and perhaps deeply symbolic events that were set in motion by the delivery of the invitation to the police commissioner in the first place.

Foreshadowing the over-the-top nature of the wedding to come, each guest's invitation card arrived accompanied by six containers filled with Lindt truffles from Europe, dried kiwi fruit from Australia, golden berries all the way from South America and other exotic goodies. When the goodies arrived at Mbombo's home one morning, 'Merriam Mbombo summoned the bomb squad to detonate the "suspicious" box'.[23]

'We got the invite, but Mrs Mbombo was not expecting an invitation,' a North West police spokesperson later told a reporter from Independent Media. 'When it arrived and when we looked at it, it looked like it had wires and we had to do our normal security checks,' the spokesperson explained.

Two sniffer dogs were then brought in. One reacted 'positively' and the other 'negatively', after which it was decided to call in the local bomb squad. Not wanting to take any chances, the bomb experts decided to detonate the package.

While the bomb squad did their duty, the Guptas were still trying to secure for their guests the pomp and officialdom that only police escorts could ensure.

'A second application that emphasised the attendance of Indian Ministers at the wedding was then presented [to senior police officials],' reads the JCPS report. 'The applicant requested that the event be categorised as High Risk.' The adjustment would at least ensure the event was afforded some degree of official police recognition, but the North West SAPS apparently remained sceptical. Eventually, 'the Deputy Provincial Commissioner: Operational Services, Major-General Mpembe, categorised the event as Medium Risk on 25 April 2013'.[24]

Major General Patrick Asaneng, SAPS cluster commander for the Rustenburg area in the North West province, convened a meeting at Sun City five days before the flight's scheduled arrival to discuss security-related issues around some of the upcoming events at the resort.

It was at this meeting that the Gupta wedding party was finally given official police recognition. An 'Operational Plan' with serial number 44/2013 dated 25 April 2013 was compiled, and it was decided that Asaneng would liaise with Major General Phumza Gela of Gauteng SAPS, the police official who would later be named in the ministerial press briefing on 3 May. This was to ensure that the two provinces' police structures were on the same page regarding the Gupta event.

On 29 April, the police's joint operational commander, Lieutenant Colonel du Plooy, 'activated the Event Safety and Security Planning Committee (ESSPC) and all relevant role players as the plan went operational in keeping with the Standard Operating Procedures'.[25]

In other words, the entire process leading up to the deployment of police officials and vehicles as security escorts for the convoy could now unfold within the bounds of the SAPS's standard and documented procedures for such an event.

After the Airbus's arrival at AFB Waterkloof, the seven helicopters and two fixed-wing aircraft left with those who must have been the most important guests. The rest were taken to the awaiting vehicles which 'were divided into four convoys of 15 vehicles each, with one police vehicle to lead [each] convoy and one traffic vehicle at the rear'.[26]

But these were not the only police cars and personnel assigned to the job. According to the JCPS report, Gauteng SAPS deployed a staggering '31 cars and 62 members for route security'. These vehicles accompanied the Gupta convoys to the border between Gauteng and North West, where 'five cars and six members' from the latter province's Flying Squad took over the task for the remainder of the journey to Sun City.[27]

Apart from the SAPS, the report found that several officials from the TMPD 'were involved in the convoy moonlighting as escorts. These Metro Police officials have now been placed on suspension by the Metro.'[28]

The JCPS report is in part a vivid description of the South African government's ability to start acting in the most decisive and urgent manner only after it has been dealt a crisis card.

The day after the landing, states the report, officials from the National Intelligence Coordinating Committee convened a five-hour-long meeting to 'coordinate a response from the [government's] security cluster'. The meeting was attended by representatives from NICOC, the State Security Agency, Defence Intelligence, DIRCO, the Presidency, the departments of home affairs and justice, SARS and GCIS.[29]

The decisions taken by the officials and listed in the report included the following: the directors general of all government departments were to advise their ministers not to attend the Gupta wedding (a directive which obviously was not taken too seriously judging by the number of ministers who attended); the Jet Airways aircraft, which still stood at Waterkloof, was to be removed from the base immediately; SARS, whose customs officials had not been present at the base when the plane landed and therefore were unable to issue the 200-plus visitors with customs declaration forms, was to travel to Sun City to issue such forms immediately; and a suitable point of departure was to be identified for the group, which could 'under no circumstances be Air Force Base Waterkloof'.[30]

The Jet Airways Airbus A330-200 was finally moved from AFB Water-kloof to O.R. Tambo International Airport on 2 May 'on the instructions of the Minister of Defence and Military Veterans'. Given that the Guptas had brazenly ignored Mapisa-Nqakula's earlier denial of their request to have the plane land at the base, it must have been with a considerable degree of satisfaction that she ordered it to leave again.[31]

On the same day, DIRCO's director general, Jerry Matjila, phoned Virendra Gupta, India's high commissioner to South Africa, to discuss the fateful event. Gupta, who has no discernible family relation to Ajay, Atul and Rajesh, told Matjila that none of the passengers who had landed at AFB Waterkloof were national ministers, but rather state ministers. Indian state ministers are akin to our provincial ministers, or MECs. The flight certainly did not transport any 'heads of state and their deputies', which are the only types of government dignitaries who, according to protocol, are allowed to land at a military base.

Gupta also told Matjila 'that the Gupta family had not asked him to assist with the arrangements for the visiting delegation'.[32]

The following day, 3 May, Virendra Gupta was called in to meet with Matjila in person 'to discuss circumstances and procedures followed regarding the landing'. Matjila told the Indian high commissioner that his embassy had failed to produce a *note verbale*, a diplomatic communication between two countries' embassies, prior to the landing in accordance with diplomatic protocol. Gupta admitted that this oversight 'had been a lapse and that the point made was a valid one'.[33]

Bringing its account of the sequence of events to a close, the JCPS report provided a summary of the 'exit phase'.

While most of the Guptas' visitors left the country via O.R. Tambo International Airport, the state ministers mentioned earlier in the report, and whose tally had now risen to seven individuals, were flown to Cape Town on a chartered flight. From there they departed South Africa on a commercial flight.

However, using the Department of Home Affairs Departure and Reconciliation List for 7 May 2013, the JCPS investigators were able to determine 'that one of the arriving visitors originally listed as [a member of flight JAI 9900's] crew had in fact not yet left South Africa'.[34] The JCPS report regarded this development as 'extremely irregular ... in the context of national security'. Furthermore, the report stated that the missing crew member's whereabouts in South Africa was the subject of an investigation, but what this person has been up to and whether he or she is still in South Africa remains a mystery to this day.

15

Pointing fingers

The JCPS report eventually identified AFB Waterkloof's Lieutenant Colonel Anderson and DIRCO chief of state protocol Koloane as the principal culprits in the Waterkloof saga.

The Guptas' role in the incident was also widely criticised in the report, but the implications for them could never compare to the threat of dismissal and even criminal prosecution that Anderson and Koloane now faced.

The report found that the Guptas' 'direct approach' to defence minister Mapisa-Nqakula and their 'request for use of a strategic entry point for a wedding was improper because this amounted to a request for untoward assistance'.[1]

The report was also highly critical of Gupta business associate Ashu Chawla and the Indian High Commission's role in furthering the request by means of 'an official diplomatic approach'. The wedding, after all, was a 'family matter' and should never have been afforded the diplomatic status it was granted. The JCPS cluster found that the 'collusion between Chawla and an individual in the Indian High Commission to abuse the diplomatic channel to request flight clearance on 4 April 2013 is of concern, and improper'. Their actions were 'a deliberate manipulation of the system to further wedding objectives couched as official business'.[2]

Chawla's contact at the high commission remains anonymous throughout the JCPS report, but it later emerged from documentation submitted during the SANDF's own inquiry that it was Captain Shaji Kutty, the Indian High Commission's defence attaché, who had been doing the Guptas' bidding. According to the JCPS report, Kutty's failure to send a *note verbale* to DIRCO amounted to a 'serious infringement of diplomatic protocol'. Furthermore, Kutty's request for 'Diplomatic Overflight and Landing Clearance' and his subsequent labelling of the flight as a 'Delegation Visit' amounted to 'a misrepresentation of the nature of the visit'.[3]

The JCPS investigators found that Kutty's request to the AFCP on 9 April 'to provide for the re-fuelling of the aircraft', in which he 'described the visit as VVIP', only 'compounded confusion as to the exact status of the pending visit' and was 'a clear misrepresentation of the facts in the extreme'.[4]

Once the Guptas' emissaries had done their work, at this point, the report concluded, Koloane 'took it upon himself to facilitate an illegal request for landing' at AFB Waterkloof. The report lists all the ways in which the chief of state protocol erred. Firstly, Koloane spoke directly to the AFCP. According to the report, 'it was not normal practice for the Chief of State Protocol to interact directly with the Command Post to enquire as to progress with a specific clearance'. Secondly, in his communication with the AFCP, Koloane misrepresented the facts when he told Sergeant Major Thabo Ntshisi that 'there would be four to five [national] Ministers on the flight'. Thirdly, and the report subjects this point to particular scrutiny, Koloane claimed that the ministers of transport and defence, as well as President Zuma, had personally given their consent for the flight 'in an effort to pressure the Command Post to issue the clearance'. The JCPS cluster found that 'this was improper and inappropriate, and amounted to abuse of political clout and office of members of the National Executive'.[5]

While Koloane himself later backtracked on this last point, the JCPS cluster officials evidently relied heavily on Zuma's own denial of these claims. 'On 13 May 2013,' according to the report, 'the Director-General in The Presidency [Cassius Lubisi] stated that at no point did the President give instructions to Ambassador Koloane or discuss the issue of the landing of the aircraft with him.' Furthermore, Lubisi 'denied that The Presidency had ever received a request for landing at Waterkloof Air Force Base from any person whatsoever'.[6] With that, any suspicion or rumour that Zuma had personally been in contact with the Gupta family or their representatives regarding the flight was seemingly quashed.

Koloane's earlier interaction with Mapisa-Nqakula's political advisor, Michael Ramagoma, on 2 April was also deemed 'improper' because the chief of state protocol had 'abused the name of the President of the Republic in an effort to exert pressure on the Political Advisor'.[7]

Somewhat predictably, the JCPS cluster investigators made a clear effort to ensure that any suggestion of President Zuma's involvement in the matter be portrayed as ludicrous and false. Following meetings with Koloane on 1 and 16 May – this last the day before the JCPS concluded its investigation – the investigators no longer had to rely on Zuma's word alone concerning his alleged role in the fiasco. By now Koloane had 'confirmed' that at no point was he influenced by 'the President nor officials in the Presidency whether junior or senior, Ministers and Directors-General in DIRCO and Defence and Military Veterans ... to assist with the landing of the aircraft'.[8]

While this would by no means be the final word on Zuma's alleged complicity in the incident, the JCPS report's inclusion of Koloane's admission at least provided the president's team with some temporary breathing space.

The report went on to condemn Koloane's conduct during his interaction with Ntshisi, the AFCP officer he contacted to have the flight cleared. According to the report, Koloane had told Ntshisi that the flight was 'a unique case' in order to 'justify a request with which [Ntshisi] was clearly uncomfortable'. Moreover, Koloane's refusal to 'put his sensitive motivation in writing [was] a clear indication that he was aware of the fact that the request was dubious'.[9]

Next up in the JCPS cluster's firing line was Lieutenant Colonel Anderson. The report found that her use of the term 'Number 1' in her conversation with Ntshisi amounted to a 'misrepresentation of the person of the President and his Office'. The investigators once again emphasised that the 'Director-General in The Presidency made it clear that no one in The Presidency ever gave an instruction in this regard'. By insinuating that President Zuma had sanctioned the flight, Anderson had brought 'the Office of the President into disrepute', the report found.[10]

Anderson was also criticised for reportedly telling Ntshisi that the granting of landing rights for AFB Waterkloof depended on 'the status of the visit' when she should have known that only flights carrying heads of state and national government ministers could be received at the base. Her transfer of 'ultimate authority for the decision to DIRCO ... amount[ed] to disregard for official policy as to the use of the base'.[11]

Colonel Maritz Visser, AFB Waterkloof's base logistics coordinator, told the JCPS investigators that on the morning of the flight's arrival, he, Anderson and another base official, Colonel Fredrikson, 'had "agreed that the flight should never have landed"' at Waterkloof. The report found Anderson's agreement with this statement to be 'ironic ... in light of the fact that she was party from inception to the planning of this visit'.[12]

She also came under fire for allowing passports to be processed 'as a batch in the absence of the visitors', a clear contravention of the Immigration Act, which 'requires that civilians entering the country present themselves physically with their passports to the immigration officials'.[13]

While the actual clearing of the flight by the AFCP was done in accordance with 'the correct clearance procedures', the report found that the request was 'based on false pretences as a result of the manipulation of the process by the Gupta family, individuals in the Indian High Commission, Chief of State Protocol Ambassador V.B. Koloane, and Officer Commanding Movement Control at the base, Lieutenant-Colonel C. Anderson, who shared a common purpose and acted in concert'.[14]

Curiously, the report's authors do not offer any suggestions as to what may have prompted Anderson and Koloane to risk their careers and reputations for the benefit of a wealthy family with whom they had no personal connection.

President Zuma and his high-level government colleagues were absolved of all blame in the report's final pages: 'Members of the National Executive were not required to issue any instructions, did not issue any instructions, and did not create the impression that they ought to have issued any instructions.'[15]

The reception of more than 200 wedding guests at AFB Waterkloof and their subsequent journey to Sun City necessitated the deployment of an astounding 194 government personnel, including from the SAAF, the SAPS and the TMPD; 296 private security officers; 88 state vehicles; and 121 private vehicles. The bill for the private security contingent was fortunately covered by the Guptas and not by the taxpayers. But the involvement of both the public and private security officers in the operation led to transgressions and oversights identified in the JCPS report.

Some of the private Range Rovers ferrying guests to Sun City, for example, had the same number plates, as did two Mercedes-Benzes, while three black BMWs had false plates. Many were fitted illegally with blue lights. In addition, the private security company that provided the vehicles and security officers was not registered as required by South African legislation. The report warned: 'These and other criminal activities uncovered in this investigation are a manifestation of a deep-seated organised crime culture waiting to be unleashed on the country.'[16]

Furthermore, the report concluded that although the 'involvement of law enforcement agencies under the auspices and leadership of the South African Police Services, in providing convoy protection services was authorised', some of the TMPD officers were moonlighting 'contrary to regulations'. They were also carrying their official firearms despite the fact that they were 'only authorised to bear their firearms within their respective Metro jurisdictions'. Overall, the report found that 'the lack of vigilance of the SAPS members deployed for escort duty ... made it possible for the cars fitted with illegal blue-lights to push people off the road, cause delays and inconvenience other road users. The public outcry that followed was therefore justified.'[17]

The report also criticised the two provincial SAPS departments, namely Gauteng and North West, for failing to properly communicate with each other during their planning for the wedding. They also ignored standard police protocol by not informing the national police commissioner of the event.

The SAPS subsequently opened criminal investigations into the misconduct of the handful of police officers and the unregistered private security company. Five cases – four in Sun City and one in Pretoria – were eventually registered, but the outcomes of these probes have been underwhelming. The private security company was let off the hook from two of the cases after paying an admission-of-guilt fine of R3 000. The two other cases opened at the Sun City police station, one relating to the contravention of the Firearms Control Act and the other to the National Road Traffic Act, were closed after the National Prosecuting Authority declined to prosecute anyone. The only case that garnered any interest from the NPA was the one lodged at the Lyttelton police station in Pretoria involving an alleged contravention of the South African Police Act. By the time this book went to print, however, the NPA had failed to provide details as to how this case was progressing.

16

The scapegoats

'The activities of Ambassador Koloane and Lieutenant-Colonel Anderson were a serious dereliction of duty in that they were advancing the objectives of this project to the detriment of their official responsibilities. Their activities also indicate the bringing to bear of undue influence on state officials, systems, equipment and infrastructure ... The activities of some of the persons involved were driven by the undesirable practice of the exercise of undue influence, and abuse of higher office.'[1]

These and other findings listed in the JCPS cluster report laid the foundation for further disciplinary action against Koloane and Anderson. While the report made no effort to establish their motive for taking part in such a plot, it roundly criticised them for abusing their seniority in their respective interactions with Sergeant Major Ntshisi.

Koloane, who was suspended by DIRCO the very week of the Waterkloof landing, seemed certain to lose his job over the fiasco. In early May, sources close to developments told the *Mail & Guardian* that he would be fired because he had broken the law in facilitating the Gupta flight.[2]

But by August it was clear that Koloane had decided to act as a fall guy for whoever gave him the instruction to request the landing, most likely in exchange for not being fired from the department. The *Sunday Independent* in that month revealed that Koloane had pleaded guilty to all of the charges relating to his role in the saga that his department had levelled against him. According to the newspaper, Koloane was charged with:

- Abusing state diplomatic channels by facilitating an illegal request for the landing.
- Misrepresenting facts during his 'facilitation' of the illegal and unlawful landing of the said aircraft.
- Compromising the processes and procedures of his employer in that

there was neither consultation nor recommendation from the relevant desk/department on the request for the landing.[3]

The most telling of the three charges is the one involving his so-called misrepresentation of facts during his interactions with, presumably, Anderson and Ntshisi, the two SAAF officers. In a clear attempt to save his own skin, Koloane was now saying that he had not been telling the truth when he told Anderson and Ntshisi that 'Number 1' had instructed him to see to it that the landing got cleared. His admission of guilt was accompanied by a relatively small penalty: he would forgo two months' salary and be demoted to a lower position within the department. But it was not long before he was rewarded for sacrificing himself as a scapegoat.

Within a year, Koloane was packing his bags for Europe after quietly being appointed South Africa's new ambassador to the Netherlands.[4]

The SANDF launched its own board of inquiry into the matter a day after the JCPS cluster probe was initiated. Tasked with finding facts and evidence and gathering written statements from any SANDF officials implicated in the scandal, the inquiry's terms of reference included establishing the 'circumstances that led to the landing' at AFB Waterkloof; determining which SANDF personnel were responsible 'for allowing the landing of such aircraft without proper authorization'; and ultimately making a call on whether any 'corrective measures, including disciplinary and or criminal steps are to be taken against any member of the SANDF and of the public'.[5]

In other words, at this juncture the fallout from the Guptas' elaborate wedding not only threatened to wreck the careers of Anderson, Ntshisi and Stephan van Zyl, but also opened them up to criminal charges, prosecution and even jail time.

A key piece of evidence unearthed during this probe, and evidently overlooked by the JCPS team, was a letter written by Captain Prashant Chowdhary, a defence advisor at the Indian High Commission, to the office of the SANDF's chief of Defence Foreign Relations (DFR) on 28 February 2013.

This letter was important because it showed that the JCPS cluster report's timeline of events was wrong. The Indian High Commission's first approach to the SANDF had occurred at the end of February, and not on 4 April as the JCPS report determined. This meant that the request for the flight had gone through official diplomatic channels from the outset and that the written request and subsequent paperwork were already being passed through official channels long before the likes of Anderson, Koloane and Ntshisi became involved in the process.

In his letter, Chowdhary claimed that 'a delegation of ministers from the government of Uttarakhand, India and members from the central government of India' were to visit South Africa and needed 'landing approval at Waterkloof'.[6]

On 5 March, Brigadier General N.F. Maphoyi from DFR faxed a letter to Colonel Nomsa Khumalo, a senior staff officer (SSO) at the SAAF's foreign relations department, requesting the latter's 'assistance for landing and departure of VIP flight on 30 April and 3 May 2013'. Chowdhary's original letter was attached to this message.[7]

The board of inquiry would show that Khumalo received further communications regarding the flight in the form of letters sent to her office. Yet despite this paper trail, Khumalo incredibly told the board that she had never received a request for the landing.

'There are two letters that were sent from the High Commission of India and one sent from Defence Foreign Relations to the office of the SSO Foreign Relations [Khumalo] and none of them is alleged to have been received, this is suspect,' reads the board's report.

Anderson, who was curiously not interviewed for the JCPS cluster report, submitted an affidavit to the SANDF board of inquiry that erased any doubt as to the identity of the mysterious and influential 'Number 1' on whose instructions the landing requests were initiated.

'During a Sunday evening between the end of March and beginning of April 2013 at about 21:00 Ambassador Koloane, chief director of state protocol department of international relations and cooperation phoned me to enquire about the capacity of Waterkloof Air Force Base for the landing of an Airbus A330 relating to a cultural event. He also mentioned that there will be two ministers on board and that Number One has knowledge about the flight,' Anderson stated.[8]

'Number One is the President of the Republic of South Africa,' she added. 'We never refer to the President in telephone conversations by name for security reasons.'

Anderson told Koloane that the AFCP would have to issue an over-flight clearance for the Gupta plane. He phoned her again around 17 April and told her that 'he had returned from the President and the President wanted to know if everything is still on track for the flight', Anderson stated. She eventually received the AFCP's clearance for the flight on 23 April.

Ntshisi, in a sworn statement submitted to the board, confirmed Anderson's claims about Zuma's involvement, as relayed to him by Koloane. DIRCO's chief of state protocol had told Ntshisi that 'four to five [Indian government] ministers' would be on board the flight and that 'the President [had] authorize[d] the landing'.[9]

But Ntshisi's own motives for his role in getting the AFCP to approve the flight would face severe scrutiny thanks to new evidence submitted to the board of inquiry.

All telephone calls to and from the AFCP are recorded as standard pro-cedure. These recordings are stored at the Bushveld Airspace Control Sector (BACS), a nerve centre located at SAAF headquarters in Pretoria where ground staff keep an eye on South Africa's airspace using radar and other surveillance equipment.

Two phone calls, made in April 2013, caught the board of inquiry's atten-tion. The first, on 8 April, was from Captain Kutty, the defence attaché at the Indian High Commission, to Ntshisi. During the conversation, Kutty told Ntshisi that 'four to five ministers' would be on board the Jet Airways flight. The second and more important call, a day later, was placed by Ntshisi to 'an unknown lady'. In their invitation to Ntshisi to make a written representation regarding his alleged wrongdoings, the board of inquiry reported that in this conversation 'you asked her to speak to Mr Koloane on your behalf about a job opportunity at DIRCO'.[10]

The board then accused Ntshisi of manipulating the flight clearance process with the intention of scoring a plush job at DIRCO courtesy of Koloane: 'You advised on the unlawful approval of the clearance with an intention to individually gain favours at the expense of the organization [SAAF] and/or the department of defence,' reads the letter.

In his written response, Ntshisi denied that the conversation with the woman in question had anything to do with Koloane or the Gupta flight. He maintained that the person on the other end of the line was Sarah

The Thabo Mbeki Foundation has vehemently denied that the former president was close to the Guptas, but there are plenty of indications that the family were familiar with him. Here is Ajay Gupta next to Mbeki, with Atul Gupta in the background. It is not clear when the photo was taken

Ajay Gupta (middle row, wearing dark glasses) was a member of the International Marketing Council of South Africa (IMC), now known as Brand South Africa. This photo of the IMC board with President Thabo Mbeki dates from circa 2006

Jacob Zuma and Ajay Gupta at a gala dinner at the Gupta home in June 2005

Proteas captain Graeme Smith (left) and bowler Makhaya Ntini at an event in Saharanpur in 2005. The Guptas persuaded Cricket South Africa to alter the Proteas' tour schedule so that the cricket team could visit their hometown

Ajay and Atul Gupta in March 2011. The duo, along with their younger brother, Rajesh, have consistently denied their involvement in state capture and corruption

Atul Gupta and Duduzane Zuma at *The New Age* newspaper's offices in March 2011. Duduzane, one of Jacob Zuma's children with the late Kate Mantsho, has greatly benefited from his interests in the Gupta business empire

Duff du Toit/Gallo Images

President Jacob Zuma and Atul Gupta during The New Age Friendship T20 Cup cricket match between South Africa and India in 2012. The Guptas were extremely influential within Cricket South Africa (CSA), but their grip on the organisation appears to have weakened

Presidency of RSA, screengrab https://www.youtube.com/watch?v=LyZ2X8GpyO0

The New Age CEO Nazeem Howa (back left), Atul Gupta and President Jacob Zuma with members of the Proteas cricket team after The New Age Friendship T20 Cup match against India in 2012. South Africa won the match

Jacob Zuma, Atul Gupta and Eastern Cape premier Noxolo Kiviet at a business breakfast sponsored by *The New Age* newspaper in Port Elizabeth in 2012. *The New Age* breakfasts became mired in controversy when it became known that state-owned companies such as Transnet and Eskom forked out millions of rands to sponsor the events

Atul Gupta, Zuma, Nazeem Howa and Malusi Gigaba, then minister of public enterprises, at the 2012 business breakfast. Gigaba, who has been rumoured to be close to the Guptas, became South Africa's new finance minister after a dramatic cabinet reshuffle in March 2017

Air Gupta: This Jet Airways plane was at the centre of a national controversy after it landed at Air Force Base Waterkloof in Pretoria in 2013. The aircraft carried Indian nationals who attended the glitzy wedding of Vega Gupta, the Gupta brothers' niece

Atul Gupta at AFB Waterkloof in 2013

All photos on this page: Barry Bateman

There was no shortage of police officials at AFB Waterkloof when the Guptas' guests arrived there. They escorted the Guptas and their guests to the wedding at Sun City

The wedding of Aakash Jahajgarhia and Vega Gupta, the daughter of the Gupta brothers' sister, Achla, became a national scandal. The wedding was a opulent affair that was rumoured to have cost about R75 million

The Sun City holiday resort, where Aakash and Vega got married, was transformed into Gupta City for four days

Then Eskom CEO Brian Molefe breaks down while talking about his relationship with the Guptas during a media conference in November 2016. Molefe, who insists that allegations against him in former public protector Thuli Madonsela's state capture report are unfounded, became a member of Parliament after he stepped down as Eskom CEO

Finance minister Pravin Gordhan (right) and his deputy, Mcebisi Jonas, before Gordhan's 2017 budget speech in Parliament in Cape Town. Gordhan and Jonas were sacked in President Jacob Zuma's cabinet reshuffle in March 2017

Ramotlalane, an employee of the Gauteng Department of Roads and Transport, and that while they had indeed discussed work opportunities, these were in no way related to the Guptas. According to Ntshisi, Ramotlalane had assisted a man at the Soweto traffic department, where she had worked previously, who turned out to be a renowned businessman. 'She realised during their conversation that [s]he is talking with the great business man in RSA that is why we end seeking for great opportunities of job,' wrote Ntshisi.[11]

His response included a sworn affidavit by Ramotlalane, who claimed to be Ntshisi's cousin: 'I told my cousin about that gentleman [the business mogul is never named]. The conversation between myself and my cousin was about getting a new job from that gentleman ... The businessman does not know anything about DIRCO or Gupta's saga cause our conversation was based on a new job that we wanted.'[12]

The board of inquiry ultimately recommended that disciplinary steps be taken against several SANDF members for their role in the landing. Its findings against Ntshisi and Anderson were the harshest. The board recommended that both be criminally charged with misuse of state property and corruption for 'colluding and assisting with the approval of a clearances [sic] to land knowing very well that doing so was unlawful'.

Colonel Nomsa Khumalo was found to have lied under oath about the three correspondences she received from the Indian High Commission regarding the flight. The board suggested that she too be charged.

The report also recommended that Lieutenant Colonel Stephan van Zyl, the senior controller at the AFCP, be disciplined for 'not checking and reviewing the recommendations forward[ed to him] by Ntshisi'.

The board also demanded that DIRCO pursue further action against Koloane.

Defence Foreign Relations was advised to 'approach' the defence attaché at the Indian High Commission 'and cordially remind him to never again write direct to any force structure element of the SANDF or to DOD individuals but [to direct requests] through the DFR'.

Following a preliminary investigation by the SANDF into the matter, Anderson, Van Zyl and Ntshisi were finally charged in October 2013 by the military's prosecuting authority. The board of inquiry's recommendation that the three face charges of corruption, misuse of state property and collusion, however, were seemingly ignored. Instead, they were charged with contravening SAAF instruction MRI: 013574, which governs the landing of civilian aircraft at air force bases. Erika Gibson, a seasoned reporter on military affairs for *Beeld* and *Rapport*, deemed the new charge 'drastically watered down'.[13] She quoted Pikkie Greeff, who had been representing Anderson and Van Zyl, as saying that the SANDF's motivation for dropping the other charges was most likely to prevent any embarrassing evidence regarding Zuma's involvement in the Gupta landing from being presented in court. The sole charge the officers now faced was an internal military matter which would not require evidence or arguments beyond those needed to prove or disprove that the three had contravened the regulations in question. For all practical purposes, it was the beginning of the end of the SANDF's prosecution of the Waterkloofgate scapegoats.

The SANDF board of inquiry and the preliminary investigation, as well as the JCPS cluster report, clearly demonstrated that the process of obtaining flight clearance was set in motion by written requests from the Indian High Commission and by additional pressure from DIRCO's Koloane. The three officers had no option but to view the flight as official, seeing as they had been told from the start that there would be government delegates on board.

The SANDF did, however, make one last desperate attempt to ensure that at least someone was brought to book for what was clearly an embarrassing fiasco. In January 2014, *Beeld* revealed that Ntshisi had turned state witness against Anderson and Van Zyl in exchange for exemption from any further legal action against him.[14]

This new development irked Greeff, who still represented Anderson and Van Zyl. In a statement on behalf of the South African National Defence Union, Greeff said:

'[T]he case has now taken a rather bizarre twist in that one of the accused, Warrant Officer Ntshisi, has apparently been offered immunity from prosecution in exchange for becoming the prosecution's main witness against his former co-accused. No explanation has been offered as to why he, in particular, has been singled out, given the fact that all three officers faced exactly the same charge of contravening an Air Force order. If anything, Ntshisi's previous evidence at other forums was full of contradictions and evidence of unseemly behaviour on his part, not the least of which was the fact that he was found to have attempted to solicit a job at DIRCO during the Gupta landing debacle. It is clear that the Military Prosecutors are, on the one hand, desperately attempting to fabricate a case against the remaining officers so as to wash the hands of their political masters and, on the other hand, unnecessarily delaying the onset of the trial, the outcome of which has the potential of political embarrassment for president Zuma a few months or weeks before national elections.'[15]

Greeff threatened the SANDF with legal action if it did not immediately set a trial date.

A source within the SANDF who had direct insight into the prosecution of Anderson and Van Zyl recently told me a story about Ntshisi's dramatic U-turn that up to now has remained under wraps. In early 2014, shortly after Ntshisi turned witness, rumours started circulating within the SAAF that he would soon enjoy a promotion that, relative to his rank, would out-shine even Koloane's rise in fortune. When Ntshisi was suddenly sent on a candidate's course to potentially become a military attaché, his colleagues were more than a little surprised.

'He held the rank of warrant officer at that time. Under normal circum-stances one would have to at least be a full colonel to be considered for training as a military attaché,' explained my source.

He added that Ntshisi had been receiving treatment for stress ever since the Gupta fiasco.

'What I suspect, and this is just me speculating, is that the SANDF put pressure on Ntshisi based on whatever was said during those taped conversations,' said my source. 'They probably told him they'd let him off the hook and even promote him if he turned state witness.'

By September 2014 Anderson and Van Zyl had been on paid sus-pension for about eighteen months, yet were no closer to having their day in court. Greeff once again put pressure on the SANDF to set a date for the trial.

Then, in January 2015, the SANDF abruptly informed the South African National Defence Union that 'the above-mentioned case was formally withdrawn by the director-military prosecutions on 19 January 2015'.[16]

For Van Zyl and Anderson, this was cause for only mild relief and cele-bration. The Guptas' abuse of AFB Waterkloof ultimately had a devastating effect on their careers and personal lives. The fact that they were suddenly free from the threat of prosecution was a rather insignificant victory considering what they had already been through.

Anderson, who reached retirement age during the saga, left the SANDF after a career of twenty-five years.

'Yes, it had an effect on me, but not only on me, also on my three children, my husband and my 86-year-old father,' she told me in an email. 'I think my husband suffered the most at that time when I sat at home. He was still a serving SAAF member and had to endure everyone's questions every day … it was very difficult for him.'

She added that she did not regret having served in the SAAF.

'I would have liked my career to have ended on a different note, but I have peace in my heart that I will be remembered for the right reasons,' she wrote.

The fiasco was equally hard on Van Zyl.

'My children were teased at school by other children,' Van Zyl told me. 'Even the teachers wanted to know from them what their father had done wrong. My daughter, who was ten at the time, kept asking me if I would be fired, and if I still had money.'

To date, neither the Guptas nor Zuma has had to endure similar pressure or persecution over the Waterkloof landing, despite the fact that there is compelling evidence that the president had knowledge of and even participated in the fiasco.

On Thursday 2 May 2013, while Sun City was still buzzing with the Guptas' wedding activities, *Beeld* reported that Zuma and his entourage of aides and bodyguards were scheduled to fly from Air Force Base Swartkop in Pretoria to Sun City in two SAAF Oryx helicopters. According to the newspaper, Zuma was to be the guest of honour at the wedding.[17] However, possibly having considered the further outrage his attendance would spark, he decided to cancel the trip at the last minute.

Ultimately, South Africa paid the greatest price for the Guptas' costly wedding festival. Apart from the financial implications of several government and military investigations, the reputational blow suffered by the country proved to be the most damaging. The saga exposed the extent to which the Zuma-led government was willing to bend and break the rules in order to satisfy the whims and desires of their friends the Guptas.

The events of 30 April 2013 and the days that followed would be remembered as the point at which many South Africans became aware that the Guptas' hold over key elements of government was far stronger and more ominous than they had ever imagined possible.

As the furore over Waterkloofgate petered out, the Guptas were left in relative peace to run their businesses. It took less than three years for that peace to be shattered, however, when the country's attention was once again drawn to a Gupta scandal of epic proportions.

But before we get to that, we must first explore some of the Guptas' deals with state-owned companies in order to understand how they profit from their activities.

PART V

CASH 'N CAPTURE

17

Horseshoes and gravy trains

Over the years, South Africa's state-owned transport and logistics oper-
ator Transnet has consistently been one of the biggest spenders among the
country's public entities. In April 2012, the company announced that it
was launching a gigantic infrastructure-expansion programme called the
Market Demand Strategy (MDS). It would see Transnet spend an astro-
nomical R300 billion between 2012 and 2019, mostly on improving or
replacing the country's ageing rail network and its equally outdated fleet
of locomotives.[1] When written out in full – R300 000 000 000.00 – the
MDS budget actually resembles a freight train. The previous year, then
minister of public enterprises Malusi Gigaba had announced that Brian
Molefe would become Transnet's new CEO. 'His understanding of capital
markets and asset management will be invaluable as the company moves
forward with its massive infrastructure development programme,' Gigaba
had said when he introduced the country's new rail boss in February 2011.[2]
Perhaps I should rather say when Gigaba *confirmed* Molefe as Transnet's
CEO, seeing as the Guptas' *The New Age* had already stolen the minister's
thunder when it reported in December 2010 that it had 'it on good authority that Molefe will be appointed CEO by the board'.[3]

Looking back at everything that has transpired since then, I cannot help
but wonder whether the Guptas orchestrated Molefe's appointment just
as Transnet was about to embark on one of the largest public expenditure
drives in South Africa's history. All indications were that the family and
Molefe had crossed paths before he became the parastatal's new boss.
In 2010 he had apparently tried to help the Guptas secure a loan from the
Public Investment Corporation, of which he was then CEO.[4]

There were other signs that suggested the Guptas were out to capture
Transnet. Shortly after Molefe's appointment, *Business Day* reported that
Gigaba had tried to have Iqbal Sharma, a Transnet board member since

December 2010, appointed as the parastatal's new chairman. The proposal, however, was reportedly shot down by cabinet over fears that Sharma 'might be too closely identified with the wealthy Gupta family, friends of President Jacob Zuma'.[5]

In March 2014, Transnet announced that it had awarded contracts totalling R50 billion to four international rail companies as part of the MDS. China North Rail and China South Rail (which have since merged into one giant Chinese state-owned rail firm), and Bombardier and General Electric clinched huge contracts to supply South Africa with 1 064 new locomotives. Collectively, the expenditure represented the 'largest-ever locomotive supply contract in South Africa's history', said Transnet in a statement. Molefe promised that the contracts would 'create and preserve approximately 30 000 jobs' thanks to the strict condition that most of the locomotives had to be built in South Africa.[6] But it did not take long for the deal's more fishy qualities to float to the surface.

The Guptas and Sharma were soon implicated in alleged dodgy dealings that seemed to confirm the widely held suspicion that the MDS was not so much intended to revive South Africa's economy as it was an opportunity to enrich politically connected deal-makers. In July 2014, amaBhungane revealed that Sharma – who oversaw the tender process as the chairperson of the Transnet board's tender committee – had apparently put himself in a position to benefit from the very tender whose winners he had helped choose. According to the report, Sharma, through a holding company, became the owner of VRLS Properties mere weeks before Transnet announced the winners of the R50-billion tender. VRLS Properties owned the premises of another company called VR Laser Services, which happened to be in a prime position to benefit from the massive locomotive tenders.[7] According to its website, VR Laser Services 'specialises in the manufacturing of a variety of steel products for a broad range of end-users, including the defence, mining, rail and transport industries'.[8]

Furthermore, amaBhungane discovered that a month before Transnet announced the outcome of the bid process, VR Laser Services – through a variety of holding companies – was acquired by Gupta associate Salim Essa, Rajesh Gupta and Duduzane Zuma. Although Sharma denied that VR Laser Services or VRLS Properties would benefit from the Transnet tender, all indications were that the steel-cutting business's order book would soon start to fill up. AmaBhungane learnt that all four of the international rail giants had visited the factory's premises 'to assess the possibility of subcontracting work to VR Laser' shortly before they won their respective stakes in Transnet's giant tender.[9] It was clear that the Guptas, President Zuma's son and their associates stood to make a fortune.

Transnet was not the only state-owned company targeted by VR Laser. In 2007, South Africa's state-owned arms manufacturer, Denel, had won a contract to produce about 270 new Badger combat vehicles for the South African military. At the time, the contract was thought to be worth R8 billion, but its value would later balloon to more than R12 billion.[10] The contract, dubbed Project Hoefyster (Afrikaans for 'horseshoe'), moved forward at a snail's pace. In 2011, *defenceWeb* reported that the Department of Defence had not yet placed a production order for the new vehicles.[11] Some industry insiders started to doubt whether Project Hoefyster would actually materialise. In July 2013, however, mere months before Essa, Duduzane Zuma and Rajesh Gupta bought their stake in VR Laser, the SANDF revived the contract by finally approving a production order.[12] Then, in April 2016, *Rapport* revealed that Denel had subcontracted the project's steel-related requirements to none other than VR Laser Services.[13] The revelation caused a fresh uproar, forcing Denel to release a statement. 'The total value of the Hoefyster Project is R12.7-billion, with VR Laser's steel fabrication and cutting component making up R400-million of this,' said the arms manufacturer. The state-owned company had no qualms about being linked to the controversial family, it seemed. 'It must be stated that there is nothing wrong with doing business with any registered, legally-trading business in South Africa, whether the Gupta family or any other,' said Denel.[14]

Furthermore, Denel did not seem fazed by the Guptas' reputation. A few months earlier, in January 2016, the company had announced that it was establishing a joint venture with VR Laser called Denel Asia.[15] According to Denel's acting group CEO, Zwelakhe Ntshepe, the new company, which was to be based in Hong Kong, would give Denel access 'to new markets for our world-class products, especially in the fields of artillery, armoured vehicles, missiles and unmanned aerial vehicles'.[16] Denel highlighted countries such as India, Singapore and the Philippines as Denel Asia's potential clients. In response to critics of the partnership, who were questioning why Denel needed VR Laser's help to market its products abroad, VR Laser CEO Pieter van der Merwe insisted his company had 'expertise in defence technology and understanding of the South East Asia defence markets'.[17]

Things then got a little peculiar. After originally indicating that its partner in Denel Asia was the South African–based VR Laser, Denel started insisting that its partner was, in fact, the Hong Kong–based VR Laser Asia, a company owned wholly by Essa. The parastatal had probably begun to realise that it would be best to keep VR Laser, whose shareholders included Duduzane Zuma and Rajesh Gupta, in the background. But Denel's protestations were in vain. In April 2016, Treasury issued a statement in which it criticised Denel for forming the new joint venture allegedly without approval from the minister of finance, as required by the Public Finance Management Act.[18] Treasury subsequently announced its intention to take Denel to court over the matter.[19]

The establishment of the joint venture was preceded by some rather disturbing developments at Denel. In June 2015, Denel board member Nkopane Motseki allegedly told Riaz Saloojee, Denel's then CEO, that he and other executives and board members were about to be axed.[20] It was never confirmed how Motseki came by this information, but what is known is that Motseki, who also happens to be treasurer general of the pro-Gupta MK Military Veterans Association, received shares in the Guptas' Shiva uranium mine in 2010.[21] His information proved accurate, and Saloojee, along with two other executives and more or less the entire board, was replaced before the end of 2015. Dan Mantsha, the new board chairperson, was rumoured to have been introduced to the Guptas by then communications minister Faith Muthambi.[22] It was widely believed that the Guptas had orchestrated the large-scale exodus of Denel board members and executives in order to replace them with individuals who would support the establishment of Denel Asia.

Denel later defended the deal in Parliament and strongly denied that it had been captured by the Guptas, saying, 'The Gupta family has no business joint venture with Denel and none of the Gupta family members or relatives are shareholders in Denel Asia.'[23] But there are ample indications that VR Laser Services was the intended beneficiary of the partnership all along. Sometime after Treasury started to probe the joint venture, I was shown a document that highlighted key findings and recommendations contained in a due diligence report on the partnership compiled by law firm ENSafrica. According to the document, the lawyers had warned Denel not to go ahead with the joint venture, seeing as there were too many 'politically exposed persons' involved. ENSafrica, which had studied the joint-venture agreement signed by Denel and VR Laser Asia, had determined that VR Laser Services would indeed benefit from the partnership. Not only would VR Laser Services be a preferred supplier for any Asian contracts secured by Denel Asia, but it would also be paid as a consultant on such deals, the document showed.

Back to Transnet. Neotel, one of South Africa's two major national operators for fixed-line telecommunication services, has been a supplier to Transnet since 2008. But in mid-2015 it emerged that while Neotel was providing the parastatal with goods and services worth billions of rands, it was also paying 'success fees' to an obscure company with some interesting links to the Guptas. Homix (Pty) Ltd, a registered company that consisted of little more than an abandoned office in an indistinct building in Wierda Park, Centurion, received its first payment of R30 million from Neotel in April 2014, amaBhungane revealed. The payment appeared to be a 10 per cent 'commission' for IT equipment worth R300 million that Transnet had bought from Neotel. It later transpired that Homix had written a letter to Neotel in which it claimed that it could help Neotel secure the lucrative contract from the state-owned rail company, in return for which it wanted 10 per cent of the contract value. Another payment was an apparent 2 per cent 'success fee' of R41 million plus VAT paid to Homix for a R1.8-billion network-management contract that Transnet had awarded to Neotel at the end of 2014. By April 2015, after Neotel had committed to paying Homix fees totalling about R100 million, Deloitte, Neotel's auditor, informed the company's board that its payments to Homix were suspicious. There were, after all, no indications that Homix had actually done any work to justify the millions it was receiving. The transactions were subsequently reported to the Independent Regulatory Board for Auditors and the police, as required by law. When Deloitte probed Neotel's payments to Homix, one Ashok Narayan identified himself as Homix's CEO. As it turned out, Narayan was a former manager at the

Guptas' Sahara Systems.[24] Company records showed that Narayan was also a former business partner to known Gupta associates such as Oakbay Investments' acting CEO Ronica Ragavan, and Jagdish Parekh, Oakbay's former managing director.

In October 2016, amaBhungane revealed the full extent to which Homix was being used as an alleged recipient and launderer of apparent kickbacks. According to documents obtained by the team of investigative journalists, another four companies who were contractors of Transnet and other state-owned entities made payments to Homix totalling R90 million. But this was clearly just a fraction of the money Homix had received. In 2014 and 2015, Homix made payments to equally obscure local and over-seas-based companies worth an eye-watering R250 million. This included payments of just under R190 million to Bapu Trading, a company that appeared to exist only on paper and whose sole director could not be traced. But what linked Homix to the Guptas were payments totalling R51 million made by Homix to two companies based in Hong Kong: YKA International Trading Company and Morningstar International Trade. The latter shared its registered address in Hong Kong with none other than VR Laser Asia, which is, of course, linked to VR Laser Services, the company owned by Essa, Duduzane Zuma and Rajesh Gupta.[25]

A company that was found to have paid Homix even more money than Neotel was Regiments Capital, a financial advisory firm that, according to a *Sunday Times* report, billed Transnet to the tune of R800 million in 2014 and 2015 alone.[26] As shown in one of the amaBhungane reports, Regiments paid Homix R84.3 million during the same time frame.[27] Another 10 per cent 'success fee'?

Neotel, in the meantime, kept winning lucrative contracts from Transnet. However, seeing as its auditors were asking uncomfortable questions about the payments to Homix, the telecoms firm needed a new channel through which it could pay its 'success fees'. Neotel's solution to the problem would bring to light the clearest indication to date that the Guptas themselves were directly squeezing kickbacks from the benefactors of government contracts. In 2014 and 2015, Neotel secured contracts totalling R834 million to supply Transnet with CCTV cameras.[28]

According to documents filed in a messy court battle involving Regiments Capital, Neotel's latest 'success fee' to the Guptas was apparently channelled to their newspaper, *The New Age*. In an affidavit filed as part of the court proceedings, Litha Nyhonyha, a founding director of Regiments, described how his firm had sent 'fake' invoices to the value of R15 million to a company called Techpro.[29] Techpro, it turned out, had been sub-contracted by Neotel for the Transnet CCTV contracts.[30] 'Regiments had nothing to do with Techpro, had rendered no services to it and Techpro did not owe Regiments the R15 million, plus VAT,' Nyhonyha stated in his affidavit. *The New Age* then sent Regiments 'three matching fake invoices for R15 million, plus VAT, which pretended falsely that this newspaper had provided advertising services to Regiments', read the affidavit. But according to Nyhonyha, 'Regiments did not advertise, and has never advertised in *The New Age* newspaper, much less did it owe it R15 million'. Nevertheless, Techpro paid Regiments R17.1 million (the R15 million plus 14 per cent VAT) and Regiments subsequently paid *The New Age* R17.1 million, according to the affidavit. 'The effect was to launder R17.1 million through Regiments' account,' concluded Nyhonyha.[31]

The above-mentioned court proceedings formed part of a battle for control over Regiments Capital. Litha Nyhonyha and his partner Magandheran Pillay wanted the High Court to declare their former partner, Eric Wood, delinquent as a director. In other words, they wanted the court to rule that Wood no longer legally qualified to be a director of the company. At the same time, Wood lodged a delinquency application against Nyhonyha and Pillay. Wood's relationship with the Guptas appeared to be a key element in the spat between the former partners. 'At one stage, Pillay, at Wood's instance, was driven to a meeting at one of the Gupta residences,' alleged Nyhonyha in his affidavit. 'A proposal was made at this meeting for the Gupta family to acquire the majority shareholding in Regiments.' The family evidently wanted a far larger slice of the huge advisory contracts Regiments was getting from Transnet – larger, at least, than the 'success fees' that were being paid to Homix. But Nyhonyha and Pillay were opposed to the takeover, which, according to Nyhonyha, was a 'primary source' of the subsequent falling-out with Wood. 'It subsequently became apparent that even while still employed at Regiments, and from early on, Wood began planning his exit to Trillian Capital Partners, a company which has strong connections to the Gupta family,' maintained Nyhonyha.[32]

By the time Wood was formally appointed as a director of Trillian in

March 2016, the company was already majority-owned by Salim Essa, who had bought his 60 per cent controlling stake in Trillian in September 2015.[33] It seems that the Gupta-linked Trillian then effectively took over the work Regiments had been doing for Transnet. In December 2015, the parastatal paid Trillian Asset Management, a sister company of Trillian Capital Partners, almost R94 million for supposedly facilitating a loan Transnet had secured for its R50-billion locomotives tender. Invoices later obtained by amaBhungane showed that Trillian had done a further R74 million worth of work for Transnet by the end of June 2016.[34]

In May 2016, Treasury started probing Transnet's contracts with Regiments and Trillian as part of a far-reaching investigation into alleged state capture and rent-seeking activities in the awarding of contracts by state-owned entities. According to a source at Treasury, these transaction and financial advisory services oftentimes represent some of the most flagrant abuses of public funds. 'Transnet's own financial people could easily be doing most of this work, but I guess it's become pretty clear why a lot of it is being outsourced,' said the source.

18

Dirty money

Coal is a dirty business. Mining the sooty fossil fuel has been known to cause black lung and other pulmonary diseases.[1] Coal mines also spew sulphurous water into nearby rivers and streams, sometimes irrevocably damaging these precious water resources.[2] When coal-fired power stations burn the hard black rock to generate electricity, its effect on the environment, and on human health, is even worse. The toxic concoction of carbon dioxide and other pollutants that are released is a significant contributor to global warming.[3] Given coal's grimy qualities, it is almost fitting that the sale of it in South Africa has become equally grubby, at least as far as the Guptas' coal activities are concerned.

The family's intention to move into coal mining can be traced to 2006, when a group of known Gupta associates registered Tegeta Exploration and Resources, Tegeta Resources, and Idwala Coal. These entities subsequently obtained prospecting rights in Mpumalanga, Limpopo, the Free State and KwaZulu-Natal.[4] Company documents, including annual reports, would eventually confirm that all three coal-mining entities were owned by the Guptas' Oakbay Resources & Energy, and by extension Oakbay Investments.[5] News that the Guptas, or at least their associates, had entered the industry would only surface in 2011, when the *Sunday Times* reported that Idwala Coal had started coal-mining activities near a sensitive wetland on the Vierfontein farm in Mpumalanga without the requisite water-use licence. Ravindra Nath, a director of several Gupta-owned companies and then chief financial officer of Sahara Computers, was named as an investor in Idwala Coal. Evidently sensitive about the mine's links to the Guptas, Nath denied that they were involved but refused to say who exactly owned Idwala Coal. 'I am just a silent investor in that [company]. The owner of the company is a BEE consortium and an overseas investor. It has nothing to do with the Gupta company [Oakbay],' Nath told the newspaper.[6]

In the meantime, Idwala Coal continued to wreak havoc on the environment. In 2013, the *Sunday Times* reported on documents submitted to the Department of Environmental Affairs that shed light on the mine's harmful activities. The sensitive wetland near the mine was damaged to such an extent that, according to the documents, 'there exists the possibility that protected species were destroyed'. Idwala had also released 'contaminated water' into the ecosystem.[7] Apart from a notice issued in 2011 by the then Department of Water Affairs over its continued mining activities without a water licence,[8] the authorities seemed unwilling to act against Idwala. At one stage, the Department of Environmental Affairs stated that those involved in the illegal mining operation could face 'administrative action or criminal prosecution',[9] but this never happened.

In 2014, the *Mail & Guardian* reported that Tegeta's Brakfontein Colliery in Mpumalanga had also started mining coal illegally. Local farmers told the newspaper that polluted water from the mine was draining into an adjacent wetland before ending up in a nearby river. This time, the Department of Water Affairs issued a directive to the mine for 'failing to take reasonable measures to prevent pollution and for using water without authorisation'.[10] Again, the authorities' bark proved to be worse than their bite, seeing as Brakfontein was allowed to continue its operations without significant resistance.

Eskom, South Africa's state-owned power utility, is the country's largest consumer of coal.[11] Each year, the company spends R45 billion on coal for its thirteen coal-fired power stations,[12] which provide the country with about 90 per cent of its electricity needs.[13] When the Medupi and Kusile coal-fired power plants finally go live, Eskom's coal bill will be even higher. These two new power stations have been plagued by problems and are expected to be fully operational only in 2021.[14]

Given Eskom's huge appetite for coal, it is no wonder that the Guptas viewed the power utility as a potential cash cow. In 2014, the *Sunday Times* reported that the family had allegedly leant on Zola Tsotsi, Eskom's then chairperson, to approve a R500-million coal-supply contract with Idwala Coal in Mpumalanga. But the deal did not go through after some senior Eskom executives expressed concern over Idwala's illegal mining operations.[15] This, however, would be the last time that Eskom rejected the Guptas.

In December 2014, President Jacob Zuma's cabinet announced that almost the entire Eskom board of directors would be replaced.[16] An amaBhungane investigation would later reveal the shocking extent to which the new appointments represented a takeover of the board by the Guptas and their associates. Of the nine new board members, four had discernible business or family links to either the Guptas or Salim Essa. The latter owned 21.5 per cent of Tegeta Exploration and Resources through a company called Elgasolve.[17] In some instances, the links between the new board members and the broader Gupta network were astonishingly overt. Mark Pamensky, for instance, was a director of Oakbay Resources & Energy. And Dr Ben Ngubane, who would later become Eskom's chairperson, had previously been a co-director with Essa in a private company.[18]

Three months after the new Eskom board was formed, the Guptas finally got a foot in the door at the power utility when their Brakfontein mine secured a coal-supply contract worth R400 million a year.[19] Despite not having a water licence, Brakfontein was contracted to supply coal to Eskom's Majuba power station in Mpumalanga for a period of ten years, bringing the total contract value to R4 billion. The *Sunday Times* later revealed astonishing details about events that transpired at Eskom before and after Brakfontein got the contract. As it turned out, Tegeta Exploration and Resources had been trying to land a deal with Eskom since 2011. However, no fewer than four laboratory tests on Brakfontein's coal had showed that it was not of a high enough quality to be used at Majuba. A fifth test, done in March 2015, found the coal to be marginally within specification, but still risky. To Eskom, though, the latest assessment was more than sufficient grounds to finally award the contract to Brakfontein. That Eskom allowed the mine's coal to be retested so many times was out of the ordinary. It suggested that Eskom was only too keen to find a reason to award the contract to the Guptas' mine. A source at Eskom told the *Sunday Times* that the power utility normally only tested a mine's coal once or twice before making a call on whether to sign it up as a supplier. After all, each test cost around R100 000. 'To do it three, four, five times, that's unusual ... It's expensive. I mean, in whose interest is it?' the Eskom insider told the newspaper.[20]

It would also transpire that whoever labelled Brakfontein's coal as 'risky' had been spot on. Just two months after the Majuba power station started burning the mine's coal in its boilers, Eskom rejected it because of its poor quality. In August 2015, Eskom informed Tegeta that it was suspending the coal-supply contract to further investigate inconsistencies in the laboratory results. Incredibly, Eskom lifted the suspension only five days later. The *Sunday Times* investigation found that Matshela Koko, at the time Eskom's group executive for generation, had bypassed company protocol by personally getting involved in the matter. He allegedly questioned the Eskom employees who had found inconsistencies in the lab results, after which four of them were suspended. It seemed Eskom was getting rid of the very people whose job it was to protect the power utility by rejecting poor-quality coal. On top of that, Eskom also decided to suspend the services of two laboratories that had been contracted to test Brakfontein's coal.[21] The mine was again free to continue with its R4-billion coal-supply contract.

While the Guptas' Brakfontein and Vierfontein mines were allowed to get away with breaking the law, the owner of one of Eskom's longest-standing coal suppliers was being exposed to such harsh treatment from Eskom and the Department of Mineral Resources that it was ultimately left with no choice but to sell its assets to the Guptas. This is the tale of Gupta-owned Tegeta Exploration and Resources' acquisition of Optimum Coal Holdings. It contains perhaps the most frightening manifestations of state capture in the broader Gupta saga.

The story begins in 1993, when Eskom signed an agreement with the Optimum Colliery to supply coal to the Hendrina power station in Mpumalanga for a period of twenty-five years.[22] It was a fixed-price contract that would see Optimum supply coal to Eskom at a cost of R150 per tonne until 2018.[23] The mine, at that stage, was owned by international mining giant BHP Billiton.

In 2008, BHP Billiton sold the Optimum mine, along with a right to export 6.5 million tonnes of coal per annum from the Richards Bay Coal Terminal, to a group of businessmen that included Eliphus Monkoe, a former chief operating officer of one of BHP's South African subsidiaries.[24] Monkoe and his partners formed a holding company called Optimum Coal Holdings to house the mine and the Richards Bay coal export right. They also later bought Koornfontein, another coal mine that would eventually become a supplier to Eskom, from BHP Billiton.[25] The Optimum mine again changed ownership in 2012 when multinational mining company Glencore and its BEE partner, Cyril Ramaphosa's Shanduka Group, acquired the majority of Optimum Coal Holdings' shares.[26] Ramaphosa would later sell his shares in Shanduka when he became the country's deputy president in May 2014. Glencore reportedly paid $783 million for Optimum Coal Holdings.[27]

If Glencore expected to inherit a trouble-free coal-supply contract with Eskom, they were in for a nasty surprise. The company soon learnt that the 1993 agreement to supply coal to the Hendrina power station, which was still in place, was forcing them to sell their coal at a loss. In a letter sent to Eskom in July 2013, Optimum Coal Mine, a subsidiary of Optimum Coal Holdings, claimed that it would lose R881 million in that year as a result of its contract with Eskom. Optimum was also unhappy about provisions in the original coal-supply agreement that allowed Eskom to impose massive penalties on the mine in the event that it supplied the power utility with poor-quality coal. The letter was unearthed during former public protector Thuli Madonsela's state capture investigation in 2016. Its purpose was to formally invoke the coal-supply agreement's 'hardship clause', which essentially stated that Eskom and Optimum could enter into negotiations if either party ever felt that the coal-supply agreement was no longer in its best interest. After months of negotiations, the mine and the power utility signed a 'Co-Operation Agreement' in May 2014. The agreement did not in itself resolve any of the problems Optimum said it was experiencing, but instead paved the way for the possible conclusion of a new coal-supply agreement that would not see Optimum lose money.[28]

In April 2015, public enterprises minister Lynne Brown announced that Brian Molefe would leave his position as Transnet boss to become Eskom's acting CEO.[29] After his appointment, Molefe almost immediately became involved in the spat with Glencore's Optimum Coal Mine. According to the public protector's report, Molefe met with Optimum's CEO in May 2015 to inform him that Eskom would not conclude a new deal with the mine. The power utility would instead continue enforcing the original coal-supply agreement. But Optimum kept asking Eskom to revise the agreement. In July, the mine asked Eskom if it would consider paying R300 per tonne of coal delivered to Hendrina until the end of 2018, and then R570 per tonne between 2019 and 2023. Instead of considering the request, Eskom notified Optimum that it would impose on it a fine of R2.1 billion for supplying poor-quality coal. 'Optimum has for a consecutive period from 1 March 2012 to 31 May 2015 ... failed to supply and deliver to Eskom coal which meets the quality parameter contemplated by [the coal-supply agreement],' Eskom's lawyers said in a letter sent to Optimum on 16 July 2015.[30] Eskom finally slapped Optimum with the fine in August, ironically the same month in which it lifted the suspension on coal sourced from the Guptas' Brakfontein mine after it too had been found to be of poor quality.

Glencore, in the meantime, warned that at least a thousand of its South African employees would lose their jobs if Optimum was forced to close because of the 'financial hardship' it was suffering.[31] In July 2015, while Optimum and Eskom were still bickering over the coal-supply agreement, Glencore announced that it had started retrenching some 380 employees in an effort to cut costs.[32] Less than two weeks later, the DMR pounced on Optimum by suspending its mining licence. The department claimed that the mine had carried out the retrenchments in an 'inhumane manner' and that it had not complied with the relevant labour laws.[33]

At the beginning of August, Glencore announced that Optimum Coal Holdings and Optimum Coal Mine were being placed under business rescue. The company openly blamed Eskom for the development. 'In June 2015, Eskom informed Optimum that it is not willing to renegotiate the [coal-supply] agreement and terminated the framework agreement. The framework provided the platform on which the renegotiation discussions were being conducted and interim supply of coal to Eskom was being made,' Glencore said in a statement. 'Eskom is enforcing specifications in the supply agreement which Optimum is unable to meet on a sustainable basis and which were the subject of the recent renegotiation discussions.'[34] Glencore appointed Piers Marsden and Peter van den Steen as Optimum's joint business rescue practitioners (BRPs). According to auditing firm Mazars, 'business rescue refers to proceedings to facilitate the rehabilitation of a company that is financially distressed, with the aim of maximising its chances of continuing to exist as a solvent business'.[35]

The Guptas, meanwhile, had clearly been following the public spat between Eskom and Optimum with great interest. In July, shortly before the two Optimum entities were placed in business rescue, auditing giant KPMG approached Glencore with an offer from an 'anonymous' client to purchase Optimum Coal Mine for R2 billion, according to the public protector's state capture report. KPMG subsequently confirmed that its client was the Guptas' Oakbay Resources & Energy, after which Oakbay itself got in touch with Glencore in August. At that juncture, Glencore told Oakbay that it was not ready to sell Optimum.[36]

Eskom and the BRPs, in the meantime, continued discussions around the possible conclusion of a more favourable coal-supply agreement. The BRPs informed Eskom that if the parties could not reach an agreement, Optimum would have to be liquidated. If this were to happen, Optimum would no longer supply coal to the Hendrina power station, something that would seriously jeopardise Eskom's already troubled power network. In a letter to Optimum Coal Mine dated 5 November 2015, Eskom's Matshela Koko noted 'with grave concern' the 'threat of liquidation'. By now the power utility had started to take an interest in Oakbay's offer. According to the coal-supply agreement, Eskom would have to approve the sale of the mine. The power utility seemed particularly keen to help Oakbay acquire Optimum. 'We note that you have an offer on the table,' Koko wrote in the same letter in November. 'Eskom is happy to engage in a roundtable discussion with the interested party and yourselves to establish the veracity of the offer. You have repeatedly emphasized the limited time available to explore such options and Eskom would be willing to enter in such discussions provided that it aims to find a solution.'[37]

When Eskom, Optimum Coal Mine and Oakbay finally met at the end of that month, Koko seemed to be the one dictating the terms of the negotiations. He said Eskom was concerned that if Oakbay bought Optimum Coal Mine as a stand-alone entity, the company might not be able to sustain it. Optimum Coal Holdings, however, had a far better chance for survival. The company owned the lucrative Richards Bay coal-export right as well as the Koornfontein mine, which was by then supplying coal to Eskom's Komati power station. In other words, whoever bought all of Optimum Coal Holdings' assets would be able to offset any losses it might incur through the Hendrina coal-supply contract with the profits earned from the Koornfontein mine and the Richards Bay export right. According to the meeting's minutes, Koko said that Eskom would only approve the sale if it included Optimum Coal Holdings and not just Optimum Coal Mine.[38]

Glencore was apparently unconvinced that selling Optimum Coal Holdings was in its best interest. Enter mining minister Mosebenzi Zwane. When President Zuma appointed the former Free State MEC for agriculture as South Africa's new minister of mineral resources in September 2015, there were already sufficient grounds to suspect that he was a Gupta appointee. As mentioned previously, Zwane's former provincial government department played a key role in getting the Gupta jet carrying wedding guests cleared for landing at AFB Waterkloof in 2013. Less than a month after the debacle, the Free State Department of Agriculture was again linked to the Guptas when *Volksblad* revealed that Zwane's department was sponsoring a controversial dairy project that benefited Linkway Trading, a company in which Rajesh Gupta used to be a director.[39] AmaBhungane, who discovered further links between the Guptas and the Estina dairy farm, later reported that the department intended spending R570 million on the controversial project.[40] A *City Press* report following Zwane's appointment as the new mining minister described how even senior ANC members were taken by surprise by Zuma's decision. 'We were aware of his presence in Parliament over the last few weeks and anticipated that he was being positioned for a Cabinet post,' one NEC member told the newspaper. 'We thought it would be a post like agriculture as part of a bigger reshuffle. We did not expect it to be such an important portfolio.'[41] At the time, amaBhungane reported that a large motorcade that looked like Zuma's was seen at the Gupta compound in Saxonwold two days before Zuma announced Zwane's appointment.[42]

In December 2015, about three months after taking up his new position at the DMR, Zwane travelled to Switzerland to meet with Ivan Glasenberg, Glencore's CEO, allegedly 'to help facilitate a deal for a Gupta-linked company to buy the distressed Optimum Colliery in Mpumalanga', according to a later report in the *Sunday Times*. During his three-day stay in Zurich, Zwane mostly had meetings and dinners with Glasenberg in the city's upmarket Dolder Grand hotel. Furthermore, the newspaper alleged, the Guptas may have been present. 'Zwane arrived in Zurich on an Emirates flight, via Dubai, on November 30 last year [2015]. A Bombardier ZS OAK, a plane owned by the Guptas, is known to have been in Zurich at the same time,' the paper reported. 'A week later, the sale of Optimum coal mine to the Gupta family was announced.'[43] Zwane has, on several occasions, denied that the Guptas accompanied him to Switzerland.[44] He has also defended his relationship with the family – on one occasion, ironically, during a *The New Age* Business Briefing.[45] But according to Madonsela's state capture report, she received confirmation from an 'independent source' that Rajesh Gupta and Salim Essa were indeed present at the meetings in Zurich.[46]

Mere days after Zwane's return to South Africa, Optimum's BRPs concluded a conditional transaction that would see Oakbay's Tegeta Exploration and Resources acquire Optimum Coal Holdings' assets for R2.15 billion, 'the proceeds of which will be used to part settle the existing bank debt of Optimum Holdings of approximately R2.55 billion', according to *Mining Review Africa*. Glencore had also agreed to advance R400 million to Optimum to settle the rest of the debt.[47] Glencore, which paid about R7 billion for Optimum Coal Holdings in 2012, was now forking out a fortune to get rid of it. Perhaps they were only too eager to dump an asset that had brought them nothing but pain and problems. Or perhaps the mining conglomerate was somehow compensated by the South African government for its loss. Apart from Zwane, the Guptas and Glencore, only the walls of the Dolder Grand know the exact details of the deal.

In February 2016, *City Press* revealed that if Tegeta's purchase of Optimum Coal was approved, President Zuma's son Duduzane stood to benefit from the Eskom coal contracts. 'Just two days after Economic Freedom Fighters leader Julius Malema coined the catchy new phrase "Zuptas" for the commercial romance between the Zuma and Gupta families, the Competition Commission revealed that Duduzane Zuma is one of the buyers of the Mpumalanga coal mine, along with the Guptas' Oakbay Investments,' wrote journalist Susan Comrie, before explaining that one of Tegeta's major shareholders was Mabengela Investments, 'whose two directors are Duduzane Zuma and Rajesh Gupta'. 'The disclosure of Zuma's stake in the Optimum deal adds to accusations that have already been made that the Guptas' political influence has been at play in securing not only the Brakfontein contract with Eskom but also the Optimum deal,' concluded Comrie.[48]

Thuli Madonsela referred to this apparent conflict of interest in her criticism of Zwane's role in the whole saga in her state capture report. 'It is potentially unlawful for the Minister to use his official position of authority to unfairly and unduly influence a contract for a friend or in this instance his boss's son [read 'Duduzane Zuma'] at the expense of the State. This scenario would be further complicated if his actions were sanctioned by the President,' she wrote in the report.[49] Referring to the Zurich trip, Madonsela noted that 'if Minister Zwane travelled in his official capacity to support Tegeta's bid to buy the mine his conduct would give Tegeta an unfair advantage over other interested buyers'.[50]

Another troubling aspect of Zwane's role in the negotiations was the fact that two of his advisors during that time could be linked to the Guptas: Malcolm Mabaso, Zwane's personal advisor, and Tegeta's Salim Essa were once co-directors in the same company.[51] Even more disturbing, though, was the public protector's discovery that Kuben Moodley, a special advisor to the minister, had apparently bought into Optimum Coal Holdings as the Glencore deal was being concluded. According to the state capture report, a company called Albatime, of which Moodley is the sole director, contributed R10 million towards Tegeta's acquisition of Optimum Coal Holdings. Furthermore, Moodley's wife, Devapushpum Viroshini Naidoo, who at one point listed herself as an employee of Albatime, was one of the new Eskom board members appointed in December 2014.[52]

Although the Guptas and their partners still had to scrape together the R2.15 billion to conclude the deal, Tegeta Exploration and Resources took over Optimum's mining operations in January 2016. It would be the start of an unbelievable turnaround for the once-struggling coal mine. Thanks to Optimum's earlier contract to supply coal to the Hendrina power station, the mine was reportedly losing around R100 million a month when Tegeta took over. But in April, Eskom awarded Tegeta a contract worth R700 million, including transport costs, to supply coal from the Optimum mine to its Arnot power station, *City Press* later revealed. At R470 a tonne, it was one of the most expensive coal contracts on Eskom's books.[53] But that was not the contract's most dodgy aspect.

On 1 July 2016, Optimum's BRPs submitted a report to the Hawks that suggested Eskom's board had literally helped the Guptas pay for Optimum Coal Holdings by means of the Arnot contract. According to the report,

Oakbay CEO Nazeem Howa phoned Piers Marsden on 11 April 2016 to request a meeting at Tegeta's offices. It was two days before Tegeta had to pay the full purchase price of R2.15 billion for Optimum Coal Holdings in terms of the sale agreement. At the meeting, Howa told Marsden that Tegeta was R600 million short on the purchase price. Howa wanted Marsden, in his capacity as one of Optimum's BRPs, to approach a consortium of banks to apply for a bridging loan to cover the shortfall. After meeting with the banks on the same day, Marsden informed Howa at about 15:00 that the banks were not prepared to lend Tegeta the R600 million. And yet, on 14 April, the BRPs were informed that Tegeta had made payment in full. According to their report, Marsden and Van den Steen became suspicious of how Tegeta had managed to secure the R600 million shortfall when they saw episodes of *Carte Blanche* that were broadcast on 12 and 19 June, as well as a full-length interview with Howa that was made available on the show's website.[54]

In his interview with *Carte Blanche*, Eskom's Matshela Koko admitted that the power utility had made a pre-payment to Tegeta for the purchase of coal to the tune of R586 million, and that the coal was to be procured from Optimum Coal Mine and delivered to the Arnot power station. Koko initially denied the pre-payment, but after *Carte Blanche* showed him a document proving the transaction, he was forced to backtrack. 'Let's say I made a mistake,' Koko told the programme's presenter.[55]

In their report to the Hawks, Marsden and Van den Steen stated: 'We have come to learn from the Episodes, Interview and Articles that the Pre-Payment was approved by a committee of Eskom representatives at a meeting held at 21h00 on 11 April 2016. This meeting was held on the same day on which the request for the bridging finance was made to, and rejected by, the Consortium of Banks.' But this was not all that troubled them. Howa's *Carte Blanche* comments on the pre-payment raised further suspicions. 'Pursuant to the Interview, Howa remarked that the Pre-Payment had been made on the basis that OCM [Optimum Coal Mine] was in business rescue and required money for its liquidity and for the start-up of equipment,' they wrote. But, as Optimum's BRPs, the duo would have known if such a payment had been made to the mine. At the time of the approval of the pre-payment – 11 April – Optimum Coal Mine was still owned by Optimum Coal Holdings and managed by the BRPs, whose obligations would only come to an end on 31 August 2016. 'We confirm that the Pre-Payment was not made to OCM,' they informed the Hawks.[56]

Thuli Madonsela would later confirm that the 11 April meeting of Eskom representatives did indeed take place and that the purpose of the meeting was to approve short-term coal-supply agreements. She also confirmed that a massive pre-payment of almost R660 million was made to Tegeta, and that the latter had used it to help buy Optimum. 'It accordingly appears that the urgency of the Special Board Tender Committee meeting on 11 April 2016 at 21:00 was solely for the purposes of benefiting Tegeta in order to fund the purchase of all shares in OCH [Optimum Coal Holdings],' she concluded in her report.[57]

In fact, the public protector found that of the R1.1 billion Eskom paid Tegeta between January and April 2016, which includes the pre-payment for the Arnot contract, Tegeta used R910 million to wrap up the Optimum deal. 'It appears that the conduct of the Eskom board was solely to the benefit of Tegeta in awarding contracts to them and in doing so funded the purchase of OCH and is thus in severe violation of the PFMA [Public Finance Management Act],' Madonsela concluded.[58]

Brian Molefe's fingerprints were also all over the Optimum saga. Cellphone records obtained by public protector investigators showed that between 2 August 2015, two days before Glencore placed Optimum in business rescue, and 22 March 2016, less than a month before Eskom approved the pre-payment to Tegeta, Molefe phoned Ajay Gupta a total of forty-four times. Gupta, in turn, made fourteen calls to Molefe during the same period. Molefe also had frequent contact with Ronica Ragavan, the Gupta associate who later replaced Howa as Oakbay's CEO. Cellphone records showed that Ragavan phoned Molefe seven times between 9 and 12 April. This included a call made on 11 April, the day on which the Eskom board approved the pre-payment.[59] It is interesting to note that in September 2015, cabinet appointed Molefe as permanent CEO of Eskom (he had been acting CEO since April).

Data obtained from Molefe's cellphone also showed that he had been in the vicinity of the Guptas' estate in Saxonwold on nineteen occasions between 5 August and 17 November 2015.[60] When later asked at an Eskom media briefing to explain why he had been such a frequent visitor to the suburb, he famously intimated that he visited a shebeen in the area. 'There is a shebeen there, I think it's two streets away from the Gupta house. Now, I will not admit or deny that I was going to the shebeen, but ... because I haven't ... my young wife is not aware that there's a shebeen there. But there's a shebeen there,' stuttered an emotional Molefe, shortly before breaking down and wiping tears from his eyes.[61] Perhaps the accumulated *dronkverdriet* (drinker's remorse) brought on by nineteen pub visits in less than two weeks had finally got the better of him. Despite my own and others' ongoing efforts, the now infamous Saxonwold shebeen has still not been located.

In September 2016, word got out that Tegeta was in the process of selling Optimum Coal Terminal, the Optimum Coal Holdings subsidiary that owned the valuable right to export coal from the Richards Bay Coal Terminal.[62] Ajay Gupta would later tell the public protector that Tegeta stood to make a profit of $150 million, or about R2 billion, from the deal. Eskom, which previously would not allow Optimum Coal Holdings and its subsidiaries to be sold separately during the negotiations with Glencore, kept quiet. 'It is unclear as to why Eskom has now allowed Tegeta to sell an asset which it previously deemed vital to subsidise OCM,' wrote Madonsela in her report. 'Eskom had made its point clear in that OCM, Koornfontein and Optimum Coal Terminal needed to be kept together and cannot be sold separately.'[63]

In November 2016, public enterprises minister Lynne Brown admitted in Parliament that Tegeta had not yet paid the fine of more than R2 billion that Eskom had imposed on the Optimum mine before it was sold and which, according to the sales agreement, Tegeta had inherited when they bought the mine from Glencore.[64]

PART VI

THE UNRAVELLING

19

Pandora's box

Google has an analytical tool that measures how frequently its users enter certain words or phrases into the search engine over particular periods of time.

When visualised as graphs, the Google Trends search histories in South Africa for 'Guptas' and 'the Guptas' show two massive spikes in the last four years. The first, in May 2013, was a result of the Guptas' audacious exploits at AFB Waterkloof on the last day of April. By July, the public's interest in the controversial family had dropped to nearly the same level as it had been before the scandal.

The second dramatic spike occurred three years later, in the first three months of 2016. By March of that year the term 'state capture', which had become synonymous with the Guptas, was firmly established as a buzz-word in the South African lexicon of public discourse. In fact, the Google search histories for 'state capture' and 'the Guptas' show that both received a considerably heightened level of public interest at exactly the same time – in March 2016.

This renewed interest in the Guptas began with the news in mid-December 2015 that Tegeta Exploration and Resources had purchased Glencore's Optimum Coal Holdings. The intrigue was fuelled a few months later when it emerged that the minister of mineral resources, Mosebenzi Zwane, had apparently assisted the Guptas in acquiring the coal mine,[1] and that Jacob Zuma's son Duduzane had scored a share in the deal.[2]

But even before that, there was Zuma's controversial firing of well-respected finance minister Nhlanhla Nene on 9 December 2015, an event variously dubbed 'Nenegate' and '9/12'. Nene's shock dismissal and his replacement with the inexperienced David Des van Rooyen was nothing short of an economic calamity.

'On 9 December 2015, a little after 8pm, South African President Jacob

Zuma committed the biggest blunder of his career, at the stroke of his pen wiping half a trillion rand off the value of SA stocks and bonds,' wrote veteran business and financial reporter Alec Hogg.[3]

Zuma's decision caused the value of the rand to plummet to a then record low of R15.38 to the US dollar. Local and international business and political commentators were dumbfounded. What could have prompted the president to take such a seemingly reckless gamble with the country's economy?

Zuma, faced with mounting criticism over Nene's axing, was forced to make an embarrassing U-turn. Four days after his appointment, Van Rooyen was replaced with Pravin Gordhan, Nene's predecessor.

'I have received many representations to reconsider my decision. As a democratic government, we emphasise the importance of listening to the people and to respond to their views,' Zuma said in a statement on 13 December, in which he announced Gordhan's appointment to finance and Van Rooyen's reshuffling to Gordhan's old post in the Department of Cooperative Governance and Traditional Affairs.[4]

It did not take long for allegations to emerge that the Guptas had been behind the disastrous appointment of Van Rooyen.

In an opinion piece in which he urged 'all South Africans to stand up against the Gupta syndicate', EFF deputy president Floyd Shivambu claimed that 'the reason why Nene was removed and replaced with Des van Rooyen is because Saxonwold said so'. According to Shivambu, Nene was fired because of his opposition to South Africa's pending nuclear power expansion programme, as well as his criticism of other government transactions that allegedly would benefit the Guptas.[5]

Nene's criticism of the country's potential investment in new nuclear power stations stemmed from his concerns over the projected cost – anywhere between R700 billion and R1.4 trillion – which he genuinely feared would cripple the country's finances.[6]

But the Guptas were desperate for the transaction to go ahead, according to Shivambu, because Shiva Uranium, owned by the family's Oakbay Resources & Energy, would be in a prime position to supply the new nuclear power plants with uranium.

A week after Gordhan's dramatic appointment as finance minister, *Rapport* revealed that just hours after his short-lived tenure began, Van

Rooyen showed up at National Treasury in Pretoria with two special advisors. They were named by the newspaper as Mahommed Bobat and Ian Whitley, both from the private financing and banking sectors.[7]

In February 2016, *Africa Confidential*, a London-based subscription news service that covers the continent, released a report in which it claimed that Bobat and Whitley were 'Gupta allies' and that both men 'have associations with the Guptas and their businesses'.[8]

A few days later, *Business Day* reported on claims made by 'ANC and government sources' that Bobat had 'worked closely with the Gupta family and had taken their tender documents to government departments'. But when asked, Bobat had strongly denied that he had ever been a Gupta lackey. 'The fact that I am Indian does not mean we are related. I did no such thing as deliver documents or had any interactions with them,' Bobat told the paper.[9] (Both Bobat and Whitley continued working for Van Rooyen when he became minister of cooperative governance and traditional affairs.)

Rumours about the Guptas' alleged role in Nenegate continued to circulate until Luthuli House, headquarters of the ANC, could ignore them no longer. So it was that the family was summoned to meet with top ANC leaders in downtown Johannesburg.

According to the *Sowetan*, a delegation including Ajay Gupta and Duduzane Zuma representing the family's interests met with ANC top brass, including President Zuma and the party's secretary general Gwede Mantashe, 'where they were asked about their influence on ANC leaders'.[10]

While the headline claimed that the Guptas had been hauled 'over the coals', the article contained little evidence that the meeting had been anything more than a jovial gathering of old friends. It would have been highly unlikely in any event for a meeting presided over by the president to be used as an opportunity to reprimand the very family with whom he was said to have improper ties. The fact that the attendance of Zuma's own son, in his capacity as a Gupta associate, was not seen as a conflict of interest casts further doubt over whether the Guptas received even the slightest of wrist slaps.

Mantashe, with characteristic gruffness, told the *Sowetan*, 'We did not meet a family, we met a company.' To his credit, however, about a month earlier the secretary general had been candid with the newspaper by giving his opinion on the issue of state capture following Van Rooyen's appointment as finance minister. In the interview he admitted that there was a possibility that individuals within the ANC, but not the organisation as a whole, had succumbed to the influence of certain businesspeople.[11]

But worse was still to come for the beleaguered Mantashe. While the Waterkloof scandal had made South Africans painfully aware of the fact that the Guptas had the ability to influence the state, the revelations that surfaced in March 2016 presented an even more disturbing possibility: the Guptas did not just influence the government; to some extent they had *become* the government.

The *Financial Times* dropped a major state capture bombshell when it reported early in March that deputy finance minister Mcebisi Jonas had been offered the position of finance minister by the Guptas prior to Van Rooyen's appointment.[12]

The claim, despite its potentially massive repercussions, was curiously buried in a lengthy exposition of the Guptas and their relationship with Zuma in the wake of Nene's axing, and the family's dubious coal mine deal. About halfway through the article, the *Financial Times* dropped the following nugget:

'The family also denied a claim, made to the FT, that weeks before Mr Van Rooyen's appointment they had asked Mcebisi Jonas, deputy finance minister, if he was interested in the Treasury's top post at a meeting at the Gupta home.

'"There have been an extraordinary number of allegations around the Gupta family in recent weeks, several of which have involved the finance ministry," a family spokesman said. "To be absolutely clear: there was no meeting at all."

'The Treasury and Mr Jonas declined to comment, neither denying nor confirming the existence of the meeting.'

If the Guptas thought the story would die there, they were wrong.

On the Sunday following the *Financial Times* report, the *Sunday Times* ran a story that provided seemingly concrete details of the meeting between Jonas and the Guptas.[13] According to the article, Jonas met with the Guptas and Duduzane Zuma at a hotel in Sandton, Johannesburg, towards the end of November 2015. Senior sources in National Treasury informed the newspaper that Jonas was told that the job of minister of finance was his if he wanted it. However, the offer was conditional: he would have to perform two key tasks. The first involved ensuring that South Africa's pending multibillion-rand nuclear procurement programme continued unhindered. The second concerned firing key Treasury officials who were fierce critics of the country's nuclear energy aspirations due to the vast financial burden it would place on the state's coffers.

The report added fuel to Shivambu's earlier allegation that Nene had been fired because of his opposition to the nuclear deal. It also provided grounds for further speculation about Van Rooyen's advisors, Bobat and Whitley, and the role they would have played at Treasury had their boss's tenure as finance minister not been cut short. And, of course, it raised fresh questions about Zuma's motivation for firing Nene and appointing the inexperienced Van Rooyen in his place, heightening the already established suspicion that the Guptas had somehow played a role in the whole fiasco.

In a statement issued by Oakbay Investments on behalf of the Guptas, the family denied the *Sunday Times* claims regarding Jonas: 'We challenge the faceless purveyors of these lies to provide evidence of any of these allegations. To be absolutely clear: there was no meeting at all. Further, Atul Gupta was not even in South Africa on the date of the alleged meeting.'[14]

On the Wednesday following the *Sunday Times* report, Jonas himself stunned the country by releasing an official statement through the finance ministry in which he finally broke his silence on the matter: 'Members of the Gupta family offered me the position of Minister of Finance to replace then-Minister Nene. I rejected this out of hand. The basis of my rejection of their offer is that it makes a mockery of our hard-earned democracy, the trust of our people and no one apart from the President of the Republic appoints ministers.'[15]

The Guptas, who could no longer blame 'faceless' individuals for spreading 'lies' about them, hit back with a statement denying Jonas's claims: 'These latest allegations are just more political point scoring between rival factions within the ANC. To be clear: any suggestion that the Gupta family or any of our representatives or associates have offered anyone a job in government is totally false,' read the statement. 'We challenge Minister Jonas to provide a full account of the supposed meeting that took place, under oath, in a court of law. Minister Jonas is attempting to cover up and divert attention away from his own relationships and practices. We are confident questions about his own ethical standards will be exposed.'[16]

But details about the family's approach to Jonas continued to seep into the public domain. On the same day as Jonas's statement and the Guptas' subsequent denial, *City Press* published a story on its website revealing a conversation between the newspaper's then editor Ferial Haffajee and Jonas three weeks before. In the article, *City Press* revealed that Jonas 'confirmed the information we had from three sources which was that he had received the approach from the Guptas. We could not publish until he spoke out on record which he has now done.'[17]

According to the newspaper, Jonas was 'invited to a coffee date with Duduzane Zuma', who asked him 'if he could meet with presidential emissaries'. Curious, Jonas agreed to the meeting, which took place at the Guptas' compound in Saxonwold. It was here that he was told, 'The old man [Zuma] wants to make you finance minister.'

'A stunned Jonas listened as two of the Gupta brothers told him that if he agreed to "work with us", he would be enriched. "We'll fix you up," he was told. The family said they would provide staff for him, and that he should get rid of certain senior Treasury staff,' stated the article.

In the meantime, a second member of the ANC had come forward with a similar claim.

On the Monday evening following the *Sunday Times* revelation about Jonas and the job offer, Johann Abrie of the Democratic Alliance entertained a lively discussion on his Facebook page about the claims made in the newspaper.

'The Minister of Finance did not confirm or deny the fact that the Gupta brothers approached his deputy, Mcebisi Jonas for the job as Finance Minister,' Abrie wrote. 'For those of you able to read between the lines, this mean [*sic*] that deputy minister Jonas is the second person (after Minister of Sport Fikile Mbalula) who were [*sic*] approached by the Guptas for a job as Minister instead of by President Zuma. It is now clear that Zuma abdicated his job of appointing Ministers to the Guptas.'

Hours later, ANC member of Parliament (MP) Vytjie Mentor responded to the post with yet another startling claim. 'But they hap [*sic*] previously asked me to become Minister of Public Enterprises when Barbara Hogan got the chop, provided that I would drop the SAA flight-route to India and give [it] to them. I refused and so I was never made a Minister. The President was in another room when they offered me this in Saxonwold,' she wrote.

Abrie's response to the post summed up the disbelief with which many South Africans would view the latest revelations about the Guptas: 'Dear God Aunty Vytjie. Please tell me you are joking,' he replied.

Zuma's axing of Hogan and several other cabinet members occurred on 31 October 2010. At the time, Mentor was chair of Parliament's Portfolio Committee on Public Enterprises. It is therefore not inconceivable that Zuma may have viewed Mentor as a good candidate to replace Hogan. However, the Presidency – in an unusually terse media statement – denied Zuma's involvement, saying, 'President Jacob Zuma has no recollection of Ms Mentor. He is therefore unable to comment on any alleged incident in her career.'[18]

The Guptas also denied the latest claim about their alleged meddling in state affairs. 'No meeting has ever taken place between ANC MP Vytjie Mentor and any member of the Gupta family or their representatives and no job offer was made. Facebook is not the appropriate forum to air such a complaint and we can only assume it is an attempt to gain personal profile and media attention,' The New Age quoted 'the family' as saying.[19]

The Guptas had also prepared a lecture on the soundness of the country's political mechanics: 'South Africa has a robust Constitution and a strict process governing the appointment of ministers and deputy ministers. We have every faith that if anybody tried to abuse power around appointments, they would be rebuffed by our Constitution and our strong political leadership.'[20]

But then a 2010 Sowetan article surfaced which revealed details of a trip to China which Mentor had undertaken alongside Zuma in August of that year,[21] casting doubt on the president's apparent inability to remember her. Clearly shaken, the Presidency soon released a follow-up statement, hilariously titled 'Presidency maintains no recollection of Ms Mentor'.

'The Presidency refutes the misleading media reports stating that the former ANC MP, Ms Vytjie Mentor, "accompanied" President Jacob Zuma on a state visit to China in 2010,' read the statement. 'Such reports are an attempt to dispute the Presidency assertion that the President has no recollection of the former MP. Ms Mentor was definitely not part of the official delegation to the People's Republic of China, should she have travelled to the country during the State Visit.'[22]

But Mentor, who was on holiday in Thailand at the time of her revelation, was having none of the president's sudden amnesia. In another Facebook post, she explained in detail how she and Zuma had previously worked together in Parliament: 'I chaired the ANC National Parliamentary Caucus when President Zuma was a Deputy President. He sat next to me and spoke through me and with me in Caucus each Thursday when Parliament was in session. I sat with him in the ANC's Political Committee each month too. He is the one [who] was sent by the [ANC] Top 6 then to tell me that the ANC has [deployed] me to be the Chair of Caucus then. He is the one who introduced me to the ANC Caucus then as a new Chair of Caucus. I had a bi-monthy [sic] with him in his Tuynhuis Offices then. He knew me right from when he arrived from exile. He met me frequently on the ground in the Northern Cape on many occasions.'[23]

No counterclaims were forthcoming from the Presidency following Mentor's second Facebook volley.

Hogan too decided to enter the fray by claiming that while she was public enterprises minister she had been put under pressure to meet with Jet Airways, an Indian airline based in Mumbai, regarding SAA's flight route to India. Jet Airlines wanted SAA to drop its flights between South Africa and India and to give that route to them.

'The issue that Vytjie Mentor raises about Jet Airways, I cannot tell you how much pressure I was put under to meet with Jet Airways for commercial reasons,' Hogan told Talk Radio 702's John Robbie. 'And I refused; I said their relationship is with the SAA ... it's got nothing to do with me. So I'm absolutely not surprised that Vytjie Mentor is confirming this.'[24]

Netwerk24 later revealed that the Guptas were Jet Airways shareholders at the time Hogan was being put under pressure to meet with the airline. According to unnamed former SAA employees quoted in the report, the office of Malusi Gigaba, Hogan's successor as minister of public enterprises, pressurised SAA's executive management to drop the route.[25]

Earlier reports on the Guptas' alleged attempts to capture the state airline made these latest claims seem even more plausible. In 2013, the *Sunday Times* had reported that Vuyisile Kona, at the time SAA chairperson and acting CEO, had also once been summoned to Saxonwold.[26] The meeting, which reportedly took place shortly after Kona's appointment in October 2012, was allegedly facilitated by an advisor to Gigaba and attended by Rajesh Gupta, Duduzane Zuma and Tshepiso Magashule, son of Free State premier Ace Magashule. The Guptas allegedly offered Kona R500 000, which he declined. The article made no mention of what the Guptas had wanted from Kona in exchange for the cash. Given Mentor's and Hogan's later claims, it is not difficult to imagine the return favour.

A few days after her Facebook revelations, Mentor appeared as a guest on Gauteng-based radio station Power FM. The interview with radio host Onkgopotse J.J. Tabane lasted nearly forty minutes, and Mentor gave detailed information on the events that occurred in October 2010 before the cabinet reshuffle that saw Barbara Hogan axed.[27]

'When I left Cape Town on my crutches on an early-morning flight I was doing so because I was made to believe I was going to meet the president,' Mentor began her account. Upon landing at O.R. Tambo International Airport, she was picked up in a car driven by 'a guy with dark glasses'. 'The younger one', perhaps a reference to Rajesh Gupta, was also in the car. Mentor was perplexed, especially when she realised that she was not being taken to the Union Buildings in Pretoria, where she had expected to meet Zuma, or to Luthuli House in downtown Johannesburg.

She became irritable and angry when instead her hosts drove her to an office building bearing the logo of the Guptas' Sahara Computers. Her fellow passenger apparently told her that they had stopped at the offices in order for Mentor to 'say hello' to his brother. 'I said I did not come here to say hello to anybody, your brother etcetera ... And for an hour I was there, I was very angry actually, I thought we were leaving to see the president,' Mentor said in the interview.

In an interview with the *Sunday Times* shortly after her radio appearance, Mentor shed further light on the events of that day in 2010.[28]

'We stopped at Sahara's premises and the one guy, who turned out to be the younger Gupta brother, said I would meet the president but he was held up ... at Luthuli House,' Mentor told the newspaper. 'I was then taken to meet a biggish guy who turned out to be Atul Gupta. We did not really know how to relate and made chit-chat.'

After the stop at Sahara, Rajesh took Mentor to the Guptas' estate in Saxonwold. A while later, Atul arrived and Mentor and the two brothers had a private meeting during which the latter made their unbelievable offer.

In her Power FM interview, Mentor said that the two Gupta brothers, in a meeting that lasted no longer than fifteen minutes, told her the following: 'Influence the cancellation of that route [SAA's route between India and South Africa] and then you could become the minister of public enterprises.' Should she choose to accept the offer, she 'could be a minister within a week's time or so'.

Mentor recalled being 'shocked, flabbergasted, frozen'. 'I said to them: "You know what, excuse me, I don't play these games, and you don't have the authority actually to appoint ministers."'

After this, Mentor finally got to see Zuma, who, according to her, was 'in the same house' at Saxonwold.

'There was an uneasiness, you know, but I said to him I've just been asked to do this, and this is improper,' she said on air. 'I immediately said to the president this is what's been put to me and I'm not accepting this. To his credit the president did not get angry.'

In fact, Mentor recalls that Zuma took her refusal rather well.

'He said in Zulu: "It's okay, *ntombazana* [girl]." He then even said "take care of yourself" and "you are even on crutches"; he was sympathetic to the fact that I had come all the way there on crutches.'

Zuma then escorted her out of the Guptas' house and into the vehicle that would ferry her away. '"Look after yourself, and take care actually." That is the last word [Zuma] said before I climbed into a black twin cab, with heavily tinted windows, to be taken to the airport.' Then, mere days after her visit to Saxonwold, her blood 'coagulated' when she heard in a radio broadcast that Hogan had been axed as minister of public enterprises.[29]

Hogan's replacement with Malusi Gigaba formed part of a massive cabinet reshuffle that involved the appointment of no less than twenty-six new ministers and deputy ministers.[30]

During a media briefing at the presidential guesthouse in Pretoria, Zuma said: 'We had to change the way government works in order to improve service delivery. Our mission was guided by improving the quality of the lives of South Africans.'[31]

But Mentor knew that at least one of the myriad changes to Zuma's cabinet had little to do with improving service delivery or the quality of ordinary South Africans' lives. The Guptas' sway over Zuma and the shocking amount of power they wielded was now very clear to her.

'I was hoping against hope that [the Guptas] were trying to trick me into a situation; there's no way they could know [about the cabinet reshuffle] ahead of time. It only really dawned on me when that was announced. I was sitting in that car with the radio, the announcement about the reshuffle was being made, then I realised that indeed [the Guptas] knew their story,' Mentor told Power FM.[32]

The commotion around the claims made by Mentor and Jonas encouraged Julius Malema, the live-wire leader of the EFF, to publicly revisit a story he had been telling for years regarding the appointment of the equally boisterous Fikile Mbalula as South Africa's minister of sport and recreation.

Mbalula replaced Makhenkesi Stofile as sports minister during the very same October 2010 cabinet reshuffle that claimed Hogan's political scalp. Malema first started making noise about the events surrounding Mbalula's appointment after his own dramatic expulsion from the ANC in 2012.

In 2013, shortly after the Waterkloof debacle, Malema told the *Sunday World* that since 2011 he had been warning 'the public and the ruling party about the power the Guptas had over Zuma'.[33]

'Mbalula also told the ANC national executive committee meeting that the Guptas told him he was going to be appointed a minister before the president informed him,' Malema told the newspaper. 'He was attacked in the NEC, accused of ill-discipline and [asked] why is he not talking to the president privately.'

On 16 February 2016, a month before the storm around Jonas's and Mentor's claims hit, Malema repeated the allegation in a speech in Parliament: 'In my previous life, when I was a friend of the Minister of Sport and Recreation, he received a call from the Guptas. He was still the Deputy Minister of Police, and they told him that he was going to be the Minister of Sport and Recreation. That was during the time he still had courage. He went to the National Executive Committee, NEC, of the ANC and raised this matter. He was so angry and he even cried about it asking why we were being appointed by unelected leaders into positions of responsibility. I hope, one day, my former friend will find himself and continue to fight this just cause.'[34]

In March, right in the middle of the furore around Jonas and Mentor, Malema, ever the belligerent strategist, again reminded the country about the Guptas' alleged involvement in Mbalula's appointment: 'Hope @MbalulaFikile will also confirm that he was offered the sports ministry by the Gupta's [sic] & unlike Jonas he accepted it & complained later,' he tweeted to his more than one million Twitter followers.

It was the opening salvo of the type of Twitter interaction that makes users of the social media platform reach for their proverbial popcorn.

Mbalula retorted: 'What you are saying is simply provocation. I was never offered any job by anyone. I'm not accountable to you but to ANC NEC @Julius_S_Malema.'

Malema countered: '@Mbalula_Fikile you are accountable to South Africans, stop being a coward. You love a [political] position more than the country, history will judge you.'

Malema's onslaught could not have come at a worse time for the sports minister, who was busy defending South Africa's 2010 FIFA World Cup legacy following the massive corruption scandal that had hit the world football governing body the previous year and that implicated South African football officials.

At a media briefing on the FIFA issue shortly after his Twitter war with Malema, a journalist asked Mbalula about allegations that he was appointed by the Guptas. The minister angrily brushed off the question, failing to deny that the incident took place. 'We are not governed by the Guptas, we are not run by the Guptas, we are here for sport,' Mbalula growled at the reporter. 'If you want to ask me about the Guptas, ask me out of this press conference.'[35]

What followed was one of his famously nonsensical rants. 'If I felt the need to clarify any issue, it would be substantive,' he said. 'And the fact of the matter is that I owe nobody any explanation, the onus is on those who make such allegations to prove them. I am not going to join the chorus [when] I don't know who is the conductor. I am in charge of my own destiny and I don't just dance to music that I've never composed.

I compose my own sound. So for those who have composed the Guptas' chorus, let them sing for it ... Those who have composed the chorus of the Guptas, let them dance to it, I don't dance to that tune.'

The following day, the Guptas weighed in on the matter in an article in *The New Age* in which Ajay Gupta and Oakbay CEO Nazeem Howa attempted to explain how the 'urban legend' around Mbalula's supposed appointment by the family had originated. 'I read a speculative report in a weekend newspaper that Fikile is being named as a possible minister,' Ajay told the paper. 'When I bumped into him a few days later I jokingly congratulated him on his possible appointment.' According to Howa, 'Fikile then tweeted that he was told by a Gupta that he is heading for the Cabinet.' This, the newspaper concluded, was how the story started.[36]

Meanwhile, during a question-and-answer session in Parliament held on the same day as Mbalula's press conference, and a day before the ANC's scheduled NEC meeting to be held from 18 to 20 March in Irene, Pretoria, Zuma had to fend off accusations that he had delegated his power to appoint ministers to the Guptas.

Mmusi Maimane, leader of the opposition DA, had submitted a written question to Zuma in which he asked the president whether any third parties had influenced his decision to replace finance minister Nene with Van Rooyen. Zuma responded with a lecture on the president's constitutionally mandated prerogative to appoint and dismiss ministers and their deputies as he or she pleased. 'The constitution does not require me to consult anyone before I appoint or remove a minister or deputy minister,' Zuma told Parliament.[37]

Maimane was not impressed with Zuma's vague answer. He put a follow-up question to the president, forcing him to provide an unscripted answer.

'Mr President, deputy minister Mcebisi Jonas has already confirmed that the Guptas offered him the position of finance minister before it was even offered to Minister Des van Rooyen,' Maimane began. 'In fact, your former caucus chairperson, Vytjie Mentor, has already been on record, the woman you claim you don't know, has already been on record saying, in fact, that she was also offered a cabinet position by the Guptas. Mr President, it has become quite clear that power does no longer sit at the Union Buildings. In fact, worse, it does not even sit at Luthuli House.

It now sits at Saxonwold. And so, Mr President, you and your family are getting richer while South Africans are getting poorer and losing work. So my question to you, Mr President: whether the Gupta family has ever offered anybody a cabinet position in your term of office as president, or is Minister Jonas in fact lying? Because if in fact he is, or he is not, is the president willing to take accountability for the decision [to fire Nene] and resign in front of the people of South Africa?'

Zuma, after a characteristic giggle and a clearing of the throat, again refused to be drawn into any specifics around Mentor's and Jonas's claims.

'Honourable speaker, I appointed Jonas as a deputy minister, that is what I offered Jonas, I never offered Jonas ministry, that is why he is a deputy minister,' said Zuma.

Somewhat ironically, he then passed the buck to the Guptas: 'If Jonas says he was offered [a ministerial position] by the Guptas, I think you'll be well placed to ask the Guptas or Jonas, don't ask me, where do I come in? I had no business with that, I had absolutely no business.'

'I am in charge of the government,' he concluded. 'I appoint in terms of the Constitution, there is no minister who is here who was ever appointed by the Guptas or by anybody else. Ministers who are here were appointed by me.'

Zuma and the Guptas had barely enjoyed two days of peace following their denials when yet another scandal involving the family and their alleged meddling in government affairs broke in the media.

On the Sunday following Zuma's question session in Parliament, the *Sunday Times* introduced South Africa to another high-ranking former government official who was willing to put on record startling claims about the president and the Guptas. Themba Maseko, former CEO of the GCIS, the state entity that oversees government communications, was once urged by Zuma to meet the Guptas and 'help' the family, the newspaper reported.[38]

According to Maseko, the Guptas started contacting him towards the end of 2010 to try to set up a meeting. He eventually agreed. The very day he was due at their estate in Saxonwold, Maseko received a phone call from Zuma. After greeting him, Zuma said, in Zulu, 'The Gupta brothers need your help. Please help them.' When Maseko informed the president that he was already on his way to Saxonwold, Zuma responded, 'It's fine then.'

Maseko was not pleased with the call from Zuma and the prospect of meeting the Guptas. 'I was so pissed off and a bit unsettled,' he told the *Sunday Times*.

Maseko met with Ajay Gupta and another brother whose name he could not recall. 'After niceties, Ajay said: "We are setting up a newspaper called *The New Age*. I want government advertising channelled to the newspaper,"' recalled Maseko. According to the *Sunday Times*, 'as GCIS CEO, Maseko was in charge of a media-buying budget of just over R240-million a year'.

Maseko told the Guptas that things did not quite work like that; GCIS merely selected the appropriate media platforms on behalf of government departments, which controlled their own budgets for advertising. But Ajay brushed off his concerns, allegedly saying, 'Don't worry ... tell us where the money is and tell departments to give you money and if they refuse we will deal with them. If you have a problem with any department, we will summon ministers here.'

Maseko was rattled by Ajay's comments. 'I was extremely perturbed. He [Ajay] said if the ministers were not co-operating, they [the Guptas] have a way of dealing with them. [He said] they have regular weekly meetings with the president,' Maseko told the *Sunday Times*.

Several weeks after the meeting, Maseko said a senior staffer at *The New Age* phoned him to request an urgent meeting. It was a Friday afternoon and Maseko was already on his way to Sun City, where he planned to spend the weekend relaxing and playing golf. He told the staffer to call his office on Monday. The staffer allegedly replied, 'I'm not asking you. I am telling you. The meeting has to happen. It is urgent because of the launch of the TNA [*The New Age*].'

An hour later, Ajay Gupta called, demanding that Maseko cancel his plans in order to meet with him. 'He [Ajay] said: "I am ordering you to meet tomorrow." I said he must go and f**k himself,' Maseko recalled. 'I told him that there were ANC leaders who owned media companies and they never behaved like that or gave me such instructions. He said: "I will talk to your seniors in government and you will be sorted out." He said: "We will get you, we will replace you with people who will co-operate."'[39]

A year after this incident, Maseko was removed from his position as CEO of the GCIS to make way for Jimmy Manyi, president of the Black

Management Forum. In 2013, Manyi, who over the years had been described as a friend of the Guptas, accepted a job as a television host on the Guptas' twenty-four-hour news channel, ANN7.[40]

All indications were that the Guptas had indeed found a more 'cooperative' person to fill Maseko's position, although Manyi, who only lasted as GCIS boss until the end of 2012, vehemently denied that the family interfered in any way at the entity while he was at the helm.[41]

Repeated denials from the Guptas, Zuma and other state officials implicated in allegations of state capture could not stem the tide of public dissent over the family's apparent transgressions. Nevertheless, the Guptas made a spirited effort to convince South Africa that they were the innocent victims of an unfair witch-hunt.

On 18 March 2016, the Friday on which the ANC National Executive Committee meeting was due to start in Irene, where the issue of state capture would be on the agenda, Oakbay Investments placed a double-page advertisement in *The New Age* proclaiming the family's innocence. It stated: 'As the global economic slowdown began to bite, the family became the scapegoat for every calamity and misfortune that South Africa has faced. We have been quiet until now but given the recent xenophobic and hate speech against us, now is the time to set the record straight.'[42]

Among other points, the advertisement repeated a previous assertion that the Guptas' main holding company derived less than 1 per cent of its revenue from government contracts. Furthermore, it denied that the family exerted undue influence over any government officials, saying, 'Like any other South African business, we interact with the government. In fact, friendship with the previous president was as strong.'

But these protestations would do little to stymie the ever-growing barrage of criticism and dissatisfaction over the Guptas' 'friendship' with Zuma. Much to the ANC's consternation, objections were increasingly being raised from within its own ranks and from organisations aligned with it. In a media statement released on the eve of the NEC meeting, the South African Communist Party, one of the ANC's long-serving alliance partners, claimed that another 'Gupta-inspired cabinet shuffle' was imminent. This time, trade and industry minister Rob Davies would make way for someone who would favour the Guptas in a steel manufacturing deal.[43]

'The SACP has called for a broad spectrum investigation into the phenomenon of corporate state capture and a judicial commission of enquiry to reveal the nature, character and extent of the problem, and to contribute on the way forward to deal decisively with the problem,' read the statement. 'The SACP will seek engagement with the ANC and the alliance as a whole to discuss the problem in general, and specifically growing evidence of the manipulation of political appointments by the Gupta family.'

There was scepticism at the SACP's sudden criticism of the Guptas. Only a day before, senior SACP member Senzeni Zokwana had publicly questioned the veracity of Vytjie Mentor's story about being offered a ministerial position. 'We don't think that there is any truth in that because no family can have such power to decide who becomes a minister or not,' Zokwana was quoted as saying.[44]

As the NEC meeting got under way on 18 March 2016, another struggle hero and ANC stalwart voiced his strong disapproval of the Guptas' apparent influence over government. Former ANC treasurer Mathews Phosa stated that the country needed 'a very serious judicial commission of inquiry to investigate not only the Guptas, but all others who may be involved in this [sic] illegal and corrupt activities of capturing the state'.[45]

Meanwhile, some of the country's most prominent activist bodies and civil rights organisations were also making their voices heard. The public criticism of three organisations named for respected and revered ANC struggle heroes – namely, the Oliver and Adelaide Tambo Foundation, the Nelson Mandela Foundation and the Ahmed Kathrada Foundation – had to have been a painful blow to the ruling party.

In a joint open letter to the ANC NEC and secretary general Gwede Mantashe, Dr Frene Ginwala (acting chairperson of the Oliver and Adelaide Tambo Foundation), Professor Njabulo S. Ndebele (chairperson of the board of trustees of the Nelson Mandela Foundation) and Derek Hanekom (on behalf of the Ahmed Kathrada Foundation) stated:

'We are deeply concerned about the current course on which our country is headed ... We read disturbing stories in newspapers and other media about "state capture"; we see important institutions of democracy such as Parliament under great strain; we hear what ordinary South Africans tell us through our work, and are challenged by friends and comrades who witness cumulative fragmentation of the ANC, a great organisation our

Founders helped build and sustain over generations. In the spirit of our Founders, we cannot passively watch these deeply concerning developments unfold and get worse by the day.'[46]

The ANC NEC meeting was in its final day and the three foundations urged the party's leaders to 'take note of the mood of the people across the country, to reflect deeply on their solemn responsibilities, to make urgent choices, and to take urgent corrective actions in the best interest of South Africa and its peoples'.

20

Clipped wings and failed probes

The criticism from alliance partners, struggle icons and prominent foundations meant that the ANC could no longer ignore the growing discontent over the Gupta matter. It therefore came as no surprise that the Guptas featured prominently when Mantashe briefed the media on some of the key decisions made at the NEC meeting.

'The ANC NEC had frank and robust discussions on the serious allegations surrounding the Gupta family and its purported influence in the appointment of ministers, their deputies and other positions in key state owned entities in their interests,' Mantashe stated on behalf of the NEC. 'Such actions can have no place in the ANC or its government as they have the potential to undermine and erode the credibility and confidence of our people in the leadership of their organization, the ANC and its government. We reject the notion of any business or family group seeking such influence over the ANC with the contempt it deserves while also recognizing the need to act to protect the integrity of our government and our organization.'[1]

He also gave his undertaking that the party would thoroughly investigate the matter: 'The ANC NEC mandated the Officials and the NWC [National Working Committee] to gather all pertinent information about the allegations to enable the ANC to take appropriate action on this matter. The ANC calls on all members who have information to approach the Secretary General's Office.'

Mantashe harshly criticised the manner in which the Guptas had brushed off state capture allegations by characterising them as the manifestation of infighting within the party. 'In addition, the NEC expressed its utmost disgust at the arrogance, disrespect and reckless journalism displayed by the New Age Newspaper (18, 19 March 2016), ANN7 News Channel (16–18 March 2016) and representatives of the Gupta-family,' Mantashe scolded.

'They have characterized the ANC as a group of factions for and against President Zuma.'

The ANC seemed to be aligning itself with the broader public's sentiment towards the Guptas, much like it had done after the Waterkloof fiasco.

Ignoring the ANC secretary general's rebuke, the Guptas, in a statement issued by Oakbay Investments, said they supported the ANC probe: 'The Gupta family welcomes the decision of the ANC to investigate the alleged capture of the state by any business entities. We welcome this process which should ultimately allow the truth to be recognised and end this current trial by innuendo and slander. We will fully cooperate with the Office of the Secretary General during the information gathering process.'[2]

When deputy president Cyril Ramaphosa publicly spoke out against the threat of state capture soon after the ANC probe was launched, many South Africans saw it as a sign that the party was aligning against the Guptas and, by extension, Zuma.

'The ANC is not for sale ... the ANC refuses to be captured,' Ramaphosa told delegates at a summit in Sandton the Wednesday after the NEC meeting. 'We will not be captured. Those who want to capture the ANC and make it their own and influence it to advance personal or corporate interest, you have come to the wrong address.'[3]

He continued: 'It is not only the Gupta family [that has allegedly captured the state]. There are a number of others as well, there are others who have either captured the state or are in the process of capturing the state, and we are saying to all and sundry, stop in your tracks, we are not going to allow you to capture this glorious movement, we will not allow that.'

But such enthusiasm for the investigation was not universally shared.

'It is debatable whether the office of the secretary-general of the ANC is the appropriate place to exclusively gather this information and analyse it,' Saki Macozoma, the president of Business Leadership South Africa, told *Business Day*.[4]

Themba Maseko, the former GCIS CEO, took to Twitter to voice his concerns. 'The decision to invite everyone with a Gupta bullying story to come forward is welcome but what next. Is there a commitment to act?' he tweeted after Mantashe's announcement. Maseko nevertheless added that 'Gwede Mantashe's process must be given a chance' and that he had 'confidence in the process'.

The DA insisted that the Gupta matter be investigated by Parliament, and not just by the ANC, and put pressure on Jackson Mthembu, the ANC's chief whip in Parliament, to support the establishment of an 'ad hoc committee to investigate revelations regarding the Gupta family and their illicit influence over the Presidency and Executive'.[5]

Noting Mthembu's supposed support for the ANC's Gupta investigation, the DA stated: 'If the former ANC spin doctor and newly-appointed chief whip is serious and not merely offering lip service, he and his caucus will support this motion in the NA [National Assembly] next term and work with the opposition to ensure that this ad hoc committee is free of political influence and not another ANC whitewash to protect President Zuma.'

But Mthembu made it quite clear that his party would not support the DA's motion to establish a parliamentary ad hoc committee to investigate the Guptas' alleged state influence. He justified his refusal by saying that 'the allegations relating to the so-called "state capture" are before some state institutions, such as the Hawks and the public protector, following requests for investigations by certain formations and individuals ... Parliament should not find itself in a situation where it is conducting parallel investigations.'[6]

It soon became evident that the ANC's probe would be nothing more than a weak effort by the ruling party to at least appear to be genuinely interested in investigating the complaints and claims about the Guptas.

Towards the end of April 2016, *City Press* would later report, Maseko and a large group of other former senior government officials had clearly lost faith in the ANC probe, as evidenced by their decision to formally ask finance minister Pravin Gordhan and public service and administration minister Ngoako Ramatlhodi to launch a public inquiry into the Guptas' capture of government entities, departments and employees.[7]

The newspaper reported that the group of forty-five former directors general wrote to Gordhan and Ramatlhodi on 22 April, asking the ministers to ensure that an independent inquiry, in accordance with the Promotion of Administrative Justice Act, be established to determine the extent to which government officials had been breaking the law in order to benefit the Guptas.

Asked by *City Press* why the group did not take their grievances to

Mantashe, Roger Jardine, a former director general of the Department of Arts, Culture, Science and Technology, said that 'as former directors-general, we are mindful of not falling into a situation where we conflate party and state'.

Another member of the group, who spoke to the newspaper on condition of anonymity, hinted that they simply did not view the ANC probe as a safe platform. 'There are many who are willing to talk about their experiences, but are afraid. They want a space in which they are protected,' said the former official.

At the end of May, suspicions about the ANC's dedication to unearthing the Guptas' misdemeanours were proved justified when, after another NEC meeting, Mantashe unceremoniously pulled the plug on the party's Gupta probe.

'Following the call by the ANC for comrades to provide any information about alleged business influence on the state, a number of comrades came forward to engage with the Office of the Secretary General,' Mantashe said in a statement at a press conference in Johannesburg. 'It was unfortunate that only one person could make a written submission on the matter. The allegations made were serious, they cannot be treated lightly and many warrant a comprehensive investigation. The NEC has advised comrades to formalise their complaints to institutions that deal with complaints of this nature.'[8]

Mantashe told reporters that eight people had approached his office with information on the Guptas, but because only one of them had been willing to put his or her claims on paper, the party viewed the probe as a 'fruitless exercise'. 'When they don't come forward to the ANC, the ANC will not force them,' said Mantashe. 'It doesn't mean that we are walking away from it, but if you make allegations then you must be bold enough to take [the matter] through.'[9]

Journalist Ranjeni Munusamy, writing for the *Daily Maverick*, scoffed at Mantashe's advice. 'When the allegation is that the state has been captured, which department in the state, including the South African Police Service, would view evidence in this regard neutrally?' she asked.[10]

In her autopsy of the ANC's failed probe, Munusamy wrote: 'Mantashe's open invitation to ANC members to come forward with information appeared to be a constructive step towards finally uncovering whether allegations that had been circulating for years about the Guptas' interference in state affairs were in fact true. But only once people went to the ANC headquarters did they realise there was no formal investigation and that Mantashe did not have any powers or capacity to process any information and evidence they brought forward.'

Business Day political editor Natasha Marrian, writing in the *Financial Mail*, noted that it was the ANC's NWC that made the call to pull the plug on the Gupta probe. She described the NWC as 'a structure which is packed to the brim with Zuma loyalists'.[11]

The SACP again growled at its alliance partner. The party's deputy general secretary, Solly Mapaila, labelled the ANC probe a 'whitewash' and made it clear that the SACP would not abandon the issue.[12]

Themba Maseko would later indicate in a post on Twitter that it was he who had handed in the lone written submission to Mantashe's office.

Ultimately, the abandonment of the probe proved that the ANC's own internal structures were not fit to properly examine an issue that had the potential to do the party great damage. The disappointing outcome validated the scepticism of those who from the outset had predicted that the probe would come to nothing.

When Mthembu poured cold water on the DA's request for a parliamentary inquiry into the Gupta matter, he justified his decision by saying that the Hawks and the public protector were already conducting state capture investigations. However, it would soon become apparent that the Hawks were no more serious about probing the Guptas than the ANC had been.

The Directorate for Priority Crime Investigation, as the Hawks are formally called, was prompted to launch Gupta probes after the DA and fellow opposition party the Congress of the People (COPE) laid separate criminal charges against the family in March 2016.

In a statement on 17 March, the DA announced that it had 'laid criminal charges against members of the Gupta family in terms of Section 4 of the Prevention and Combating of Corrupt Activities Act, 2004'. Referring to the allegations made by Mcebisi Jonas and Vytjie Mentor, the DA stated: 'These revelations of undue executive influence by the Guptas amount to a *prima facie* case of corruption.'[13] The party also laid a charge of corruption against Duduzane Zuma, who, according to Jonas, had facilitated his meeting with the Guptas.

On the same day, COPE laid separate charges of corruption and treason against the Guptas and President Zuma, saying that the Guptas needed to be arrested so that a court of law could rule on the veracity of such claims as those made by Jonas.[14]

The DA's David Maynier, who had laid the charges at the Cape Town Central Police Station, later indicated that the SAPS had provided him with a case number and had transferred the case to the Hawks' anti-corruption unit.[15] Two days later, the Hawks confirmed that they had started processing the complaints from the two political parties, although they incorrectly stated that both were laid by the DA. 'We therefore appeal to the members of the public and the media alike to give us space to conduct our investigations without undue interference, and we also urge those who are allegedly involved in the matter to cooperate with our investigators so that the investigations can be expedited,' said the Hawks in a statement.[16]

In June, the *Sunday Times* revealed that Vytjie Mentor had opted to lay corruption-related charges with the police against three cabinet ministers and the Gupta family rather than submit a written statement to Mantashe. She had been lukewarm about the ANC's Gupta probe, telling the *Sunday Times*: 'I decided not to take part in the ANC internal investigation because it is ridiculous and it was clearly not an earnest effort. The intention is to pull the wool over people's eyes, to buy time and to test how much people know.'[17]

Nevertheless, according to the *Sunday Times*, Mentor was 'not optimistic about the prospects of her charges reaching the courts'. In March, she actually told *City Press* that she 'thought that investigations by the Hawks into the Guptas were doomed because she believed that the investigative unit was "corrupt". "The Hawks say they will investigate the Guptas, but it is compromised by [Major General Berning] Ntlemeza, who is at the helm of the unit. The Hawks believe their role is to serve the president and not the interests of the country," Mentor claimed.'[18]

Mentor filed her corruption-related charges – against public enterprises minister Lynne Brown, trade and industry minister Rob Davies, defence minister Nosiviwe Mapisa-Nqakula, state-owned weapons manufacturer

Denel and the Industrial Development Corporation – in May. All the charges were understood to be related to the Guptas.[19]

In July, *City Press* revealed further details from Mentor's so-called Gupta files, including a statement she had made before top Western Cape police officer Major General Jeremy Veary.

'I am of the conclusion that the Gupta family, the son of the president (Duduzane Zuma), and some ministers I have named in this statement – as well as the president, to a certain extent – all have [a] corrupt relationship that gives unfair advantage to the Gupta family and their associates at the expense of the state, using state resources and agencies all the way for their own benefit,' Mentor wrote in the statement, which also contained allegations around funding that the Guptas received from the IDC.[20]

Mentor's submission also contained further detail on the family's nuclear power endeavours, as well as additional information about her visit to the Gupta estate in Johannesburg.

Hawks boss Berning Ntlemeza told the newspaper that the complaints lodged by Mentor, COPE and the DA had been merged into one probe and that a team of investigators had been assigned to the investigation. The deadline for the probe, said Ntlemeza, was December 2016. When asked how he felt about investigating friends of the president, Ntlemeza told *City Press*, 'When I am investigating a case, I stick to my mandate, which is to serve without fear, favour or prejudice, no matter whose friend is involved. To me it is immaterial.'[21]

When I contacted the DA and COPE in August 2016, five months after they laid their criminal charges, it did not seem as if the Hawks had been tackling the probe with much fervour or commitment. Dennis Bloem, COPE's spokesperson, said at the time that the only contact he had had with the Hawks was when a general of the unit interviewed him a month after the charges were brought. 'Since then nothing has happened,' he told me. 'We are not going to leave it like this, we are going to follow up.' Similarly, DA leader Mmusi Maimane's spokesperson, Mabine Seabe, said that his party's complaints seemed to have received little attention.

Brigadier Hangwani Mulaudzi, spokesperson for the Hawks, seemed irked when asked for an update on the investigation. 'We are on record that the matter is being handled by the DPCI; however, we are not at liberty to discuss anything regarding the case,' he told me. 'Therefore, no further comments will be entertained on this matter from the media.'

With their commitment to the Gupta investigation in doubt, the Hawks were far more enthusiastic about their involvement in another issue that dominated news headlines throughout most of 2016. Enter Pravin Gordhan and the now infamous SARS 'rogue unit'.

While the SARS rogue unit saga is too complex to analyse in any detail here, an overview is necessary because the controversies surrounding the Guptas and Gordhan are in fact intertwined.

The genesis of Gordhan's troubles is to be found in the so-called SARS Wars, the media's catchphrase for the controversies that began plaguing South Africa's tax-collecting authority towards the end of 2014. Starting in August of that year and continuing well into 2015, a team of *Sunday Times* investigative journalists wrote some thirty articles detailing the existence of a so-called rogue intelligence unit within SARS. The claims were startling: the rogue unit had broken into President Zuma's Johannesburg residence to illegally plant listening devices;[22] had set up a brothel to spy on top ANC leaders; and had infiltrated ANC leaders' security details as paid bodyguards.[23]

The rogue unit, at one point formally known as the National Research Group, consisted of a team of investigators who were initially mandated to help identify tax dodgers and other tax offenders. But according to the *Sunday Times*, the unit had become a reckless, dangerous and uncontrollable gang of rogue intelligence operatives who seemed to have taken it upon themselves to run dubious covert projects, none of which appeared to involve uncovering tax-related transgressions.

The reports would ultimately have far-reaching and devastating consequences for a range of people, including members of the rogue unit, top SARS executives under whose watch the unit was established, and even key *Sunday Times* staffers.

The newspaper's first rogue unit reports coincided with the appointment of Tom Moyane as the new SARS commissioner. Using the allegations contained in the reports, Moyane facilitated a purge of those SARS officials accused of wrongdoing. Johann van Loggerenberg, the National Research Group's former head, was placed on special leave following the initial reports. Shortly thereafter, on the recommendation of a panel inquiry led by Advocate Muzi Sikhakhane, deputy SARS commissioner Ivan Pillay and strategic planning and risk division head Peter Richer were suspended. Moyane made no secret of the fact that the *Sunday Times* articles served as the basis for his actions.[24]

A string of other top SARS officials either willingly left the organisation or were suspended following the departure of Pillay and Richer. The latter two, along with Van Loggerenberg, would later resign from SARS.

Moyane brushed off accusations that he was driving a purge of highly qualified SARS officials and continued to focus on the rogue unit, appointing auditing firm KPMG to conduct yet another investigation into the matter. Tellingly, it was the *Sunday Times* investigative journalists who were allowed an exclusive look at a draft version of the completed KPMG report that had been submitted to Moyane in September 2015. The newspaper reported that the auditing firm recommended that Pravin Gordhan, at the time still minister of cooperative governance and traditional affairs, be probed over the establishment and activities of the rogue unit, as it allegedly came into existence in 2007, when Gordhan was SARS commissioner.[25]

But it later emerged that Moyane had taken it upon himself to lay criminal charges against Gordhan and other former SARS officials implicated in the rogue unit matter in May 2015, months before he received the KPMG report.[26]

In February 2016, two months after his reappointment as finance minister and mere days before he was to deliver the country's crucially important budget speech, the Hawks sent Gordhan a list of twenty-seven questions about his role in and knowledge of the SARS rogue unit's operations. They demanded that he respond by 2 March. The deadline arrived with no word from Gordhan. Instead, his lawyers sent a letter to Hawks boss Ntlemeza in which it was made clear that the finance minister would not dance to their tune.

'You are aware of the national importance of the Budget Speech, and that he [Gordhan] was not able to permit any distractions to jeopardise the Budget process,' stated the letter. 'He will respond in due course, once he has properly examined the questions and ascertained what information, of the information you request, he is able to provide.'[27]

When Gordhan finally responded, at the end of March, he said that as far as he was aware 'the unit lawfully performed its functions'. 'In respect of the legality of the investigation unit established during my time as Commissioner of the South African Revenue Service, I believed that the Unit was lawfully established to perform very important functions for and on behalf of SARS,' he maintained.[28]

After receiving complaints from Gordhan, Van Loggerenberg and Pillay, the press ombudsman, South Africa's independent press regulator, ruled that the *Sunday Times* had to apologise to all three men for having reported as fact the findings in the draft KPMG report. The ombudsman also ordered the newspaper to retract all of its rogue unit stories.[29]

In April 2016, following the departures of Piet Rampedi, one of the investigative journalists who had helped write the stories, and Phylicia Oppelt, the editor who had overseen them, the *Sunday Times* published an admission that its reporting on the matter had been problematic. 'Today we admit to you that we got some things wrong,' wrote the paper's new editor, Bongani Siqoko. 'In particular, we stated some allegations as fact, and gave incomplete information in some cases. In trying to inform you about SARS, we should have provided you with all the dimensions of the story and not overly relied on our sources.'[30]

While it appeared that the former SARS officials implicated in the saga, including Gordhan, had been vindicated, the Hawks continued to pursue the issue. In May 2016, fresh rumours began to circulate that the Hawks were on the verge of arresting Gordhan and eight other former SARS officials said to have been involved in or who had knowledge of the so-called rogue unit's activities.[31] The *Daily Maverick* claimed that the Guptas seemed to be privy to information regarding the Hawks' probe. 'It appears that the politically connected Gupta family had special insight into the Hawks investigation and possible changes to the Cabinet as a result of the imminent arrests,' wrote Ranjeni Munusamy. 'At a meeting in Johannesburg on 6 May, Ajay Gupta allegedly informed people dealing with his family's companies that the Hawks would soon be making a number of arrests in connection with the SARS spy unit. He said those who would be arrested included Gordhan, [Trevor] Manuel and Pillay.'[32]

At the time, both the Hawks and the NPA denied the pending arrest of Gordhan,[33] but then in August the *Daily Maverick* revealed that Gordhan, Pillay and other former SARS officials had been summoned to present themselves to the Hawks in Pretoria, where they would receive warning statements.[34] Warning statements are given to accused persons before they are charged with an offence and to warn them of their rights in terms of the Constitution. The news that the Hawks seemed to be once more on the verge of arresting Gordhan was met with disbelief and even panic, as evidenced by an immediate depreciation of the rand.[35]

The *Daily Maverick* suggested that the Hawks' targeting of the finance minister may have been at least partly influenced by the Guptas: 'Gordhan has for some time, since his reinstatement as Minister of Finance in December after President Jacob Zuma's disastrous firing of Nhlanhla Nene, been viewed as an obstacle thwarting the interests of individuals linked to Zuma including SAA's Dudu Myeni, current SARS Commissioner Tom Moyane as well as the Gupta family's interest in the country's nuclear deal, among others,' wrote Marianne Thamm.[36]

Gordhan, too, reportedly felt that the Guptas were behind his persecution. At a Treasury staff meeting held soon after the news about the warning statements broke, Gordhan allegedly told his colleagues that the Guptas were attacking him because of his opposition to some of their business ambitions.[37]

After reclaiming the reins of finance minister and doorkeeper to the Treasury's riches in December 2015, Gordhan's tough and disciplined stance towards wasteful expenditure and corruption saw him become an obstacle to more than one Gupta business endeavour. One of the first indicators of how he would be dealing with the family in his second stint in the Department of Finance was his refusal to do his post-budget media briefing at one of the infamous breakfast events hosted by the Guptas' *The New Age*.[38]

This was followed by the Treasury's scrutiny of two lucrative deals between state-owned entities and companies belonging or linked to the Guptas – namely, state-owned weapons manufacturer Denel's partnership with Gupta-linked VR Laser Asia, and the contentious agreement between the Guptas' Tegeta Exploration and Resources and Eskom for the supply of coal.

While the Guptas have never been linked to attempts to directly influence the Hawks' investigation, they certainly had motive for encouraging their friends in power to see to it that the Gordhan matter be concluded in their favour.

21

Battle with the banks
and closing shop

On 10 April 2016, as the public debate around state capture reached fever pitch, *City Press* and *Rapport* reported that the Guptas had fled South Africa. According to the newspapers, Ajay and Atul Gupta, along with a small entourage, had quietly left the country in their private jet following a decision to resign their directorships in all their South African companies.[1]

'Just hours after an emotional meeting with his executives on Thursday [7 April 2016], where he told them he was resigning from his business empire, Ajay Gupta left for Dubai with his brother Atul on their luxurious private jet,' reported the *City Press*. 'At 11pm that night, and with a mountain of luggage loaded on to the business jet ZS-OAK, the brothers, together with one of their wives and five of their assistants, left Lanseria Airport – likely for good.' Rajesh, the youngest brother, had already been living in Dubai for several months, it seemed.

The reports were perhaps a little premature. At the beginning of May, a source who was once close to the brothers informed me that Ajay and Atul were in fact back in South Africa, staying at their mansion in Constantia, one of Cape Town's most affluent suburbs.

Developments before and after these reports, however, seem to indicate that the family had made a decision to extricate themselves from South Africa, at least to some extent, most likely as a result of the intense public scrutiny to which they had been subjected.

A report in the *City Press* in May shed light on the incredible amounts of money the Guptas had been spending in Dubai to establish a new base abroad. Investigative reporter Susan Comrie travelled to the United Arab Emirates to have a look at the spectacular mansion which the Guptas had apparently bought for a jaw-dropping R445 million. 'Decorated in marble and gold, and with 10 bedrooms, 13 bathrooms, nine reception rooms, a double grand staircase, hand-painted dome, space for 11 cars, and chandeliers in virtually every room, the house is extravagant even by Dubai's standards,' she wrote.[2]

Given the string of financial setbacks the Guptas' companies had endured following the incriminating claims made against the family in March, it seemed plausible that the brothers were considering leaving the country for a less hostile environment. On 1 April 2016, *Fin24* revealed that auditing firm KPMG, who audited the Guptas' businesses, had decided to terminate their business relationship with the family's empire.[3]

The news site had obtained an internal email sent by KPMG Southern Africa CEO Trevor Hoole to staff and partners in which he explained the reasons behind the firm's decision. 'The recent media and political interest in the Gupta family, together with comments and questions from various stakeholders ... has required us to evaluate the continued provision of our services to this group,' Hoole wrote. 'We have decided that we should terminate our relationship with the group immediately. I can assure you that this decision was not taken lightly, but in our view the association risk is too great for us to continue. It is with heavy hearts that we have reached our conclusion, and there will clearly be financial and potentially other consequences to this, but we view them as justifiable.'[4]

Banking and financial services group Sasfin followed KPMG's example, confirming to *City Press* two days later that it too had decided to part ways with the family's businesses.[5] Sasfin had acted as one of Oakbay Resources & Energy's sponsors for its listing on the Johannesburg Stock Exchange. Sponsors are financial firms that have been approved by the exchange to provide companies with the required advice and guidance to ensure that they comply with the JSE's rules and regulations. Without a sponsor, Oakbay Resources & Energy risked being booted off the JSE. According to the JSE's listing requirements, 'the applicant issuer [listed company] has 30 business days to appoint a new sponsor from the date of resignation of the sponsor, unless the JSE decides otherwise'.[6]

Because the JSE requires companies to submit audited financial statements, Oakbay also faced having its listing terminated if it did not find a replacement for KPMG.

In a Stock Exchange News Service (SENS) announcement a few days later, Oakbay attempted to explain the situation: 'The reason for KPMG's resignation is solely based on their assessed association risk and KPMG have indicated that there is no audit reason for their resignation, whereas the termination of Sasfin's services follows a recent decision by Sasfin to align the strategic objectives of Sasfin's Corporate Finance Division more closely with that of the broader Sasfin group.'[7]

In the *City Press* report on Sasfin, it was also revealed that ABSA, which had been Oakbay's bank when the company listed on the JSE in 2014, had already terminated its ties with Oakbay Resources, but would not say when or why.[8]

The day following Oakbay's SENS announcement, news broke that First National Bank (FNB) had closed Oakbay Investments' company accounts. In a statement, Oakbay revealed that ABSA had inexplicably done the same in December 2015.[9] These dramatic developments clearly infuriated Nazeem Howa, who accused the financial institutions of being part of what ANN7 described as a 'carefully orchestrated political campaign' against the family. Lashing out at FNB, Howa said, 'We are already in the process of moving our accounts to a more enlightened institution.'[10]

The Oakbay CEO's resolute stance created an expectation that the Guptas would regroup and fight back against what they believed was a secret plot against them. Days later, however, Howa admitted that Standard Bank and Nedbank had also severed all ties with the holding company.[11] All of South Africa's so-called big four banks had now abandoned them. After a week of high drama, on Friday 8 April Oakbay Resources made what must have been one of the most unexpected SENS announcements the JSE had ever seen. Atul Gupta, Oakbay Resources' non-exective chairperson, Varun Gupta, Oakbay Resources' CEO, and Duduzane Zuma, non-executive director of Oakbay subsidiary Shiva Uranium, would all resign with immediate effect.[12]

'This decision follows a sustained political attack on the Company, and the concern that the jobs and livelihoods of nearly one thousand employees would be at immediate risk as a result of the outgoing director's association with the Company,' read the announcement. 'Accordingly, the outgoing directors are of the view that it would be in the best interests of the Company, its shareholders and employees for them to step down with immediate effect.'

If the Guptas thought that their departure from Oakbay would some-how restore investors' confidence in the company, they were wrong. When the accouncement was made, Oakbay Resources & Energy's shares were trading at R24 each on the JSE. By the following Wednesday, the share price had plummeted to R18.50. This 23 per cent drop in share value represented a R6.6-billion decline in Oakbay's market value.[13] In fact, a broader look at Oakbay Resources & Energy's share price indicates just how devastating the series of scandals was to the company's value. In May 2015, Oakbay had reached its peak of R50 a share. By the end of October 2016, it was down to just R19 a share – a staggering decline of 62 per cent.

In a follow-up SENS announcement later on 8 April, Oakbay tried to convince the public, specifically its shareholders, that the termination of the major banks' services would not affect the company negatively. 'Despite the cessation of the provision of services by the major local banks, the Group continues to be serviced by a major Asian bank with a presence in South Africa, which bank has requested that the Company not commu-nicate their name in this update,' Oakbay declared, without the slightest acknowledgement of the awkward reality that the sole bank still willing to do business with them apparently did not want to be seen doing so. 'Con-sequently, the terminations will not impact the operations of the Group and the Company is confident that the remaining banking relationship is sufficient to fully service the operational requirements of the Group.'[14]

This bravado was in sharp contrast to the contents of a letter Howa wrote to Oakbay Investments employees, and which was leaked to *Times-Live*, on the day Oakbay made its SENS announcements. 'It is with deep regret, that following a period of sustained political attack on the Gupta family and our businesses, and by extension, you our employees, we have come to the conclusion that it is time for the Gupta family to step down from all executive and non-executive positions,' Howa wrote. 'In doing this, the family hope to end the campaign against Oakbay and save all of our jobs. The closure of our bank accounts has made it virtually impossible to do business in South Africa. Without bank accounts we may find ourselves in a position where we are unable to pay you, our valued employees.'[15]

Howa went on to add that Oakbay had taken their grievances to the Guptas' most senior friends in government: 'To this end we have been in direct contact with the ministries of labour, finance, mineral resources and the Office of the President to express deep disappointment over the decisions of our banking partners and to make it very clear that livelihoods are at risk if we are unable to restore these important banking relationships.'

Somewhat unsurprisingly, the upper echelons of government were as zealous as ever to assist the Guptas in their latest plight. Mere weeks after Howa's letter was made public, minister in the Presidency Jeff Radebe announced at a media briefing that Zuma's cabinet would support the appointment of an inter-ministerial committee (IMC) to investigate the banks' termination of the Guptas' accounts. 'Whilst Cabinet appreciate the terms and conditions of the banks, the acts may deter future potential investors who may want to do business in South Africa,' Radebe said.[16] Considering the near-cataclysmic impact of Zuma's appointment of Van Rooyen on South Africa's economy a few months earlier, it seemed suspicious that cabinet was now suddenly concerned about investor confidence.

According to Radebe, the IMC would consist of the ministers of finance, mineral resources and labour. The presence of Pravin Gordhan and Mosebenzi Zwane on the same committee was bound to cause friction, as it was crystal clear that the two ministers held vastly differing views when it came to the Guptas. But what was particularly concerning about this development was the fact that government had chosen to side with the Guptas despite indications that the banks had chosen to part ways with the family's business empire for reasons that appeared to relate to possible financial illegalities.

After it become known that the banks had deserted the Guptas, the Banking Association of South Africa (BASA), an industry body for the banking sector, released a statement implying that the banks may have cut ties with the family's companies for some very worrying reasons. In a statement released on 14 April, BASA said: 'Amongst the array of regulations banks must be governed by are those related to the current Financial Intelligence Centre Act (FICA), impending amendments to this Act and anti-money laundering regulations ... These regulations make it incumbent on banks to conduct a detailed due diligence on clients, particularly those of a substantive nature and those that are in the public domain ... A bank will take these matters into account when considering ongoing relationships with clients, and will take appropriate action, based on circumstances.'[17]

About two months later, in an interview with *Carte Blanche*, Howa rather surprisingly read from a confidential letter Standard Bank had written to Oakbay in which it clarified its reasons for dropping the Guptas as clients. It appeared as if Howa intended to use the letter's contents to somehow prove his and the Guptas' assertion that there was a conspiracy against the family and their businesses. Howa's ploy, however, backfired. In the letter, Standard Bank cited fears of being party to alleged financial crimes as its reason for distancing itself from Oakbay.

'Without waiving our right not to furnish reasons for our decision, without inviting any debate about the correctness of our decisions, I point out the law, inclusive of South Africa's Companies Act, regulation 43, the Prevention of Organised Crimes Act, the Prevention and Combating of Corrupt Activities Act, the Financial Intelligence Centre Act, as well as the USA's Foreign Corrupt Practices Act, and the UK's Bribery Act, prevents us from having dealings with any person or entity where a reasonably diligent and vigilant person would suspect that such dealings could directly or indirectly make us a party to or accessory to contraventions of that law,' Howa read from Standard Bank's letter. 'We have conducted enhanced due diligence of the Oakbay entities and, as required by the Financial Intelligence Centre Act, have concluded that continuing with any banker/ customer relationship with them would increase our risk of exposure to contravention of the abovementioned law to an unacceptable level.'[18]

Howa would later express his regret at sharing the contents of Standard Bank's letter. 'That was one of the major mistakes I made, reading out that letter,' he told journalists at the JSE in September 2016.[19]

Little more than a week after Radebe's announcement about the IMC, the *Sunday Times* reported that Zwane had for all intents and purposes been abandoned by Gordhan and labour minister Mildred Oliphant as far as the committee's work was concerned.[20] Undeterred by his colleagues' seeming lack of cooperation, Zwane told a media briefing in May: 'This matter should be resolved. We are the government of the people. We will not allow our people to just lose their jobs.' Zwane indicated that he had already met with some of the banks.[21]

Towards the end of May, however, Radebe stated in a response to a question in Parliament that the committee had not yet reported back to cabinet, meaning that the IMC had missed its first deadline, which was initially set for a cabinet meeting on 11 May.[22]

Zwane, in the meantime, kept insisting that the banks would be made to account for cutting ties with the Guptas and that government would not stop pursuing them over the matter. 'We are government, banks must actually realise that,' he told reporters in June. 'We engage until we find a solution. We will continue pursuing them. Everybody including Oakbay must enjoy their equal rights ... We will continue pursuing this matter, even if it means government coming up with a state bank, we will do so.'[23]

The mining minister's unfettered and open support for the Guptas continued to escalate in the following months until the beginning of September, when he eventually overstepped his boundaries in such spectacular fashion that Zuma, of all people, had no choice but to rein him in.

On 1 September 2016, Zwane, in his capacity as chairperson of the IMC, released a media statement through the Department of Mineral Resources in which he claimed that cabinet had tabled the IMC's report and had made a number of resolutions based on the committee's recommendations.[24]

'Cabinet established an Inter-Ministerial Committee (IMC) to consider allegations that certain banks and other financial institutions acted unilaterally and allegedly in collusion, when they closed bank accounts and/or terminated contractual relationships with Oakbay Investments,' wrote Zwane in his statement.

Seizing the opportunity to take a swipe at Gordhan, Zwane said: 'Although the Minister of Finance was a member of the constituted IMC, he did not participate in its meetings.'

According to Zwane, cabinet had decided to 'recommend to the President that given the nature of the allegations and the responses received, that the President consider establishing a Judicial Enquiry in terms of section 84(2)(f) of the Constitution'. In addition, cabinet had agreed to 'consider the current mandates of the Banking Tribunal and the Banking Ombudsman', two key watchdogs in South Africa's banking sector.

'Evidence presented to the IMC indicated that all of the actions taken by the banks and financial institutions were as a result of innuendo and potentially reckless media statements, and as a South African company, Oakbay had very little recourse to the law,' stated Zwane. 'Looking into these mandates and strengthening them would go a long way in ensuring that should any other South African company find itself in a similar situation, it could enjoy equal protection of the law, through urgent and immediate processes being available to it as it [*sic*] required by the Constitution.'

Furthermore, Zwane declared, cabinet had approved a review of the Financial Intelligence Centre Act and the Prevention and Combating of Corrupt Activities Act, two key pieces of legislation when it comes to fighting financial crimes, 'as evidence presented to the IMC was unclear on whether the various banks and financial institutions as well as the Reserve Bank and Treasury complied with these and other pieces of legislation'.

Lastly, cabinet was considering the 'establishment of a State Bank of South Africa' because 'evidence presented to the IMC suggested that all of South Africa's economic power vests in the hands of very specific institutions'.

The very next day, the Presidency issued a statement in which it unequivocally denied that Zwane's statement in any way represented decisions formally made by cabinet. 'The statement issued by the Minister of Mineral Resources ... was issued in his personal capacity and not on behalf of the task team or Cabinet. Minister Zwane is a member of the task team. He does not speak on behalf of Cabinet and the contents of his statement do not reflect the position or views of Cabinet, the Presidency or Government. The unfortunate contents of the statement and the inconvenience and confusion caused by the issuing thereof, are deeply regretted,' said Zuma's office.[25]

The ANC took an even harsher line against Zwane. 'This type of ill-discipline has brought the name of government into disrepute. We call on President Zuma to discipline Minister Zwane because [it is] this kind of reckless and careless statement that sends wrong signals about our cabinet,' said ANC spokesperson Zizi Kodwa.[26]

To make matters worse for Zwane, near the end of September *Fin24* revealed that Bell Pottinger, a British public relations firm appointed by Oakbay Investments in the middle of the Mcebisi Jonas storm, had been in possession of the IMC's 'confidential' recommendations months before the minister released them in his statement.[27]

It turned out that a Bell Pottinger employee working on the Gupta account had leaked an extract from the document to *Fin24* journalist Matthew le Cordeur back in July, ostensibly to ensure that the IMC's recommendations be put in the public domain. According to the news report, the Bell Pottinger source even gave Le Cordeur two cellphone numbers for Zwane, claiming that the minerals minister would be happy to confirm the document's authenticity. Le Cordeur reached out to Zwane's spokesperson, who would not comment on the matter, and eventually *Fin24* decided against publishing the story because there was no proof that the document was authentic. After Zwane's ill-fated press release in early September, however, *Fin24* now knew that the document they had been leaked months before was in fact real. So they approached Bell Pottinger to find out how a Gupta-linked PR firm had managed to obtain a confidential government document before its official release.

In response, the PR firm claimed that it 'did not seek to obtain this information, but was made aware of it. Given its relevance to the issue of Oakbay's closed accounts, the public interest and the ongoing media coverage of the story, Bell Pottinger contacted Fin24/News24 to put the information into the public domain. It is no secret that Bell Pottinger has advised Oakbay Investments on its corporate communications since March this year. Bell Pottinger abides by strict professional ethics. Its source was not the Gupta Family as News24 implies and Bell Pottinger has never met with or spoken to Minister Zwane or any of his advisors.'[28]

However the firm came by the document, the fact that it had it was highly suspicious and indicative of the cosy relationship between Zwane and the Guptas. Yet despite these fresh concerns over his relationship with the family, and despite the fact that Zuma had distanced himself from the IMC recommendations, the mining minister refused to back down. In a written reply to a parliamentary question put to him by DA MP David Maynier, Zwane insisted that he had not been 'speaking in his personal capacity but in his capacity as Chairperson of the IMC' and that four of the committee's recommendations had indeed been approved by cabinet while the fifth had been referred to Zuma for his consideration.[29]

While the claims and counterclaims flew in government, the Guptas began making alternative arrangements to ensure their businesses could continue to operate. Mere weeks after news broke that KPMG and Oakbay had parted ways, Oakbay appointed a new auditor, SizweNtsalubaGobodo.[30] It took a while longer to find a new JSE-approved sponsor, which was crucial for Oakbay Resources & Energy to remain on the stock exchange. Finally, in a SENS announcement on 1 September, the company introduced the River Group as its new sponsor.[31]

Meanwhile, it had become known that the 'major Asian bank' to which Oakbay had referred in an earlier SENS announcement was in fact the Bank of Baroda, an Indian bank majority-owned by the Indian government. The bank's South African branch 'boasts a strong network and a global reputation',[32] something that would be tested thanks to their association with the Guptas. In June 2016, the *Sunday Times* revealed that the South African Reserve Bank (SARB), together with the Financial Intelligence Centre (FIC), had approached the Bank of Baroda to request information on the Guptas' financial activities. The probe reportedly stemmed from suspicions that the family was using the Indian bank as a means to illegally move money out of South Africa, possibly to Dubai.[33]

Despite their best efforts to plug a sinking ship, things got worse for the Guptas once Gordhan named them in late August as role-players in the saga around his persecution over the SARS rogue unit matter.[34] The finance minister's accusation seemed to act as a catalyst for what came next.

A day after Gordhan allegedly told colleagues that the Guptas were covertly attacking him, the family released a statement in which they expressed their 'deep disappointment' over the allegations. 'We have repeatedly pointed out that our family has been a victim of a political campaign against it. A narrative has been constructed against us, which has been perpetuated by many media titles, and that flawed perception has become the truth in the eyes of some,' read the statement. Despite this, the Guptas added, 'we remain fully committed as shareholders to ensuring that our business[es] are run on sound business lines with all transactions being done on a transparent, arms-length basis'.[35]

But mere hours later, the Guptas released another statement, announcing their 'intention to sell all of our shareholding in South Africa by the end of the year'. 'As a family, we now believe that the time is right for us to exit our shareholding of the South African businesses which we believe will benefit our existing employees, and lead to further growth in the businesses,' the statement read. 'We are already in discussions with several international prospective buyers and will soon be in a position to make further announcements.'[36] The Guptas, it seemed, were done.

22

Pravin's bomb

The year 2016 had been an eventful one for finance minister Pravin Gordhan, to put it mildly. His persecution by the Hawks and the NPA, which was initially informed by the SARS rogue unit matter, took a dramatic and surprising turn on 11 October. In a statement that would once again send South Africa's currency into a downward spiral, NPA head Advocate Shaun Abrahams announced that Gordhan, Ivan Pillay and former SARS commissioner Oupa Magashula were being charged with fraud. The charges related to SARS's granting of early retirement to Pillay in 2010, and his rehiring as deputy commissioner on a fixed-term contract in 2014, as well as the fact that SARS had paid the R1.1-million penalty triggered by his early retirement on Pillay's behalf.[1]

Pillay's early retirement had been granted during Gordhan's first tenure as finance minister, and he was the one who signed off on it. But, as many legal experts pointed out, Pillay's early retirement was not unique. It also did not appear to remotely justify the charges of fraud that were thrown at Gordhan by the NPA. 'Closer examination shows that the NPA is bringing a case it cannot win ... This case may therefore have less to do with the law than with the pursuit of a political agenda,' wrote law expert Cathleen Powell on *The Conversation*, a news, opinion and analysis website.[2]

The conclusion reached by the media and experts alike was that the NPA had brought the charges against Gordhan out of sheer desperation. It appeared as if the SARS rogue unit issue had failed to provide Abrahams and his colleagues with even a remotely sound legal argument to charge Gordhan, leaving them clutching at straws in order to find something that stood even the slightest chance of holding up in court.

Gordhan made no secret of the fact that he viewed the Guptas as active agents in the plot to have him charged by the NPA. As previously mentioned, National Treasury, which is controlled by the finance minister, had been clamouring about reining in the type of questionable government deals that the Guptas exemplified, a crusade that coincided with Gordhan's reappointment after Nenegate. One such deal was the cushy coal contract awarded to Gupta-owned Tegeta Exploration and Resources by the state-owned power utility Eskom.

As long as Gordhan was in charge of the country's coffers, the likes of the Gupta family would find it increasingly difficult to do business with the state. This, Gordhan seemed to suggest, was why the Guptas were behind the Hawks' investigations of him.

But as dire as Gordhan's situation seemed to be throughout 2016, the finance minister proved to be a tough opponent. The first hint of Treasury's intention to put up a fierce fight against Gordhan's foes came in the form of an article by seasoned financial journalist Alec Hogg at the end of August. According to Hogg, a highly placed source had told him that Treasury was in possession of sensitive information about the financial dealings of those viewed as Gordhan's adversaries. Given that Treasury had at that stage been battling with state-owned entities over their dealings with Gupta-linked companies, it would be reasonable to assume that Treasury's file of financial sins included information involving the Guptas. The information, according to Hogg's source, was known as the 'nuclear bomb'. If it appeared that Gordhan's demise was imminent and that the country's financial resources would once again become vulnerable to wholesale looting by Zuma's allies, Treasury would enact the 'nuclear bomb option'. This involved making public the damning information they had stockpiled.[3]

And then came the NPA's shock announcement that Gordhan would be charged with fraud. With the uproar still echoing across the country, the finance minister made a move that suggested phase one of the 'nuclear bomb option' had perhaps been activated. Three days after NDPP Abrahams's statement, Gordhan filed a court application in the North Gauteng High Court that would ensure the Guptas, and not him, would be in the spotlight over allegedly dodgy transactions.

Gordhan wanted the court to grant him a declaratory order in which it would be stated in no uncertain terms that, in his position as finance minister, he had no legal power or obligation to help the Guptas in their ongoing battle with South Africa's major banks, who had closed their accounts earlier that year. But the most explosive aspect of Gordhan's application was the attached list of 'suspicious' transactions from the Guptas' accounts, flagged by the Financial Intelligence Centre and totalling nearly R7 billion.[4]

While it had been clear from the outset that mining minister Mosebenzi Zwane and his IMC had been roped in to fight for the Guptas' cause, the extent to which the family had also hounded Gordhan to assist them only became fully apparent in the court application, which included a series of letters sent to Gordhan by the CEOs of various Gupta-owned companies.

The first was penned by Nazeem Howa, Oakbay Investments' then CEO, and reached Gordhan on 8 April, mere days after news broke that the banks had terminated their business relationships with the Guptas. While not an overt plea for assistance, the letter did seek to draw the minister's attention to what Howa called 'an anti-competitive and politically motivated campaign designed to marginalise our businesses'. Howa maintained that the banks, as well as KPMG and Sasfin, had given Oakbay 'no justification whatsoever' for dumping the Gupta-owned companies. 'As the CEO I now hope to draw a line under the corporate bullying and anti-competitive practices we have faced from the banks,' Howa wrote.[5]

This letter, and others, strongly emphasised the potential job losses that could accompany the closing of the businesses' bank accounts. But, as Gordhan pointed out in his affidavit, Oakbay itself seemed unsure about the number of 'affected individuals', 'which Oakbay has variously estimated at 6 000, 7 500 or 15 000'.[6]

On 17 April, Gordhan received another letter from Howa assuring him that the correspondence was nothing more than 'a plea to you as political head for the financial sector to assist us in avoiding this huge impact on the lives of around 50 000 people, if we include families of our employees'. As in his previous letter, Howa emphasised the fact that the Guptas themselves had 'resigned all executive and non-executive roles in our group as a move to address the concerns of the parties about possible association risk'. The banks, however, were 'intransigent', Howa complained, before urging Gordhan to intervene 'given your strong relationship with the captains of industry'.[7]

Gordhan's court application included his responses to these and other letters. One was a summation of a meeting between the finance minister, Treasury officials and the Oakbay CEO on 24 May. In his follow-up letter,

Gordhan made it clear to Howa that 'banks operate in a highly-regulated environment, and a range of factors could give rise to a bank's decision to close an account'. He then reiterated that 'there are legal impediments to any registered bank discussing client-related matters with the Minister of Finance, or any third-party. Further, the Minister of Finance cannot act in any way that undermines the regulatory authorities.' In addition, Gordhan told Howa that Oakbay had not 'exhausted all legal remedies, including approaching the court for appropriate relief'.[8]

This last consideration formed a key part of Gordhan's court application, in which he argued that if Oakbay genuinely believed the banks had closed the accounts without sufficient reason, the company could simply have launched its own court application to have the decision reviewed on legal grounds.[9]

In a written response, his third letter to Gordhan, Howa stated that the company had good reason to believe that such a court application would fail. 'I thought it prudent to place on record that following detailed discussions with several legal advisors, we are of the strong view that given the contractual rights the banks have, any legal approach may indeed be still-born,' he wrote.[10]

Howa had chosen to share a startlingly sensitive bit of information with Gordhan. He was basically admitting that Oakbay's own lawyers had come to the conclusion that the banks may have had grounds to close the accounts. At the same time, however, Howa insisted that 'no bank has given us any indication of any wrongdoing on our side'. Howa also claimed that he understood the 'legal impediments' and 'challenges presented by the current regulatory framework' which prohibited Gordhan from getting involved in the matter. Yet he again asked the minister to get back to him regarding 'any possible assistance you are able to offer us in these trying times'.[11]

Towards the end of June, Gordhan received another letter, this time from Stephan Nel, CEO of Sahara Computers. Nel complained that 'vital banking services have still not been restored neither to us, nor for that matter other businesses across the Oakbay group'. 'I now find myself in a precarious position where I am forced to make a number of important strategic decisions concerning the future of our business – decisions which will inevitably lead to further redundancies,' he wrote. 'The decisions ...

will not only affect the livelihoods of the remaining 103 employees at Sahara, but their families and dependents too.' The Sahara CEO also claimed to have been 'the recipient of a threatening phone call aggressively warning against further appeals to you regarding the reopening of Oakbay's bank accounts'. Nel said he hoped Gordhan would 'publicly condemn acts of intimidation, which are using your name'.[12]

In yet another letter to Gordhan, dated 25 July 2016, Howa again claimed that Oakbay had no idea why the banks had deemed it necessary to close their accounts. By now Gordhan had begun asking questions as to why Oakbay was still making such a claim, seeing as Howa himself had publicly acknowledged in an interview on *Carte Blanche* on 19 June that at least one of the four major banks (Standard Bank) had provided what seemed like a compelling and deeply concerning explanation for its actions.

In his defence, Howa now wrote Gordhan that 'in detailing the contents of the Standard Bank letter in my TV interview with *Carte Blanche*, I was merely trying to illustrate that these were the allegations that were being made, but without being provided with a shred of evidence'. According to Howa, none of the four banks had provided Oakbay 'with a single example of where we have transgressed any of the legislation mentioned in their letters'. He then vowed to provide Gordhan with 'my full file of all the correspondence with the banks so that you can understand our frustration at not getting a proper explanation for their unprecedented action'.[13]

Gordhan had been asking for this 'full file' ever since Oakbay had lodged their first complaint with him. In his response to Howa's latest letter, the finance minister expressed his frustration at Oakbay's continued failure to hand over these documents. 'Every opportunity has been provided for Oakbay to do so since your first approach to me in April,' Gordhan wrote, before giving the CEO a final deadline of 12 August 2016 'to honour the undertaking'.[14]

In his last letter to Gordhan, dated 9 September, Howa was still promising to send Gordhan the documents as requested. 'It makes for interesting reading,' Howa wrote.[15]

In the end, Gordhan never received Howa's 'full file of all the correspondence with the banks'. But the finance minister had files of his own up his sleeve. Also included in his court application was a document that suggested the banks had every reason to close the Guptas' company accounts.

The document, a certificate from the FIC, listed R6.8 billion in 'suspicious and unusual' transactions involving the Gupta family and their companies over the past four years.[16] It was the inclusion of this explosive annexure which suggested that Gordhan and Treasury may have activated the 'nuclear bomb option', a strategy that entailed the release of information potentially devastating to the likes of the Guptas.

The FIC, which was brought into life by the Financial Intelligence Centre Act 38 of 2001, is a government body that gathers and analyses financial information with a mandate to identify the proceeds of crime and to combat money laundering and the financing of terrorism.[17] Once it has received and processed such information, the FIC may then pass it on to law enforcement agencies such as the SAPS, to SARS or to any of a variety of local and international supervisory bodies, including the International Monetary Fund and even the United Nations Security Council.[18]

Under section 29 of the Financial Intelligence Centre Act, anyone, including financial institutions, who suspects a business of conducting unlawful financial activity is compelled to report it to the FIC. The Act lists several examples of what it deems 'suspicious and unusual transactions', including anything that points to possible money laundering, tax avoidance or the financing of terrorism, or 'has no apparent business or lawful purpose'. It was on the grounds of this last consideration that some of the banks reported Gupta company transactions to the FIC as suspicious or unusual.[19] It essentially meant that the banks, and in turn the FIC, could not find any obvious justification, such as paying suppliers or receiving payment for goods or services, for any of the listed transactions.

According to Gordhan's affidavit, at the end of July he wrote to the FIC asking 'whether or not the registered banks have indeed reported to the Financial Intelligence Centre ("FIC") as indicated ... by Mr Howa [when he read from the Standard Bank letter on *Carte Blanche*] or whether no such reports have been made'.[20] It was in response to this request that FIC director Murray Michell compiled a report listing transactions by Gupta family members and entities that banks had reported to the FIC between December 2012 and June 2016. However, legislation did not permit Michell to share the details of the banks' original reports.

'The disclosure of information concerning reports under the FIC Act is strictly governed by, among others, section 40 of the Act. By virtue of these provisions the Centre is allowed to disclose such information only in limited circumstances and only to a limited group of potential recipients,' Michell wrote to Gordhan. However, he added: 'The FIC Act, in section 29(4)(c), provides for an exception to these controls where such information is to be used for the purposes of legal proceedings ... Given that your letter indicates your intention to approach a court for a definitive ruling on certain questions of law, and by virtue of my powers under the FIC Act, I have decided to issue a certificate under section 39 of the Act, relating to possible reports that may have been made in relation to the entities mentioned in your letter. I must emphasise that such a certificate is only to be used for the purpose of introducing evidence in legal proceedings and will only confirm or refute the receipt of reports pursuant to the FIC Act. Such a certificate will not disclose any information concerning the content of any particular report which the Centre has received.'[21]

The FIC certificate that Gordhan included in his court application, in other words, merely showed that the FIC had received a total of seventy-two reports from the banks detailing 'suspicious and unusual transactions' relating to the Guptas' company accounts. The certificate listed the date on which the FIC had received each report, the individual or company that was the subject of each report, and, in most cases, the rand value associated with the report. Twenty of the listed reports did not include a rand value but instead showed that there had been 'multiple transactions' linked to the relevant subjects.

Although some media reports at the time indicated that the FIC certificate detailed payments made by the Guptas and their companies, the document did not in fact specify whether the reported values reflected money received by the Guptas or money paid to other parties, or both. Such finer details, including where each payment had come from or where it ended up, could only be drawn from the banks' original reports. The Financial Intelligence Centre Act, however, did seem to include a loophole that would make the sharing of such information possible in the future. In a subsequent letter to Gordhan, Michell explained that 'a certificate issued by an official of the Centre ... is on its mere production in a matter before court admissible as evidence of any fact contained in it of which direct oral evidence would be admissible'.[22] This indicated that once court proceedings had begun, Gordhan's legal team could possibly derive further details on each 'suspicious' transaction from an FIC official.

Even though the FIC certificate was scant on details, the revelation of the enormous amounts of money that had been flowing through Gupta-linked bank accounts made for very interesting reading. As explained in the document, the FIC had gone through its records to identify 'suspicious transaction reports' (STRs) relating to nine members of the Gupta family, including the three brothers, their wives and some of their children, and twenty-six companies in which the family had an interest.[23]

The first of the seventy-two STRs received by the FIC was dated 10 December 2012, while the most recent was dated 3 June 2016. Some of the red-flagged transactions were transfers to or from an account held by Atul Gupta, totalling more than R93 million. Other notables included nearly R1 billion that had flowed either into or out of the bank account of Shiva Uranium, the main asset of JSE-listed Oakbay Resources & Energy. These transactions were particularly interesting seeing as Oakbay Resources & Energy's entire revenue in the 2014–2015 financial year had been only R165 million.[24] This raised questions regarding the origin and purpose of such large sums.

The largest chunk of the listed transactions involved Optimum Coal Mine and some of its subsidiaries. According to the FIC certificate, the watchdog had received reports on 21 April 2016 highlighting a transaction worth R1.3 billion in Optimum Coal Mine's account, and another worth R1.2 billion involving the account of Koornfontein Mines. The FIC certificate also showed a R1.3-million transaction in the account of the Optimum Mine Rehabilitation Trust on 11 May 2016, as well as a further three transactions involving three different Optimum subsidiaries and amounting to R174 million.

In his affidavit, Gordhan invited Oakbay to share with the court the full details of each of the transactions that had made the banks uncomfortable. Such information 'would confirm whether there is any substance to the serious contentions advanced by Oakbay that the banks have acted improperly in closing the accounts', he argued.[25]

Gordhan's court application also included a letter sent from Werksmans Attorneys to the SARB on 27 June 2016 that focused on the impending transfer of about R1.5 billion from the Optimum Mine Rehabilitation Trust's Standard Bank account to accounts held with the Bank of Baroda, the Indian bank that was still doing business with the Guptas. Werksmans, acting on behalf of Optimum's business rescue practitioners, wanted to know whether the SARB had any 'reservations or concerns' about the impending transfer, seeing as there had been reports in the media that the SARB was busy probing the Bank of Baroda. The letter also noted the fact that the Department of Mineral Resources, headed by the pro-Gupta Zwane, had already approved the transfer.[26]

When details about Gordhan's court application emerged, a former trustee of the Optimum Mine Rehabilitation Trust told me an interesting story. When the Guptas' Tegeta Exploration and Resources officially took ownership of the Optimum group, the trustees were all replaced. It is not clear who these new trustees were, but the fact that Tegeta was so quick to get rid of the old guard does raise questions about the Guptas' intention for the rehabilitation fund.

When Oakbay Investments hit back with a series of press releases after the details of Gordhan's court application became public, they claimed the FIC certificate did not prove any wrongdoing by the Guptas or their companies. In one statement, on 17 October, they highlighted the Optimum Mine Rehabilitation Trust transaction as proof of this, saying that no monies had been removed from the fund, but simply transferred due to Standard Bank's closure of its accounts. The statement contained a link to a certificate issued by the Bank of Baroda in which it confirmed that more than R1.4 billion belonging to the trust was now being kept in four different Bank of Baroda accounts.[27]

Despite their bravado, that same day, in a separate statement, Oakbay announced that CEO Nazeem Howa was stepping down 'due to health issues' and on 'medical advice'. Ronica Ragavan, Oakbay's then financial director, would take over as acting CEO while the company searched for Howa's 'permanent successor'. 'In time, Oakbay will be recognised as the type of company South Africa needs: innovative, job-creating, tax paying and law-abiding. I look forward to that day,' Howa said in his parting statement.[28]

The following day, Oakbay Investments released another statement. 'The Gupta Family and Oakbay Investments are delighted to have been cited as respondents to the application from the Finance Minister. At last, the Gupta Family and Oakbay can begin to formally clear their names,' said Van Der Merwe & Associates, the Gupta family lawyers, in the statement. This time Oakbay vowed to deal 'in full' with 'each and every entry' in Gordhan's court application. But, they added, the application was 'fundamentally flawed'. For a start, the six transactions linked to Optimum and totalling just over R4 billion had been done before the Guptas' Tegeta Exploration and Resources took control of Optimum and its associated companies, Oakbay maintained. The rest of the transactions were 'perfectly legitimate' and 'not suspicious in any way'. And besides, all seventy-two transactions 'were approved and cleared by the respective banks processing the transactions'. In closing, Oakbay took a final swipe at Gordhan: 'Whilst we thoroughly welcome this application, it is undiluted nonsense and appears to be little more than the usual political games.'[29]

The next day, Oakbay Investments put out yet another statement, saying that their lawyers, Van Der Merwe & Associates, had 'notified the Minister of Finance's attorneys of their client's (the Oakbay Group of companies) intention to oppose the application issued under case number 80978/16 on 14 October 2016 – unless the Minister of Finance withdraws the application and tenders costs by this afternoon – Wednesday 19 October'. Furthermore, read the statement, the lawyer's letter had 'noted that the Minister of Finance's affidavit implicated its clients in inappropriate and unlawful conduct' and found this to be 'uncalled for, malicious and nothing but vexatious'.[30]

Gordhan would not be cowed. He informed Oakbay that same morning that he would not be withdrawing his application and tendering costs. Van Der Merwe & Associates responded by notifying the finance minister's attorneys that they would oppose the application in court.

Oakbay Investments' headquarters is located in an office park on the outskirts of Sandton's central business district. Compared to the flashy glass towers nearby that house some of South Africa's largest corporations, their offices are rather drab. But there are telltale signs of the power that lies within. On the day in question, standing near the entrance to the office block were four neatly dressed men. Were they not built like professional front-row rugby players or heavyweight boxers, you could mistake them for office personnel. As I made my way to the building's entrance, the four men, members of the Guptas' security detail, turned their heads towards me, but the stares did not last long. I was expected, after all, and I clearly posed no physical threat.

I had come to Oakbay's headquarters at the invitation of Gert van der Merwe, the Guptas' lawyer, and representatives of Bell Pottinger, the UK-based PR firm that had been roped in by the Guptas at the start of 2016. Oakbay was willing to share with me some of the Optimum group's bank statements dating from 14 April 2016, the day on which Tegeta Exploration and Resources officially became the owner of Optimum Coal Holdings and its associated companies. The bank statements, Oakbay maintained, would prove that the approximately R4 billion worth of transactions linked to Optimum and its subsidiaries and listed in the FIC certificate were concluded before the Guptas took control of the coal-producing company.

In the meeting attended by Ronica Ragavan, Oakbay's then newly appointed acting CEO, Trevor Scott, Oakbay's chief financial officer, and two Bell Pottinger employees, I was allowed to study the bank statements of five of the Optimum entities that featured on the FIC certificate.

According to the document annexed to Gordhan's court application, a suspicious transaction report relating to a transfer of R1.3 billion to or from the account of Optimum Coal Mine had been lodged with the FIC on 21 April 2016. This was, of course, a week after Tegeta Exploration and Resources' acquisition of Optimum was officially concluded. But, as the Oakbay representatives explained to me, the date on which the FIC receives an STR is not necessarily the date on which the transaction actually took place. In fact, the FIC might only receive a report months after the transaction is flagged by the relevant bank. To prove their point, Oakbay challenged me to try to find the R1.3 billion in any of their bank statements after 14 April 2016. Sure enough, the amount did not show up in the statements. This was also the case for the red-flagged transactions linked to Koornfontein Mines and Optimum Coal Terminal, worth R1.2 billion and R173 million respectively, as well as for the significantly smaller transactions involving Optimum Vlakfontein Mining and Exploration and Optimum Overvaal Mining and Exploration.

The team from Oakbay and Bell Pottinger naturally expected me to conclude that the Optimum transactions on the FIC certificate indeed had nothing to do with the Guptas, seeing as the listed amounts were not reflected in any of the companies' accounts on or after 14 April. But there were simply too many unanswered questions to come to that conclusion. Where exactly had the huge payments listed on the FIC certificate come from, or where had they ended up? And why would Gordhan include them in his application if they really had nothing to do with the Guptas?

Given the confidential nature of the original FIC reports, these questions may never be answered. Unless, of course, South Africa's law enforcement agencies take an interest in them. But given the Hawks' apparent unwillingness to properly probe the Guptas, this seems unlikely.

The potential loophole in the FICA legislation outlined by Murray Michell made me wonder whether Gordhan's court application was really just about him asking the court to declare that he could not intervene in the closing of the Guptas' bank accounts. Or was it part of a cleverly crafted strategy that would ensure the Guptas' dirty laundry was one day aired in public? Whatever the real motivation, the stage had been set for what promised to be an explosive legal battle involving the Guptas.

In January 2017, Oakbay filed its response to Gordhan's court application. In an affidavit deposed on behalf of the company and its subsidiaries, Ragavan slammed the minister's application as being 'riddled with factual and legal errors'. She stated that the Guptas and their associates had never insisted that Gordhan was legally obliged to intervene in their battle with the banks. For this reason, Ragavan asked the court to dismiss Gordhan's application.[31]

Oakbay's response also included a report from Nardello & Co., a firm of forensic auditors that had been tasked by Oakbay to probe the seventy-two 'suspicious' transactions listed in the FIC certificate. After perusing bank statements and other documents linked to the Guptas and their companies, the auditors allegedly could only locate fifteen transactions with a combined value of just over R127 million that may have corresponded to transactions listed on the FIC certificate. In the end, Nardello & Co. concluded that the FIC certificate did not contain sufficient information in order for it to make any definitive findings on the origins or purpose of any of the transactions. The firm did, however, question whether transactions worth nearly R4 billion involving Optimum and its subsidiaries could be linked to Oakbay or the Guptas, seeing as the FIC certificate seemed to indicate that they were concluded before Tegeta Exploration and Resources finalised its purchase of Optimum. But again, Nardello & Co. concluded that it could not make any final findings on any of the seventy-two transactions without seeing each of the suspicious transaction reports.

In her affidavit, Ragavan maintained that there was nothing suspicious about the transfer of money from the Optimum Mine Rehabilitation Trust, as the money had simply been moved to a new account held with the Bank of Baroda.

The acting Oakbay CEO could not resist the temptation to bring up the alleged politically motivated plot against the Guptas in her affidavit. She claimed that several 'credible sources' had told her that at a meeting on 29 January 2017 Gordhan had urged the local business community to 'clip the wings' of the Gupta family. This, Ragavan concluded, set in motion an 'orchestrated effort by business in South Africa (including the banks) to close out the Oakbay Group and the Gupta Family'.

The furore over the Guptas' 'suspicious' transactions would ultimately be in vain. In March 2017, the North Gauteng High Court struck the FIC certificate from Gordhan's application, saying the transactions were not relevant to the case. It seemed that the public would forever be in the dark over the multibillion-rand transfers that had for some reason drawn the attention of the major banks.

23

Thuli's last tango

As public criticism continued to be levelled at the Hawks due to their perceived lack of enthusiasm for the Gupta investigation, people turned to the Office of the Public Protector as seemingly the most reliable state entity with investigative powers to properly examine the family's dealings with government.

The office of Advocate Thuli Madonsela, whose legally mandated term as public protector would come to an end in October 2016, received myriad complaints about the Guptas in March 2016, following Mcebisi Jonas's claims about his dodgy job offer. The Office of the Public Protector would eventually focus its attention on three sets of complaints, submitted by the Dominican Order (a Catholic religious order), the DA and 'a member of the public' whose name was withheld.

The Dominican Order had asked the public protector to probe the claims made by Jonas and Mentor, as well as possible links between the Guptas and Zuma's shock appointment of Van Rooyen as finance minister in December 2015, Madonsela's office explained in a statement. 'In addition to these issues, the Dominican Order asked the Public Protector to look into all business dealings of the Gupta family with any of the government departments to determine whether there were irregularities, undue enrichment, corruption and undue influence in the award of tenders, mining licenses, government advertisements in the New Age Newspapers and any other government services,' read the statement.[1] The request was incredibly wide-reaching and had the potential to place a vast array of the Guptas' dealings with the state under Madonsela's magnifying glass.

After laying its criminal complaint against the Guptas, the DA had approached the Office of the Public Protector to determine whether Zuma had breached the Executive Members' Ethics Act by virtue of his connection to the Guptas. 'The DA contends that the Public Protector should investigate whether President Zuma violated Paragraph 2(b) of the Executive Ethics Act by: (i) Exposing himself to any situation involving the risk of a conflict between his official responsibilities and his private interests; (ii) Using his position or any information entrusted to him, to enrich himself or improperly benefit any other person; (iii) Acting in a way that may compromise the credibility or integrity of his office or of the government,' the party said in a statement.[2]

In early June, Madonsela confirmed that she would investigate, 'specifically whether or not the government of South Africa and specifically the president unlawfully allowed the Gupta family to choose ministers and other occupants of high office' and whether there had been 'unlawful awarding of government contracts and licences to the Gupta businesses,' she told reporters.[3]

However, it seemed that her office's famously thin budget, to which Madonsela had alluded in the past, threatened to hamper this latest probe. She subsequently campaigned for more funding, and in July announced that she had secured an additional R1.5 million from National Treasury to be used exclusively for the Gupta investigation, which would be run in the style of a commission of inquiry. While it seemed like a victory for Madonsela's office, the amount was only half of the R3 million she had initially sought.[4]

The fact that the money would be provided by Gordhan's Treasury naturally led some Gupta allies to accuse Madonsela and the 'anti-Gupta' minister of finance of conspiracy. This particular hymn was led by Andile Mngxitama, a former EFF MP and founder of the Black First Land First (BLF) movement. Although Mngxitama's political ideology appeared to be informed by a radical variety of socialism, he had curiously become one of the biggest supporters of Saxonwold's über-capitalists. His pro-Gupta sentiments often found their way onto *Black Opinion*, a website he administered along with other members of the BLF.

'Investigating "state capture" by the Guptas while excluding similar complaints laid to her office against white capital shows how biased Thuli Madonsela is in favour of white capital,' opined a *Black Opinion* 'staff writer' (read 'Mngxitama'). 'The finance minister is also known to be anti the Guptas because of their alleged closeness to President Jacob Zuma.'[5]

Mngxitama and his BLF were not satisfied with merely hurling accusations at the public protector. In mid-July, twenty-six BLF members stormed her office in Pretoria. The group ostensibly wanted Madonsela to update them on any progress she had made with a complaint concerning state capture by 'white capitalists' and grand-scale corruption during the apartheid era. The timing of their siege, which led to the BLF members' arrest, was curious, as was the fact that the BLF was not even a formal complainant in any ongoing public protector investigations. 'The Public Protector believes that such an illegal violent act, which allegedly included intimidation of staff and taking of at least four of them as hostages, should be condemned in the strongest possible terms by all those committed to constitutional democracy and rule of law,' said Madonsela's office in the wake of the invasion. 'The Public Protector wishes to reiterate that the unruly group is not complainants in the matter provided as a basis for their actions but have recently started inquiring about an investigation lodged by Adv. Paul Hoffman of the Institute for Accountability Southern Africa.'[6]

Besides the suspicious timing of the BLF's stunt, the group's fixation with 'white monopoly capital', and especially billionaire businessman Johann Rupert, bore striking similarities to the views expressed by media outlets and individuals linked to the Guptas. In June, as the Tegeta coal deal was being debated after a *City Press* exposé revealed how Eskom was bailing out the Guptas' new mine,[7] ANN7 'exposed' how the newspaper report was supposedly part of a grander conspiracy by 'white monopoly capital' against the Guptas' mining operation. The *Black Opinion* website subsequently repeated the assertion, using the exact words and phrases that had dramatically flashed on ANN7's screen. 'Oakbay is establishing itself in the coal sector which is currently dominated by white owned companies. What is even more intriguing is that one of the companies which are major players in coal sector are those [*sic*] associated with Johann Rupert. Together with the companies linked to Deputy President Cyril Ramaphosa, who is a personal friend of Rupert, their companies have respectively milked over R8 billion from Eskom,' wrote a *Black Opinion* staff writer.[8]

Gary Naidoo, the Gupta family spokesperson, was of the same opinion. 'The Gupta family businesses are significantly smaller in comparison to the top businesses in the country and the disproportionate media focus tells you there is a hidden agenda behind targeting the family businesses,' Naidoo later told an Indian news agency.[9]

But any suggestion of a covert plot should rather have been aimed at the BLF's siege of the public protector's premises and Mngxitama's simultaneous public support of the Guptas. Given the timing of the pro-Gupta group's invasion, while the Office of the Public Protector was investigating the powerful family, one could not help but consider the possibility that the BLF, under the guise of their supposed concern for a complaint they had not even lodged, had been specifically tasked to intimidate the investigators.

During the final weeks of Madonsela's remarkable tenure as public protector, a position she was scheduled to relinquish on 14 October 2016, there was much speculation over whether her Gupta report would be finalised before her departure. In mid-September, as her investigative team was still hard at work on the state capture probe, Madonsela announced that she intended to release at least one report dealing with some of the Gupta matters before she vacated her office. 'We are doing our best to complete all investigations that are in our hands. We are not 100% sure if they will be complete but we will have a report,' Madonsela told journalists at a church conference in Johannesburg.[10]

But as she entered the final days of her term in office, Zuma, the Guptas and others whom she had investigated as part of the state capture probe made desperate eleventh-hour attempts to stop Madonsela from releasing the report.

Zuma, who had been on the receiving end of a scathing public protector report before, was the first to make noises, claiming that the process had been unfair. Little more than a week before Madonsela's final day in office, on Thursday 6 October, she met with Zuma and his legal representative to discuss some of his concerns. According to a public protector press release, the four-hour meeting had been 'cordial', but reading between the lines, it was clear there had been few niceties between the two parties. Zuma's main problem with the investigation seemed to be that he felt he 'had not had time to prepare answers with legal advice, given the investigation timelines'. But, as Zuma was reminded in the meeting, he 'had been advised in writing by the Public Protector about the allegations made against him, including his suspected breach of the Executive Ethics Code on 22 March 2016'. In other words, he had had nearly seven months to formulate replies to Madonsela's questions. Most concerning, however, was the fact that Zuma seemed desperate for the report's release to be delayed at least until Madonsela's successor took over. For the majority of the meeting, according to the press release, 'the President's legal representative argued that the investigation be deferred to the incoming Public Protector ... on the grounds that there wasn't enough time to conclude the matter properly and that there was no reason for the investigation to be prioritised'.[11]

This raised concerns over whether Advocate Busisiwe Mkhwebane, who had just been appointed as Madonsela's successor, could be trusted to be as fiercely independent as her predecessor. Why did Zuma want the report to be released by Mkhwebane and not Madonsela? It was a question that many who had been following the transition of leadership at the Office of the Public Protector were asking.

The outcome of the meeting between Madonsela and Zuma, according to the public protector press release, was that Zuma would be provided with a set of questions to which he needed to respond by means of a written affidavit.

But Zuma is an expert in evading, delaying and quashing any legal proceedings that have the potential of bringing his political career to an end or even landing him in prison. This skill set is perhaps most visible in his decade-long dodging of the 783 counts of fraud, corruption and racketeering related to the arms deal that still hang over his head.

With only five days to go before Madonsela's state capture report was to be made public, the Presidency announced in a statement that Zuma had asked the public protector to provide 'the documents and records gathered in the course of the investigation, to enable him to prepare his evidence'. Zuma had also asked Madonsela to provide him with the names of the witnesses who had implicated him, in order for his legal team to be able to question them.[12] This request prompted some commentators to accuse Zuma of trying to intimidate the witnesses who had made submissions against him. But the president's lawyers pointed out, correctly, that the Public Protector Act entitles a person implicated in a public protector report 'to question other witnesses ... who have appeared before the Public Protector'.[13]

But what was most dubious about Zuma's request was that he had chosen to make such demands on the eve of the report's release and Madonsela's departure. Furthermore, the Presidency wanted an undertaking from Madonsela 'that her office will not conclude the investigation and issue any report' until all the president's demands had been met.[14]

Madonsela fired back with another statement. This time her frustration with Zuma's conduct was palpable. 'President Zuma was on Saturday, October 01, 2016, given all copies of evidence implicating him,' the statement read. 'It is of concern to the Public Protector that the President has on two occasions undertaken to answer questions and when the time arose, he changed his mind.'[15]

On the Tuesday of her last week in office, Madonsela elaborated on Zuma's stalling tactics during a live interview with News24.[16] According to her, Zuma and his legal advisors had agreed to answer her questions in an affidavit. It had also been agreed that the parties would convene on the Monday following the 6 October meeting if Zuma required clarification on any of the questions.

'We went to the office [of the president] on the 6th with no indication prior to that that there is a problem. Only at the meeting were these issues raised. Again, we discussed it, we even gave him the questions, I read the questions onto the record to give him a sense that they're really about what he may recall and simple questions,' Madonsela explained.

'We all went home on Thursday [after the meeting with Zuma]. We had Friday, we had Saturday, we had Sunday. No indication that there was any trouble. Monday morning we sat there, we never went anywhere, waiting to be told when to come [to Zuma], and we were never told to come. We were then told that the legal advisor at some stage is going to contact us. He never did. We eventually contacted him and he said he doesn't have an answer but there's a letter that's coming. So for the first time late afternoon on Monday did we discover that the president is not in a position to answer those questions and that he would like to interview witnesses. Had he told us last week that he would like to interview witnesses we'd have arranged for him to give us the questions so that we can put them through to the witnesses.'

The following day, Gupta lawyer Gert van der Merwe sent a particularly aggressive letter to the Office of the Public Protector, adding to the pressure that Madonsela was already under over the state capture report. Like Zuma's legal team, Van der Merwe felt that his clients were being subjected to unfair treatment by Madonsela and her office. 'Despite the fact that I have insisted on your offices giving me the information I require to respond in detail to certain allegations the information was not given to me timeously,' claimed Van der Merwe, before accusing Madonsela of having a 'predetermined view of how your report should look'. 'You seem to ignore the Act responsible for your very existence and it leaves me flabbergasted,' he wrote.[17]

The Guptas' lawyer also said that he had considered bringing an urgent court application to interdict Madonsela from releasing the report, but had decided against doing so because it would only 'create a fresh media hype which will in all likelihood be interpreted as an attempt to *threaten and intimidate*" your offices'. But in the very next paragraph, Van der Merwe seemed to do just that. 'If you choose to conclude [in the state capture report] that my clients were in any way whatsoever involved in inappropriate conduct under circumstances where we have tendered evidence to the contrary and under circumstances where we had a clear right to contradict the evidence you have gathered you do so at your own peril and at your own risk,' he warned.[18]

While the Guptas would not launch a court application for an interdict to stop the report from being released, there was growing expectation that Zuma and perhaps some of the other affected parties might do so. Sure enough, the day before Madonsela was due to present her findings to the public, her office received a notice from Zuma's legal team indicating that the president had approached the North Gauteng High Court in Pretoria to seek an interdict. 'Weekend special' Des van Rooyen applied for an interdict the next day, thereby confirming that his and the Guptas' respective roles in the Nenegate saga had formed part of Madonsela's probe.

If these court applications were meant to serve as a stalling tactic, they worked. The court said it would hear the applications only on 1 November 2016. In the meantime, a preservation order issued by High Court judge Dawie Fourie ensured that the report would be kept safe until Zuma's and Van Rooyen's applications had been heard. But this preservation order set off an ancillary battle over the report that would add even more drama to the unfolding saga. In what could have been interpreted as Madonsela's distrust of her successor, Mkhwebane, the outgoing public protector decided to hand over the report to Baleka Mbete, speaker of the National Assembly, instead of leaving it under lock and key at the public protector's office in Pretoria.

Mbete, however, was quick to announce her rejection of Madonsela's plan. 'The Speaker has an obligation in terms of the Rules of Assembly to table all documents received for the information of Members, in order to ensure that the business of the Assembly is conducted in an open and transparent manner,' Parliament said in a statement. 'This report however cannot be handled in the same manner. The report will accordingly be returned to the Office of the Public Protector.'[19]

The report was duly handed back to the public protector's office, which was now officially under the leadership of Mkhwebane. The latter's approach to the whole affair raised serious questions about how the new public protector would deal with political hot potatoes such as the state capture report in the future. With little over a week left before Zuma's application was to be heard, Mkhwebane said in an affidavit that she would not oppose any applications to have the release of the report interdicted.[20] This coincided with a series of comments she made in which she expressed barely veiled criticism of the manner in which Madonsela had run things at the Office of the Public Protector.[21]

Then, on 31 October, a day before Zuma's court date, mining minister Mosebenzi Zwane also launched an application for an urgent order interdicting the release of the report. 'Minister Zwane has had no option but to now become involved in this matter, as he was not afforded an opportunity to answer allegations levelled against him,' read a statement issued by the Department of Mineral Resources.[22] Zwane's application would be heard the week after Zuma's.

The legal fight over the release of the report wrapped up sooner than anyone expected. Seeing as the new public protector would not get involved, several opposition parties applied to intervene in the matter. During proceedings on the first day, the court ruled that the DA, the EFF, COPE and the United Democratic Movement, along with Vytjie Mentor, could oppose Zuma's and Van Rooyen's applications. Judge Dunstan Mlambo, who heard the matter, also struck Van Rooyen's application from the roll 'for lack of urgency', leaving only Zuma and Zwane barring the release of the report.[23]

At the start of the following day's proceedings, however, it quickly became apparent that Zuma's legal team would withdraw his application. In fact, the Gupta-owned television station ANN7 had already announced the previous evening that 'Zuma has withdrawn his interdictory application'. At 10:00 on the Tuesday morning, Advocate Anthea Platt told the court that she had received instruction to withdraw Zuma's application, thus paving the way for the near-immediate release of Madonsela's eagerly anticipated report. 'The Public Protector is ordered to publish the report, forthwith and by no later than 5pm on 2 November 2016 – including through publication on the Public Protector's website,' ruled Judge Mlambo.[24]

24

State of capture

Despite the North Gauteng High Court's order that the state capture report be released, some uncertainty lingered over whether it would actually happen right away. According to public protector spokesperson Oupa Segalwe, Zwane's pending application for an interdict had not yet been dealt with and Mkhwebane wanted to make sure that 'all is clear' before she made the report available to the public.[1]

But by midday on 2 November, it was apparent that the new public protector would indeed adhere to the court order. It was not clear whether Zwane had withdrawn his application to allow for this to happen.

By 16:00, the report had been circulated among journalists throughout South Africa. Details about Zuma's, Zwane's and Van Rooyen's dealings with the Guptas flooded into the public domain. Madonsela, who had dedicated most of her last months in office to ensuring that the country would see the extent of the Guptas' nefarious influence, must have sighed with relief.

'State of Capture', as Madonsela named her last report, is a 355-page document that at times reads like a suspense novel.[2] There is mention of covert intelligence-gathering, piles of cash stuffed into bags and dubious bank transfers involving billions of rands. It would be an entertaining read if it did not paint such a damning picture of how key pockets of government have been completely usurped by the Guptas.

After unpacking in detail some of the shocking interactions between the Guptas and their associates and high-ranking government officials and board members of state-owned companies, the report ultimately prescribes as remedial action the establishment of a commission of inquiry to delve even deeper into the issue of state capture.

South Africans have reason to be suspicious of such inquiries, however. In April 2016, amid the latest series of scandals involving the Guptas,

President Zuma announced the findings of the Seriti commission of inquiry into the 1999 arms deal.

Headed by Supreme Court of Appeal judge Willie Seriti, the Commission of Inquiry into Allegations of Fraud, Corruption, Impropriety or Irregularity in the Strategic Defence Procurement Package was called into life in 2011. Initially, South Africans had faith in the commission's abilities to unearth some of the corruption associated with the arms deal. But the Seriti commission would soon lose almost all of its credibility amid whispers of a 'second agenda' guiding proceedings, a host of resignations by commission employees and Seriti's astounding decision to bar crucial documents from being entered as evidence.[3]

It came as no surprise when the commission eventually found that there had been no signs of wrongdoing related to the arms deal. In his statement announcing the commission's findings, Zuma somewhat gleefully declared that the commission had not received 'a single iota of evidence' pointing to bribery or corruption.[4]

When Madonsela decided to recommend the appointment of a commission of inquiry into state capture, she would have been acutely aware of the widely held belief that the arms deal commission had been nothing but a cover-up and a whitewash. She therefore found a clever way of avoiding a situation in which Zuma himself would appoint the judge or judges for the proposed commission, as he had done in the Seriti affair.

During an earlier Constitutional Court case over Zuma's failure to comply with the remedial action prescribed by a public protector report on government expenditure on his Nkandla homestead, the president had argued in his submission that he had been unable to evaluate what amount of money he needed to repay 'lest I be accused of being judge and jury in my own case'.[5] (It should be noted that Zuma did not harbour the same concerns about a possible conflict of interest when he assembled the arms deal commission.) Quoting Zuma's new-found support for an arm's-length approach when it comes to probes in which he is involved, Madonsela recommended that Chief Justice Mogoeng Mogoeng select the judge who would preside over the commission of inquiry into state capture.

The commission had to be appointed within thirty days of the release of Madonsela's report. Further to this, the commission would be given 180 days to complete its work, after which it would have to present its findings and recommendations to Zuma. Madonsela also recommended that the commission use her report, along with its supporting documents, 'as a starting point', meaning that the commission would not have to start its work from scratch.[6]

The word 'Eskom' appears a total of 913 times in 'State of Capture', much more than any other entity or individual mentioned in the report. From this we can infer that Madonsela's focus fell largely on the Guptas' dubious coal-supply agreements with the state-owned power utility. But the report also shed further light on the Guptas' role in the Nenegate saga and on the job offers made to the likes of Jonas and Mentor at the family's Saxonwold compound. Madonsela found that Zuma's alleged complicity in these developments may have constituted a breach of the Executive Members' Code of Ethics.

The code, which was brought into life by the Executive Members' Ethics Act 82 of 1998, sets guidelines, boundaries and protocols for the conduct of those elected to government positions. 'President Zuma was required to select and appoint Ministers lawfully and in compliance with the Executive Ethics Code,' reads the public protector's report. Madonsela found it 'worrying that the Gupta family was aware or may have been aware' that Zuma was going to fire Nene.[7]

Crucial evidence linking the Guptas to Nene's axing were cellphone records obtained by public protector investigators that placed Van Rooyen in Saxonwold on 8 December 2015, the very day on which Zuma informed Nene that he would be replaced as finance minister. In fact, from the cellphone records, it appeared that Van Rooyen was a frequent visitor to Saxonwold, even after his redeployment to the Department of Cooperative Governance and Traditional Affairs.

The report also contained details about Jonas's visit to Saxonwold and the job offer he allegedly received while there. In his interview with Madonsela, Jonas said that infamous local businessman Fana Hlongwane had set up his meeting with the Guptas. Given Hlongwane's role as an alleged facilitator of questionable payments linked to the arms deal, his involvement in the Jonas matter naturally raised multiple red flags. According to Jonas, Hlongwane, whom he 'knew very well as a comrade', had 'initiated discussions with him about a meeting with Mr D. [Duduzane]

Zuma'. '[Jonas] agreed to the meeting although with reservations as he was aware that Mr D. Zuma was working with members of the Gupta family for financial gain,' reads the report.[8]

Duduzane set up a meeting with Jonas for 23 October 2015 at the Hyatt Regency hotel in Rosebank, Johannesburg. But the two did not stay there long. According to Jonas's testimony, Duduzane, 'a short while into the meeting, indicated that the place was crowded and he needed to move to a more private place for a discussion with a third party ... Using Mr D. Zuma's vehicle, they travelled together to what later Mr Jonas found to be the Gupta family residence in Saxonwold.' They arrived at the 'compound like residence' at the same time as Hlongwane, and once inside were joined by Ajay Gupta, whom Jonas had never met but recognised 'from articles in the press'. Alarmingly, according to Jonas, Ajay told him that the Guptas 'had been gathering intelligence on him and those close to him'. The eldest Gupta brother allegedly told Jonas that 'they were well aware of his activities and his connections to [ANC secretary general] Mr Mantashe and the Treasurer of the ANC, Dr Zweli Mkhize'. In an apparent veiled threat, Ajay accused Jonas of being 'part of a faction or process towards undermining President Zuma'.[9]

But worse was yet to come. Ajay then allegedly told Jonas 'that they were going to make him Minister of Finance'. A 'shocked and irritated' Jonas informed his host that he had had enough and wanted to leave. 'He declined the position and informed Mr Ajay Gupta that only the President of the Republic can make such decisions,' reads the report. Duduzane and Hlongwane were present the entire time, but did not speak. 'They were told to sit down when I indicated that I was leaving,' Jonas told Madonsela.[10]

Ignoring Jonas's request to leave, 'Ajay Gupta continued to speak. He disclosed names of "Comrades" they were working with and providing protection to. He mentioned that collectively as a family, they "made a lot of money from the State" and they wanted to increase the amount from R6 billion to R8 billion and that a bulk of their funds were held in Dubai.' It seemed Ajay was getting round to telling Jonas what he wanted in return for making him minister. 'According to Mr Jonas, Mr A. Gupta further indicated that National Treasury were a stumbling block to the family's business ambitions. As part of the offer to become a Finance Minister,

Mr Jonas would be expected to remove the current Director General of National Treasury and other key members of Executive Management,' reads the report.[11]

Jonas, it seems, would not budge, even when faced with a huge bribe. 'As Mr Jonas was walking towards the door, Mr A. Gupta made a further offer of R600 million to be deposited in an account of his choice. He asked if Mr Jonas had a bag which he could use to receive and carry R600 000 in cash immediately, which he declined.'[12]

Immediately after the alleged meeting, Jonas 'informed former Minister of Finance Mr Nhlanhla Nene. I later also informed current Minister of Finance Mr Pravin Gordan [sic] and Mr Zweli Mkhize of the ANC about the offer.'[13]

Far from simply taking the accounts of Jonas and other whistle-blowers at face value, Madonsela went to great lengths to verify their claims. In an attempt to determine whether there was any truth to Jonas's story, she subpoenaed his cellphone records, along with those of Duduzane Zuma and Fana Hlongwane. The data seemed to corroborate many of the details Jonas had provided.

'Here already,' Jonas said in a text message to Duduzane on 23 October 2015, the day on which they purportedly met at the Hyatt Regency before allegedly moving to Saxonwold.

'I am on my way up Sir,' Duduzane responded.[14]

The data also confirmed that both Duduzane and Hlongwane were in the Saxonwold area on the day in question, although it could not be verified whether Jonas had been there too. This could be explained by the fact that there was no incoming or outgoing communication on Jonas's phone during the time of the alleged meeting with Ajay Gupta. 'According to the cellular network companies, there needs to be a billable event for a tower location to be recorded,' explains the report.[15]

Madonsela sought further corroboration from Nhlanhla Nene and Pravin Gordhan. Nene told her that Jonas had indeed informed him about the job offer 'by members of the Gupta family shortly after the meeting had taken place'.[16] Gordhan also confirmed that Jonas had told him about the incident.

Even Hlongwane admitted to Madonsela that a meeting involving him, Duduzane Zuma and Jonas took place at the Guptas' residence. The

Guptas' earlier assertion that they had never met Jonas or entertained him at their home was starting to look rather thin.

In his interactions with Madonsela, however, Hlongwane gave varying accounts of the meeting's purpose. In a letter sent to her on 29 September 2016, he alleged that Duduzane had told him that Jonas was telling people that Hlongwane was blackmailing him. Hlongwane then asked the young Zuma to facilitate a meeting with Jonas in order to discuss this supposed blackmail. Hlongwane wrote that it was he who suggested they move to a more private venue, though there is no mention of the Gupta compound at this stage, at least not in the excerpts of the letter quoted in the public protector's report. However, according to Hlongwane's letter, 'a Gupta family member entered the room briefly and then left'. He denied 'that there was ever a discussion or offer, by anybody, of any government position to Deputy Minister Jonas'.[17]

But Hlongwane materially altered his tale in a later interview with Madonsela. Now he told her that he had provided Duduzane with Jonas's number because the president's son had wanted to invite the deputy minister to the South African of the Year Awards, an annual event hosted by the Guptas' news channel, ANN7. Hlongwane told Madonsela that he was 'casual acquaintances' with members of the Gupta family and did not have 'a business relationship with them'. This time round, he confirmed that his meeting with Jonas and Duduzane had taken place at the Guptas' Saxonwold compound, although he did not mention Ajay Gupta by name, but he again denied that Jonas was offered a cabinet position during the meeting.[18]

In February 2017, the Guptas and their associates used the court battle with Gordhan to try to discredit Jonas's claims about the job offer, seeing as Gordhan had referred to the incident in his replying affidavit to Oakbay.

In a sworn affidavit that formed part of Ragavan's supplementary court papers, Ajay Gupta stated that 'I have never met Mr Jonas and until today I can honestly say that I have not spoken a single word to him'.[19]

The latest court filings also included confirmatory affidavits from Duduzane Zuma and Hlongwane, who both claimed that Ajay Gupta was not present at the meeting with Jonas. But seeing as Hlongwane had already confirmed that the meeting took place at the Saxonwold compound and that 'a Gupta family member' had popped in, the latest denials did little to douse suspicions. Why was the meeting held at the Guptas' residence in the first place? And who was the mysterious Gupta who briefly made his or her appearance? Both affidavits also included a fundamental flaw – instead of denying that Ajay Gupta was present during a meeting held on 23 October 2015, as alleged by Jonas, Zuma and Hlongwane incorrectly stated that the meeting had taken place on 25 October 2017.

Jonas, however, stuck to his guns. 'The correct facts regarding Mr Ajay Gupta himself is, in short, as follows. I met him at his Saxonwold residence on 23 October 2015 together with Mr Duduzane Zuma and Hlongwane,' he insisted in a sworn affidavit of his own, filed a week later. He again stated that Ajay Gupta had offered him R600 000 to take right there and then, and a further R600 million if he accepted the position of finance minister.[20]

As part of her investigation, Madonsela also asked Barbara Hogan, the former public enterprises minister who claimed to have been put under pressure to ensure that South African Airways ceded a commercial flight route to Indian airline Jet Airways, to provide more details about what she had experienced during her short tenure as minister. From what she told the public protector, 'President Zuma made it very difficult for her to perform her job'. And it appeared as if Zuma had taken a particularly close interest in the appointment of board members at the country's most prominent state-owned entities, which interfered with her responsibility as minister to make such appointments. 'President Zuma took interest in the appointment of board members at Eskom and Transnet whereas Mr Mantashe was interested in the appointment of board members at Transnet,' Hogan informed Madonsela.[21] This claim was particularly concerning given the fact that Eskom and Transnet are the two state-owned entities from which Gupta-linked companies have scored some of their most lucrative government contracts.

Regarding Maseko's and Mentor's interactions with the Guptas, the 'State of Capture' report does not contain much information beyond that which had already surfaced in the media. Their stories, however, are important elements of the state capture saga, seeing as President Zuma plays a prominent role in both of them. It was Zuma who told him over the phone that 'the Gupta brothers' needed his help, Maseko repeated to Madonsela.[22] And it was the president who appeared from an adjacent room in one of the Guptas' houses to tell Mentor 'it's okay' after she rejected their offer to become minister of public enterprises.[23]

When Madonsela gave Zuma his rightful opportunity to respond to and discuss the allegations about his involvement in these and other issues, the president 'did not respond to any of my questions', the public protector noted in her report.[24]

In fact, a transcript of Madonsela's interview with President Zuma and his legal representatives, as well as a recording of the interview itself, clearly highlights Zuma's unwillingness to engage on the allegations involving him. Most of the meeting was taken up by Zuma's lawyers protesting the manner in which the investigation was being conducted.

The release of especially the audio recording of the interview clearly infuriated Zuma. In early November 2016, the Presidency announced that it had lodged a complaint at the Office of the Public Protector, claiming that Madonsela had underhandedly 'leaked' the recording to the media after her term of office had come to an end.[25] Madonsela hit back, denying any wrongdoing. 'I released the record of the interview because, as you may remember, I was public protector until the 14th of October. I released the record on the 13th,' she told TMG Digital, adding that she had instructed her office to 'transcribe the interview after the president disputed having been given a chance to answer'.[26]

The Presidency hit back. Zuma clearly wanted Madonsela out of the picture. 'Adv Madonsela has discharged her duties as the Public Protector and has no further role to play in the process regarding the said Report,' read the latest statement. 'Her unwarranted public attacks on the President … are unbecoming and are not helpful. It would be prudent therefore, for the former Public Protector to step back and allow legal and constitutional processes to unfold unhindered.' It ended with an ironic reference to the importance of upholding the law: 'The President urges all parties to act as guided by the Constitution and respect the processes that are unfolding in respect of the report.'[27]

In December 2016, Zuma lodged an application at the North Gauteng High Court in Pretoria to review and set aside the recommendations in Madonsela's 'State of Capture' report.

The South African taxpayer would again have to cover the legal fees of a president who spent much of his two terms in power delaying a string of legal processes involving his alleged transgressions. And, once again, one couldn't help but ponder why someone so adamant that he is innocent would want to avoid what must surely be the ideal platform for a guilt-free man to clear his name.

25

Endgame

The final days of March 2017 were of the sort that drives journalists and other news junkies to bad habits. Exactly a year after the floodgate of state-capture allegations was first opened by Mcebisi Jonas, things were gearing up to get wilder. At the newsroom, espresso and Red Bull intake spiked, outdoor ashtrays overflowed with cigarette butts, and sleep-deprived members of the press shot nervous looks at one another with red eyes.

The first indication that this would be no normal week came in the form of a one-line statement released by the Presidency on the morning of Monday 27 March. 'President Jacob Zuma has instructed the Minister of Finance, Mr Pravin Gordhan and Deputy Minister Mcebisi Jonas to cancel the international investment promotion roadshow to the United Kingdom and the United States and return to South Africa immediately,' read the statement.[1]

Alhough Zuma's office did not let slip even a hint as to why the president wanted Gordhan and Jonas back in the country, the prevailing feeling was that the famously anti-Gupta minister and deputy minister were about to be axed. After all, their recall from abroad came after months of specula-tion that Zuma was planning a cabinet reshuffle that would see the firing of Gordhan and his deputy.

But it was not only Number One who wanted Gordhan back in South Africa. The court battle between the Guptas and the finance minister over his responsibilities with regard to the closing of the Gupta-linked bank accounts was due to get under way in the North Gauteng High Court on Tuesday 28 March. Ten days before Zuma recalled Gordhan and Jonas, Sahara Computers filed court papers insisting that Gordhan himself had to be physically present in court.[2]

By Wednesday it had become clear that Zuma's latest manoeuvring involved far more than just the court battle. Media reports had started to surface that suggested he was indeed planning to fire both Gordhan and Jonas. According to a *Mail & Guardian* report, at a meeting with senior ANC leaders, Zuma presented an 'intelligence report' containing damning information on Gordhan. The 'dossier' alleged that the finance minister had planned to use the overseas roadshow as an opportunity to undermine Zuma's government by colluding with the international financial community. Zuma also allegedly expressed concern over Gordhan's supposed ties with 'white monopoly capital'.[3] The term had gained considerable traction over the past year, mostly thanks to a small band of 'commentators' using Gupta media platforms such as ANN7 and *The New Age* to spread fear about the unseen hand of white capital which is supposedly ensuring that the majority of black South Africans remain marginalised from the mainstream economy.

Then, on Thursday evening, news broke that Zuma had summoned the ANC's top six to a meeting at the presidential guesthouse in Pretoria.[4] The fact that Zuma wanted to meet with deputy president Cyril Ramaphosa, ANC secretary general Gwede Mantashe and his deputy, Jessie Duarte, National Assembly speaker Baleka Mbete and ANC treasurer general Zweli Mkhize that late in the day meant he had urgent business to conclude. Soon thereafter, #CabinetReshuffle began trending on Twitter and various news outlets started to report on which ministers would be axed. By 23:30 there was no need for further speculation. The Presidency confirmed in a statement that Zuma would 'make an announcement relating to changes to the National Executive'.[5]

A follow-up statement, released well after midnight, spelled out the details of Zuma's far-reaching cabinet reshuffle. Zuma had decided to fire five of his ministers, and move five others to new portfolios. Ten deputy ministers were also either fired or moved to new departments. 'The changes bring some younger MPs and women into the National Executive in order to benefit from their energy, experience and expertise,' claimed Zuma in the statement. 'I have directed the new Ministers and Deputy Ministers to work tirelessly with their colleagues to bring about radical socio-economic transformation and to ensure that the promise of a better life for the poor and the working class becomes a reality.'[6]

The reshuffle affected some of government's most important portfolios, including police, transport and energy. But it was Gordhan's and Jonas's inclusion on the list of axed officials that drew the most attention. Many who had been following developments in 2016 feared that Gordhan would be replaced by Brian Molefe, but it was home affairs minister Malusi Gigaba who was elevated to head of the Treasury. Sfiso Buthelezi, Jonas's replacement as deputy finance minister, is an economist and businessman whose most recent public position was that of chairperson of the Passenger Rail Agency of South Africa (PRASA) board. While Buthelezi does not have any obvious links to the Guptas, his track record as PRASA board chairperson provides sufficient reason for concern. A report released by public protector Thuli Madonsela in 2015 suggests that the new deputy finance minister may have improperly benefited from a PRASA contract while at the helm of the troubled state-owned company's board.[7]

Gigaba, however, appears to be well acquainted with Saxonwold's most infamous family. As mentioned previously, in 2010, senior officials at the State Security Agency included Gigaba's name on a list of purported Gupta acolytes. This was around the time that Zuma appointed Gigaba as minister of public enterprises. If one considers Vytjie Mentor's claim that she was offered that very position in 2010 by the Guptas and turned it down, the possibility exists that Gigaba, too, was approached by the residents of 1 Saxonwold Drive. While researching this book, I managed to track down one of the Guptas' former bodyguards, who informed me that Gigaba was one of the many high-profile politicians who visited the Guptas at their Saxonwold estate, even after he had moved on to home affairs.

If Zuma had fired Gordhan and Jonas in order to further the interests of the Gupta family, it soon became apparent that he had done so at great cost to his own office. What had once been cracks in the tripartite alliance had now become seemingly unbridgeable rifts. The SACP was the first to directly link Zuma's reshuffle to the Guptas. 'The timing of Zuma's cabinet reshuffling and the deepening banking troubles faced by the Guptas is not … fortuitous,' said the SACP in a statement. 'Once more it lays bare a disturbing reality. Increasingly our country is being ruled not from the Union Buildings, but from the Gupta family compound.'[8] Solly Mapaila, the party's deputy general secretary, told *News24* that Gordhan's removal would give the Guptas 'unfettered access to the resources at Treasury'.[9]

EFF leader Julius Malema for once agreed with Mapaila. 'Malusi is a regular at Saxonwold Shebeen,' he told journalists at a press conference.

'He has never denied that. We have just placed Treasury at the gate of Saxonwold Shebeen.' He even alleged that the Guptas gave Gigaba 'corrupt money' and a house in Cape Town.[10]

The morning after the president's execution of what the DA would later label a 'midnight Cabinet cull', the main opposition party tabled a motion of no confidence in Zuma. 'South Africa is now experiencing a groundswell of opposition to Zuma and his undisguised project of state capture,' the party said in a statement.[11]

The backlash from the opposition and even from the ANC's alliance partners may have been expected. But the harsh criticism from the highest echelons within the ANC must have surprised even Zuma. The rumblings had actually started the day before the reshuffle. At a funeral service for ANC struggle icon Ahmed Kathrada, who had passed away on 28 March, some of the party's most senior leaders visibly placed themselves in the anti-Zuma camp. The president, who was not present at the funeral after the Ahmed Kathrada Foundation barred him from speaking at the event, was even berated from beyond the grave, when former president Kgalema Motlanthe read from a letter Kathrada had written to Zuma in 2016 in the wake of the controversial axing of Nhlanhla Nene. The struggle veteran had been deeply disturbed by Zuma's actions that year. 'And bluntly, if not arrogantly, in the face of such persistently widespread criticism, condemnation and demand, is it asking too much to express the hope that you will choose the correct way that is gaining momentum, to consider stepping down?' Kathrada had written.[12] Motlanthe's reading of these words prompted 'a standing ovation and thundering applause' from the audience of ANC heavyweights and other politicians, including health minister Aaron Motsoaledi and Pravin Gordhan.[13]

The backlash from the ANC's top structures gained momentum after the reshuffle. On the Friday, Ramaphosa confirmed that the 'intelligence report' on Gordhan's visit to the UK had formed the basis of Zuma's decision to axe the finance minister. Ramaphosa openly criticised Zuma's move. 'I raised my concern and objection on the removal of the Minister of Finance, largely because he was being removed based on an intelligence report that I believe had unsubstantiated allegations,' the deputy president told reporters.[14] By then, a summary of the 'dossier' had started doing the rounds on media platforms. It was indeed flimsy, if not downright amateurish. According to the dossier, Gordhan and Jonas were to hold 'secret meetings' with prominent people in the banking world in order to roll out something called 'Operation Check Mate'. This supposedly involved colluding with the world's big banks 'to fight the President'. 'They will also tell the banks that they have the support of the of many in ANC [*sic*] and other parties to force the President out,' read the badly written document. 'By having them all stand together they are attending [*sic*] to show unity so that the UK and USA banks will join in with the South African banks Against the President.'[15]

The whole affair smacked of a smear campaign, with Gordhan later calling it an 'unintelligent' intelligence report.[16] Malema, claiming his party had obtained a copy of the full report, said it was 'not coherent' and even alleged that a former Gupta employee was responsible for its drafting.[17]

I set out to try to determine whether there was any veracity in Malema's claims. A tip-off from my editor, Adriaan Basson, sent me in the direction of Zehir Omar, the lawyer for an organisation called the Society for the Protection of Our Constitution (SPOC). Omar and the SPOC were rumoured to have been behind the so-called intelligence report. Omar also happens to be a regular guest on ANN7, where he partakes in lively discussions on topics ranging from white monopoly capital to the supposed politically motivated attacks on the Gupta family.[18]

When I got hold of Omar on the phone, he happily agreed to discuss the issue of the intelligence report. He told me that the SPOC has its own 'intelligence unit', and that the organisation did indeed compile an 'intelligence report' on Gordhan's visit to the UK and the US. The information about the global banking community's diabolical plan to oust Zuma came from the SPOC's sources within Iranian, Russian and Indian intelligence agencies, Omar assured me. But, according to him, the SPOC's report was not the same as the one that appeared in the media. If there were any similarities between the two reports, it was a coincidence that could be attributed to 'the authenticity of the information', Omar told me. He insisted that the report Zuma used to fire Gordhan and Jonas was compiled by an intelligence agency of the South African government. But he also admitted that he sent the SPOC's report to several individuals and organisations before Zuma's dramatic cabinet reshuffle, including to Luthuli House. Omar added that, 'on the balance of probability', it was likely that the report on which Zuma relied was informed by intelligence gathered by the same Iranian, Indian and Russian sources on which the SPOC had based its report. Finally, Omar denied that he and the SPOC had any links to the Guptas, or that the SPOC's intelligence report had anything to do with the controversial family.

The controversy over the dubious intelligence report was but one factor in the ever-deepening crisis that Zuma now faced. By the time the cataclysmic final week of March 2017 had come to an end, the EFF and other opposition parties had indicated that they would support the DA's motion of no confidence in the president. Even more worrying for Zuma was the possibility that many ANC MPs would support the motion, if the sentiments at Kathrada's funeral and subsequent memorial service were anything to go by. Zuma's far-reaching cabinet reshuffle, and especially his choice of finance minister, had pushed his political career as close to the precipice as it had ever been. In light of Zuma's predicament, the continued survival of the Republic of Gupta seemed equally uncertain.

Epilogue

Whenever the Guptas provide their own account of their time in South Africa, they tell the classic story of the immigrant family that has achieved tremendous success in their newly adopted country through sheer determination, hard work and a knack for spotting good opportunities.

There is much to admire in this version of the family's history. The Guptas have, after all, built a diversified business empire and amassed a fortune. Considering the relatively short period of time in which they achieved their business successes, this feat seems doubly impressive.

In December 2016, the *Business Times* Rich List ranked Atul Gupta as South Africa's seventh-richest person.[1] According to the publication, Gupta's personal wealth now stands at an estimated R10 billion. The list is based on disclosed directors' holdings in JSE-listed companies. Given that it does not account for the Guptas' assets abroad, or for the personal wealth of Atul's siblings and the rest of the family, one can only speculate as to the real value of the family's fortune.

Instead of widespread admiration for Atul's achievement, the middle brother's inclusion on the rich list caused further public indignation. There are simply too many indications that the family's visible wealth may be the product of years of largely invisible dealings behind closed doors. The rags-to-riches tale that Atul and his brothers like to spin makes no mention of all the troubling developments that have on so many occasions landed the family in hot water.

When the Rich List was made public, the Save South Africa movement said it would have been astounding for anyone to have become so rich in so little time, 'but when it is Atul Gupta, a man whose every business activity is being questioned because of corruption, money-laundering and his penchant for peddling posts in public office, we really have to say: there is something fundamentally wrong'.[2]

Referring to former public protector Thuli Madonsela's report on state capture, the movement highlighted the problematic Zuma–Gupta nexus as the core reason for the public's suspicions about the Guptas' vast fortune. 'Jacob Zuma … stands at the centre of not only the Guptas' illicit economic empire, he actively facilitates it,' stated the collective of civil society groups. 'He abuses our Constitution; he consistently disrespects the rule of law, and involves members of his own family in the looting.'

If Atul, Ajay and Rajesh Gupta are to be believed, their relationship with Zuma is nothing more than an innocent friendship. They have said the same thing about their ties with some of Zuma's predecessors, one of whom – Mbeki – seems desperate to quash any notion that he was a buddy of the controversial trio.

By now, however, the string-pulling and back-room manoeuvring that accompanies these 'friendships' is blatantly apparent. Would Glencore have agreed to sell its Optimum coal mine to the Guptas were it not for the intervention of Mosebenzi Zwane, the Zuma-appointed mining minister? And would Eskom have approved a massive pre-payment to that very coal mine if the state-owned company's board had not been stacked with Gupta acolytes? I believe the answer to these questions is no. In light of the apparently dodgy deals struck by Eskom and Transnet with Gupta-owned or Gupta-linked companies, the special interest Zuma showed in the appointment of board members for these state-owned giants – as mentioned in Madonsela's report – becomes all the more troubling.

It seems unlikely that the Republic of Gupta will remain intact once Zuma leaves office, however. Ajay, Atul and Rajesh may have friends in other spheres of government, but when one considers Madonsela's report, along with the other revelations about the family contained in this book, it is Zuma's office that appears to be the glue holding the state-capture network together.

Earlier reports of a late-night exodus may have been premature, but we should not be surprised if the family does some day leave the country for good. There is, after all, no guarantee that the protection they have been afforded under Zuma's reign will continue once a new president takes power.

If the Guptas ever do turn their backs on South Africa, we should not celebrate it as the death of state capture. If this saga has taught us anything, it is that we should instead be mindful of how an entire country could fall under the sway of those wealthy and persuasive enough to infiltrate the corridors of power.

Members of the ruling party would do well to keep their eyes peeled for such influence as they ready themselves for another elective conference, and for the 2019 general election. The damage the Guptas have done to the ANC's image and reputation may still be reversible. But any further indications that the party and the country are effectively being ruled by shady characters in leafy suburbs may very well bring about the ANC's demise.

Acknowledgements

I have a host of sources and industry colleagues to thank for their support and assistance. Marida Fitzpatrick and Barry Bateman, thanks for sharing your time and stories with me. I am equally grateful to all those I cannot name. You know who you are.

To Waldimar Pelser and Adriaan Basson, my former and current editors respectively, thank you for allowing me to pursue this project. You have both played an important role in my career as a journalist.

My wonderful parents and siblings have indirectly played an equally important part in helping me get to this point in my professional life. You guys are the bedrock beneath everything I have ever achieved and each day I draw fresh inspiration from the love and respect we have for one another.

I am also vastly grateful for the team at Penguin Random House, who have helped this title see the light of day. Thank you Melt, Robert and Bronwen, and all the others who work behind the scenes to ensure that books such as this one end up in bookstores.

I am sure that I am expressing not only my own appreciation but also that of many other South Africans when I thank the likes of Mcebisi Jonas, Themba Maseko and Vytjie Mentor. Whistle-blowers such as yourselves represent the most steadfast line of defence we have against those who wish to turn this country into a hotbed of corruption.

I have saved my final words of gratitude for my beautiful, smart and wonderfully sardonic wife-to-be, Zelda. Thanks for your support and endless love. And for those indispensable cups of strong coffee. I would not have been able to complete this task without having you in my life.

Abbreviations and acronyms

ABC: Audit Bureau of Circulation
ACSA: Airports Company South Africa
AFB Waterkloof: Air Force Base Waterkloof
AFCP: Air Force Command Post
ANC: African National Congress
ANN7: Africa News Network 7
BACS: Bushveld Airspace Control Sector
BASA: Banking Association of South Africa
BEE: black economic empowerment
BLF: Black First Land First
BRP: business rescue practitioner
CCMA: Commission for Conciliation, Mediation and Arbitration
CIA: Central Intelligence Agency
CIPC: Companies and Intellectual Property Commission
COPE: Congress of the People
CSA: Cricket South Africa
CWU: Communication Workers Union
DA: Democratic Alliance
DFR: Defence Foreign Relations
DIRCO: Department of International Relations and Cooperation
DMR: Department of Mineral Resources
DOD: Department of Defence
DPCI: Directorate for Priority Crime Investigation
EFF: Economic Freedom Fighters
ELRC: Education and Labour Relations Council
FIC: Financial Intelligence Centre
FICA: Financial Intelligence Centre Act
FNB: First National Bank
GCIS: Government Communication and Information System
GDE: Gauteng Department of Education
GoL: GautengOnline

ICT: Imperial Crown Trading
ICT: information and communications technology
IDC: Industrial Development Corporation
IMC: inter-ministerial committee
IMC: International Marketing Council of South Africa
IPL: Indian Premier League
IT: information technology
JCPS: Justice, Crime Prevention and Security
JSE: Johannesburg Stock Exchange
MDS: Market Demand Strategy
MEC: member of the executive council
MK: Umkhonto we Sizwe
MP: member of Parliament
NDPP: National Director of Public Prosecutions
NEC: National Executive Committee
NGC: National General Council
NGO: non-governmental organisation
NIA: National Intelligence Agency
NICOC: National Intelligence Coordinating Committee
NPA: National Prosecuting Authority
NWC: National Working Committee
PAIA: Promotion of Access to Information Act
PIC: Public Investment Corporation
SAA: South African Airways
SAAF: South African Air Force
SABC: South African Broadcasting Corporation
SACP: South African Communist Party
SANDF: South African National Defence Force
SAPS: South African Police Service
SARB: South African Reserve Bank
SARS: South African Revenue Service
SENS: Stock Exchange News Service
SITA: State Information Technology Agency
SSA: State Security Agency
SSO: senior staff officer
STR: suspicious transaction report
TLI: Teacher Laptop Initiative
TMPD: Tshwane Metro Police Department
UCB: United Cricket Board of South Africa
USAASA: Universal Service and Access Agency of South Africa

Notes

PREFACE
1. Nickolaus Bauer, 'ANC: Nothing wrong with Zuma's call for support from business', *Mail & Guardian*, 15 January 2013.
2. Matuma Letsoalo and Qaanitah Hunter, 'Your business is in danger if you don't donate to the ANC – Zuma', *Mail & Guardian*, 9 October 2015.
3. 'Welcome to the Gupta Republic of South Africa: The new minister of mineral resources is an extension of the Gupta family', EFF press release, 23 September 2015, available at http://allafrica.com/stories/201509240331.html (last accessed 23 January 2017).

INTRODUCTION: UNPACKING STATE CAPTURE
1. Joel S. Hellman, Geraint Jones and Daniel Kaufmann, '"Seize the state, seize the day": State capture, corruption, and influence in transition', World Bank Policy Research Working Paper 2444, September 2000.
2. Joel S. Hellman and Daniel Kaufmann, 'Confronting the challenge of state capture in transition economies', *Finance & Development*, 38(3), September 2001.
3. Ibid.
4. Hellman, Jones and Kaufmann, '"Seize the state, seize the day": State capture, corruption, and influence in transition'.
5. T.S. Aidt, 'Rent seeking and the economics of corruption', *Constitutional Political Economy*, 27(2), June 2016, pp. 142–157.
6. David R. Henderson, 'Rent seeking', *The Concise Encyclopedia of Economics*, available at http://www.econlib.org/library/Enc/RentSeeking.html (last accessed 23 January 2017).
7. 'Rent-seeking', *Investopedia*, available at http://www.investopedia.com/terms/r/rentseeking.asp (last accessed 23 January 2017).
8. Ibid.
9. Richard Wong, 'Why is rent seeking so bad for competition, growth and freedom?', *South China Morning Post*, 14 June 2016.
10. John Mukum Mbaku, 'Corruption and rent-seeking', in Silvio Borner and Martin Paldam (eds), *The Political Dimension of Economic Growth*, London: Macmillan, 1998, pp. 193–211.
11. Hellman, Jones and Kaufmann, '"Seize the state, seize the day": State capture, corruption, and influence in transition'.
12. Ibid.
13. Andrej Nosko, 'Can a think tank help expose a captured state?', Open Society Foundations, 5 November 2014.
14. Hellman and Kaufmann, 'Confronting the challenge of state capture in transition economies'.

15. Mcebisi Jonas, 'State capture, possibilities for personal wealth accumulation through political office, impact on the state: Response to "The Guptas aren't the only threat to our NDR"', *Umsebenzi Online*, 15(15), 21 April 2016.
16. Ibid.
17. Maíra Martini, 'State capture: An overview', Transparency International Anti-Corruption Helpdesk, 12 March 2014.
18. Ongama Mtimka, 'Why state capture is a regressive step for any society', *The Conversation*, 7 April 2016.
19. 'Gupta brother to Themba Maseko: You will be sorted out', *EWN*, 11 March 2016.
20. Co-Pierre Georg, 'Why patronage and state capture spell trouble for South Africa', *The Conversation*, 1 September 2016.

PROLOGUE: ROUGH LANDING

1. Mandy Rossouw, 'Unease over Zuma's Gupta ties', *Mail & Guardian*, 23 July 2010.
2. Lauren Granger, 'Barry Bateman and Oscar Pistorius: Inside the Twitter explosion', *Memeburn*, 22 February 2013.
3. Cellphone recording of conversation between Barry Bateman and Atul Gupta, AFB Waterkloof, 30 April 2013.
4. 'SANDF denies it allowed private citizens to land at Waterkloof AFB', eNCA.com, 30 April 2013.
5. Sapa, 'Guptas had no authorisation to use air force base, says SANDF', *Mail & Guardian*, 30 April 2013.
6. 'Guptas slam preferential treatment claims', *City Press*, 30 April 2013.
7. 'Now government says Guptas did have permission to land', eNCA.com, 30 April 2013.
8. '#EpicFail: Government botches communication on Gupta plane', eNCA.com, 30 April 2013.
9. 'The landing at Waterkloof', statement issued on behalf of Gwede Mantashe, secretary general of the ANC, 30 April 2013.

CHAPTER 1: SUBCONTINENTAL DRIFT

1. SaharanpurLive, available at http://www.saharanpurlive.in/city-guide/about-saharanpur (last accessed 15 December 2016).
2. 'Face-to-face: The secrets behind Sahara', *IT-Online*, 13 August 2007.
3. Uday Ranal, 'Gupta bros, South Africa's "villains" are Saharanpur's "heroes"', *Times of India*, 18 December 2015.
4. Prega Govender, 'From Saharanpur to Saxonwold ...', *Sunday Times*, 27 February 2011.
5. Ibid. According to Indian company records, however, SKG Marketing, of which Atul is listed as a director, was only established in 1996, three years after Atul arrived in South Africa. Instead of importing spices, the company is said to be involved in 'other computer related activities' such as the 'maintenance of websites for other firms' and the 'creation of multimedia presentations for other firms etc.'.
6. Ranal, 'Gupta bros, South Africa's "villains" are Saharanpur's "heroes"'.
7. Govender, 'From Saharanpur to Saxonwold ...'.
8. Ranal, 'Gupta bros, South Africa's "villains" are Saharanpur's "heroes"'.
9. 'UP origin business tycoons, Gupta brothers fix cabinet berths in South Africa', *India Samvad*, 21 March 2016.
10. Kalim Rajab, 'Message to cabinet: It is NOT just a wedding', *Daily Maverick*, 6 May 2013.
11. Govender, 'From Saharanpur to Saxonwold ...'.

12. Ibid.
13. Ibid.
14. Ibid.
15. Ranal, 'Gupta bros, South Africa's "villains" are Saharanpur's "heroes"'.
16. 'Face-to-face: The secrets behind Sahara'.
17. South African Institute of Race Relations, 'South Africa survey, 1995/96', available at http://www.sahistory.org.za/sites/default/files/SAIRR%20Survey%201995-96.pdf (last accessed 19 December 2016).
18. Govender, 'From Saharanpur to Saxonwold ...'.
19. 'Face-to-face: The secrets behind Sahara'.
20. Allan Seccombe, 'The Gupta interview: The scowling "king" of the family and the soothing salary man', *Business Day*, 4 March 2011.
21. 'Face-to-face: The secrets behind Sahara'.
22. Govender, 'From Saharanpur to Saxonwold ...'.
23. Sahara India Pariwar website, available at www.sahara.in (last accessed 19 December 2016).
24. Rajab, 'Message to cabinet: It is NOT just a wedding'.
25. 'Face-to-face: The secrets behind Sahara'. In his interview with *Business Day* in 2011, Atul said: '[Sahara's] Competition used to say I created deserts for people in terms of competition.'
26. 'Face-to-face: The secrets behind Sahara'.
27. Ibid.
28. Ibid.
29. Govender, 'From Saharanpur to Saxonwold ...'.

CHAPTER 2: MAKING FRIENDS

1. 'John' is a pseudonym. The businessman in question did not want his real name to be divulged.
2. At the time of this alleged conversation, Zuma was the MEC for economic affairs and tourism in the KwaZulu-Natal provincial government.
3. 'Are the Guptas the new Shaiks?', *Mail & Guardian*, 9 July 2010.
4. Prega Govender, 'From Saharanpur to Saxonwold ...', *Sunday Times*, 27 February 2011.
5. Independent Foreign Service, 'Guptas virtually ignored in India', *Cape Times*, 10 April 2016.
6. Like 'John', 'Joe' is a pseudonym used to protect the identity of this source.

CHAPTER 3: MBEKI'S 'SECRET' COUNCIL

1. From the Brand South Africa website, available at www.brandsouthafrica.com; GCIS statement, 'Joint government/private sector drive launched to market South Africa abroad', 31 August 2000.
2. Siphiwe Mchunu, 'Mcebisi who? Ajay Gupta on Mcebisi Jonas, media capture', *The New Age*, 22 June 2016; IMC board meeting minutes, 27 November 2006.
3. Brand South Africa annual reports for 2014–2015 and 2015–2016, available at www.brandsouthafrica.com.
4. Moipone Malefane, 'Jacob Zuma dares the ANC to fire him', *Sowetan*, 22 March 2016.
5. 'Full text: Foundation responds to alleged Mbeki, Guptas link', *News24*, 11 April 2016.
6. Ibid.
7. Ibid.

8. Erika Gibson and Ferial Haffajee, 'Why Guptas left SA', *City Press*, 10 April 2016.
9. 'Watch: State capture is an imaginary concept – Ajay Gupta', *TimesLive*, 22 June 2016.
10. Ibid.
11. Marion Edmunds, 'Who's who in Mbeki's private think-tank', *Mail & Guardian*, 19 July 1996.
12. 'Too slick operators', *Noseweek*, 105, 1 July 2008.

CHAPTER 4: GAUTENG OFFLINE

1. '"I would have been further if my surname wasn't Zuma"', *City Press*, 5 March 2011.
2. Helen Grange, 'Influence in the corridors of power', *Weekend Argus*, 22 August 2010.
3. 'Gauteng to launch public ISP, give schools PCs', *ITWeb*, 13 February 2001.
4. 'Sahara wins substantial stake in GautengOnline tender', *ITWeb*, 8 December 2003.
5. Africa News Service, '1,100 Gauteng schools online by March 2004', *HighBeam Business*, 10 December 2003.
6. Ibid.
7. 'Sahara wins substantial stake in GautengOnline tender'.
8. 'ICT group wins big stake in GautengOnline tender', *Engineering News*, 9 December 2003.
9. Ibid.
10. 'Ensuring the future through education', *ITWeb*, 28 March 2002.
11. 'No shortage of innovation, style, interest at Sahara Convention', *ITWeb*, 11 January 2006.
12. Angelique Serrao, 'Gauteng Online slammed as R3bn flop', *The Star*, 29 July 2009.
13. Farzana Rasool, 'Gauteng Online provider "utterly failed"', *ITWeb*, 15 May 2012.
14. Angelique Serrao, 'Gauteng Online project at schools falls short – audit', *Pretoria News*, 8 May 2012.
15. Nontobeko Mtshali, 'R1bn later, Gauteng Online is no more', *The Star*, 19 June 2013.
16. SchoolNet South Africa, 'Project Refcomp: Refurbished computers in SchoolNet SA: A comparative case study', Final technical report, 9 October 2004.
17. 'SchoolNet SA partners', available at http://www.schoolnet.org.za/atwork/partners.htm (last accessed 20 January 2017).
18. SchoolNet South Africa, 'Project Refcomp: Refurbished computers in SchoolNet SA: A comparative case study'.
19. Ibid.
20. 'Sahara takes technology to the people', *ITWeb*, 4 August 2006.
21. 'Sahara at the forefront of ICT skills development and PC literacy', *net.work*, 15 February 2007.
22. Ibid.
23. 'Oakbay Investments annual results for the year ended 29 February 2016', press release, 8 September 2016.
24. 'The IT tender jackpot', *Moneyweb*, 29 November 2004.
25. Ibid.
26. Ibid.
27. Kaunda Chama, 'Anti-climax over seat tender', *ITWeb*, 8 December 2004.
28. 'The IT tender jackpot'.
29. South African Government, 'Teacher Laptop Initiative rollout launch', media advisory, 14 July 2010.
30. Bonnie Tubbs, 'Teacher Laptop Initiative mired', *ITWeb*, 24 January 2014.
31. NAPTOSA, 'National News Flash 2 of 2013: Teacher Laptop Initiative', 28 January 2013.

32. 'Oakbay Investments annual results for the year ended 29 February 2016'.
33. Ibid.

CHAPTER 5: CAPTURING CRICKET

1. Michael Owen-Smith, 'Newlands name-change row', *IOL*, 5 April 2004.
2. Altus Momberg, 'Sahara ready to bat in SA', *News24*, 5 April 2004.
3. 'Sahara gears up for expansion', *ITWeb*, 8 April 2004.
4. Momberg, 'Sahara ready to bat in SA'.
5. Owen-Smith, 'Newlands name-change row'.
6. Michael Owen-Smith, 'Sahara Park Newlands okay by me – Smith', *IOL*, 8 April 2004.
7. 'Sahara gears up for expansion'.
8. Owen-Smith, 'Sahara Park Newlands okay by me – Smith'.
9. 'Sahara gears up for expansion'.
10. Owen-Smith, 'Sahara Park Newlands okay by me – Smith'.
11. 'Graeme Smith reminisces on an incredible year at Sahara Park Newlands launch', *BooksLive*, 29 July 2009.
12. 'Ray Jennings executes new plan with Sahara mobile technology', *ITWeb*, 3 December 2004.
13. South Africa tour of India, 1st ODI: India v South Africa at Hyderabad (Deccan), ESPNcricinfo.com, 16 November 2005.
14. PTI, 'Proteas bowled over by fans', *Tribune India*, 17 November 2005.
15. South Africa tour of India, 2nd ODI: India v South Africa at Bangalore, ESPNcricinfo.com, 19 November 2005.
16. 'Jigsaw Production – Sahara Computer Graeme Smith TVC', uploaded 5 July 2011, available at https://www.youtube.com/watch?v=sCxJZgrb6wc (last accessed 24 January 2017).
17. 'Ray Jennings executes new plan with Sahara mobile technology'.
18. 'Sahara Computers helps train SA's future Proteas', *ITWeb*, 1 June 2005.
19. 'Sahara Computers in landmark deal to supply United Cricket Board', *ITWeb*, 19 October 2005.
20. 'Sahara Computers selected as official IT supplier to SA rugby', *ITWeb*, 9 February 2006.
21. Cricket South Africa Annual Report, 2008/09.
22. Sai Mohan, 'How Modi, Gupta brothers influenced South Africa cricket', *Yahoo! Cricket*, 5 September 2013.
23. 'CSA sacks CEO Gerald Majola', *Sport24*, 19 October 2012.
24. Amit Gupta and Subhash K. Jha, 'Ness in SA mess', *Times of India*, 19 May 2009.
25. Cricket South Africa Annual Report, 2010/11.
26. Cricket South Africa Annual Report, 2011/12.
27. 'New Age Impi plan to do it MiWay', Supersport.com, 13 February 2012.
28. Ibid.
29. MiWay T20 Challenge, 2011/12 Points Table, ESPNcricinfo.com.
30. 'CSA boots Impi out of T20', *Sport24*, 27 May 2012.
31. Luke Alfred, 'CSA's fixation with India damaging game', *Sunday Times*, 1 April 2012.
32. Stuart Hess, 'T20 expansion drive no-ball', *The Star*, 23 March 2012.
33. Cricket South Africa Annual Report, 2011/12.
34. Alfred, 'CSA's fixation with India damaging game'.
35. 'President Zuma attends The New Age T20 Cricket Friendship Cup', uploaded

17 April 2012, available at https://www.youtube.com/watch?v=LyZ2X8GpyO0 (last accessed 24 January 2017).

36. Cricket South Africa Annual Report, 2012/13.

CHAPTER 6: ZUMA'S RISE TO POWER

1. 'Sexwale, Phosa angry over Mbeki conspiracy claims', *News24*, 25 April 2001.
2. Chris McGreal, 'ANC veterans accused of plot to harm Mbeki', *The Guardian*, 26 April 2001.
3. 'Sexwale, Phosa angry over Mbeki conspiracy claims'.
4. 'Jacob Zuma cleared of rape', *The Guardian*, 8 May 2006.
5. Sibusiso Ngalwa and Wendy Jasson da Costa, 'Lekota is part of the conspiracy, says Zuma', *IOL*, 19 November 2007.
6. Moshoeshoe Monare, 'It's war by SMS at Polokwane', *IOL*, 18 December 2007.
7. Reuters and Sapa, 'Mbeki supporters booed in Polokwane', *Mail & Guardian*, 16 December 2007.
8. 'Zuma sweeps to resounding victory', *News24*, 18 December 2007.
9. 'Zuma case struck from the roll', *Mail & Guardian*, 20 September 2006.
10. Nelendhre Moodley, 'Sexwale, Zim team up in R173m Sahara deal', *Engineering News*, 19 September 2006.
11. 'Sahara Holdings in BEE deal', *Fin24*, 20 September 2006.
12. Moodley, 'Sexwale, Zim team up in R173m Sahara deal'.
13. Chimwemwe Mwanza and Sizwekazi Jekwa, 'Class double act – Zim and Sexwale join Sahara in bargain priced empowerment deal', *Finweek*, 28 September 2006.
14. 'Getting a nose in front', *Mail & Guardian*, 31 August 2007.
15. Chris McGreal, 'South Africa in turmoil as Mbeki heads for defeat', *The Guardian*, 15 December 2007.
16. Sapa, 'Tokyo backs Zuma bid', Polity.org.za, 12 December 2007.
17. Jan-Jan Joubert, 'The fall of Thabo Mbeki', *Politicsweb*, 5 February 2008.
18. 'Presidency appoints director general', South African Government News Agency, 5 June 2009.
19. 'Sahara Holdings in BEE deal'.
20. Mandy Rossouw, 'Why Zuma's top aide is leaving', *Mail & Guardian*, 15 July 2010.
21. 'Sahara keeps ANC conference connected', *IT-Online*, 19 December 2007.
22. Ibid.
23. 'Sahara helps delegates connect at ANC conference', *ITWeb*, 7 January 2008.
24. Carol Paton and Thebe Mabanga, 'Where business stands – an ear to the ground', Leader.co.za, 18 April 2009.
25. Ibid.
26. 'Too slick operators', *Noseweek*, 105, 1 July 2008.
27. Susan Comrie, 'The rise (and fall?) of Duduzane Zuma', *City Press*, 10 April 2016.
28. '"I would have been further if my surname wasn't Zuma"', *City Press*, 5 March 2011.
29. Helen Grange, 'Influence in the corridors of power', *Weekend Argus*, 22 August 2010.

CHAPTER 7: THE SISHEN SAGA

1. 'State of the Nation Address by His Excellency JG Zuma, President of the Republic of South Africa', 11 February 2010, available at http://www.thepresidency.gov.za/speeches/state-nation-address-his-excellency-jg-zuma,-president-republic-south-africa-joint-sitting (last accessed 30 January 2017).

2. Lisa Steyn, 'End of Sishen saga cast in iron', *Mail & Guardian*, 20 December 2013.
3. 'Everything you wanted to know about the Sishen row', *Mail & Guardian*, 18 August 2011.
4. Ibid.
5. Constitutional Court judgment, *Minister of Mineral Resources and Others v Sishen Iron Ore Company (Pty) Ltd and Another*, 12 December 2013, available at http://www.saflii .org/za/cases/ZACC/2013/45.html (last accessed 30 January 2017).
6. Sam Sole and Stefaans Brümmer, 'Guptas key to ArcelorMittal deal', *Mail & Guardian*, 20 August 2010; 'Everything you wanted to know about the Sishen row'.
7. Jan de Lange, 'Zuma's son linked to Sishen firm', *Fin24*, 18 April 2010.
8. Sole and Brümmer, 'Guptas key to ArcelorMittal deal'.
9. Lindo Xulu and Barry Sergeant, 'Sishen saga: Kumba lays criminal charges against ICT', *Moneyweb*, 26 October 2010.
10. Anthea Jeffery, 'Botswana has the mining law that South Africa should copy', *Daily Maverick*, 6 October 2016; amaBhungane, 'Mendelow concludes testimony at Breytenbach hearing', *Mail & Guardian*, 14 January 2014.
11. Lindo Xulu and Barry Sergeant, 'ICT: Allegedly forged signatures, stole identities', *Moneyweb*, 13 September 2010.
12. 'Everything you wanted to know about the Sishen row'.
13. Ibid.
14. Ibid.
15. Reuters, 'Timeline – Kumba, ArcelorMittal mine rights dispute', af.reuters.com, 27 July 2011.
16. Chanel de Bruyn and Terence Creamer, 'ArcelorMittal SA to buy ICT should Sishen rights be confirmed, unveils R9bn BEE deal', *Engineering News*, 10 August 2010.
17. I have put 'sell' in inverted commas because the politically connected BEE partners in these types of deals often do not pay a cent for their shares. This particular deal fell through before it could be concluded, so we will never know if the Guptas and their partners would have paid for their shares in ArcelorMittal. There were also questions at the time over whether the Guptas, who were not born in South Africa, actually qualified for BEE status.
18. De Bruyn and Creamer, 'ArcelorMittal SA to buy ICT should Sishen rights be confirmed, unveils R9bn BEE deal': 'According to legislation, BEE beneficiaries must be blacks (Africans, coloureds, Indians and Chinese) who are South African citizens by birth, descent or naturalisation prior to 1993 … The Guptas were naturalised after 1993. They were therefore not eligible to be BEE beneficiaries but could still be investors.'
19. Andile Ntingi, 'How did Guptas qualify for BEE steel deal?', *City Press*, 22 August 2010.
20. Sole and Brümmer, 'Guptas key to ArcelorMittal deal'.
21. Lindo Xulu, 'DMR backs ICT in Sishen saga', *Moneyweb*, 17 August 2010.
22. Stuart Theobald, 'Political solution is likely in Kumba-Mittal debacle', *Business Day*, 24 August 2010.
23. Ferial Haffajee and Adriaan Basson, 'For you he's a minister. For me he's a friend', *City Press*, 6 March 2011.
24. Babalo Ndenze and Sapa, 'The Gupta invite revealed', *Cape Times*, 15 May 2013.
25. Carli Lourens, 'Kumba to object to ICT mine right application', *IOL*, 16 January 2011.
26. 'Your application was fraudulent – Sandile Nogxina', *Politicsweb*, 27 January 2011.
27. 'Hawks raid DMR, ICT premises', *Politicsweb*, 27 July 2011. 'Uttering' consists of

unlawfully and intentionally passing off a false document (forged) to the actual or potential prejudice of another (https://www.saps.gove.za/faqdetail.php?fid=9).

28. 'Timeline: Glynnis Breytenbach vs NPA', *Mail & Guardian*, 28 May 2013; 'Breytenbach: ICT claims about Sishen Iron Ore fraud "seemed unlikely"', *City Press*, 6 February 2013; Mandy Wiener, 'Analysis: After NPA's epic loss, Glynnis Breytenbach must return to ALL her cases', *Daily Maverick*, 28 May 2013.
29. Agnieszka Flak, 'ArcelorMittal seeks to join case against Imperial', *Mail & Guardian*, 31 May 2011.
30. Shapi Shacinda, 'Stanlib Asset Management questions ArcelorMittal's ZEE deal', *Politicsweb*, 15 October 2010.
31. 'ArcelorMittal BEE deal with "Zuma allies" called off', *Moneyweb*, 26 September 2011.
32. Lynley Donnelly, 'Due diligence "scuppered" Arcelor deal', *Mail & Guardian*, 30 September 2011.
33. Stefaans Brümmer, 'Zuma Jnr heading for first billion', *Mail & Guardian*, 13 August 2010.
34. Terence Creamer, 'Judge favours Mittal's rights view in long-running iron-ore tussle', *Engineering News*, 15 December 2011.
35. Sapa, 'SCA dismisses Sishen challenge', *Mail & Guardian*, 29 March 2013.
36. Constitutional Court judgment, *Minister of Mineral Resources and Others v Sishen Iron Ore Company (Pty) Ltd and Another*.

CHAPTER 8: NUCLEAR FAMILY

1. Oakbay Resources & Energy Limited, Pre-listing statement, 21 November 2014.
2. 'Uranium One to place Dominion operations on care and maintenance', Uranium One Inc. news release, 22 October 2008.
3. Martin Creamer, 'Stranded Dominion uranium operation set to restart under Zuma-linked Shiva', *Mining Weekly*, 14 May 2010.
4. Oakbay Resources & Energy Limited, Pre-listing statement.
5. Creamer, 'Stranded Dominion uranium operation set to restart under Zuma-linked Shiva'.
6. Stefaans Brümmer and Sam Sole, 'Zuma "meddled in mine buyout"', *Mail & Guardian*, 14 May 2010.
7. Creamer, 'Stranded Dominion uranium operation set to restart under Zuma-linked Shiva'.
8. Ibid.
9. Brümmer and Sole, 'Zuma "meddled in mine buyout"'; Duduzane Zuma and Rajesh Gupta are both listed as directors of Islandsite Investments 255.
10. Brümmer and Sole, 'Zuma "meddled in mine buyout"'.
11. Buddy Naidu, 'Zuma defies ANC and tries to get Molefe back', *Sunday Times*, 25 April 2010.
12. Brümmer and Sole, 'Zuma "meddled in mine buyout"'.
13. Mondli Makhanya, 'The tragic fall of Brian Molefe', *City Press*, 13 November 2016.
14. Brümmer and Sole, 'Zuma "meddled in mine buyout"'.
15. Oakbay Resources & Energy Limited, Pre-listing statement.
16. AmaBhungane, 'Another state bonanza for the Guptas', *Mail & Guardian*, 5 December 2014.
17. Oakbay Resources & Energy Limited, Pre-listing statement.
18. Ibid.

19. AmaBhungane, 'Another state bonanza for the Guptas'.
20. 'Kazakh tie-in for Uranium One and ARMZ', *World Nuclear News*, 15 June 2009.
21. Peter Koven, 'Uranium One bought by top Russian shareholder ARMZ for $1.3-billion', *Financial Post*, 14 January 2013.
22. 'Address by President Jacob Zuma at UN Climate Change Conference, Copenhagen, 18 December 2009', available at http://www.dirco.gov.za/docs/speeches/2009/jzum1221.html (last accessed 1 February 2017).
23. Lily Gosam, 'Zuma, the Guptas and the Russians – the inside story', *Rand Daily Mail*, 2 February 2016.
24. Lionel Faull, 'Battle for South Africa's R1-trillion nuclear contract', *Mail & Guardian*, 7 October 2011.
25. 'Russia and SA sign agreement on strategic partnership in nuclear energy – ROSATOM', *Politicsweb*, 22 September 2014.
26. Allister Sparks, 'At home and abroad: Is now the time for Vesuvius of Zupta scandals to erupt?' *Business Day*, 13 April 2016.

CHAPTER 9: SPOOKED

1. Much of the information in this part of the chapter was sourced from individuals who were part of South Africa's intelligence community at the time. Considering the sensitive nature of their work, I cannot provide much detail about their identities beyond saying that they were all privy to the State Security Agency's probe into the Guptas.
2. Mandy Rossouw, 'Unease over Zuma's Gupta ties', *Mail & Guardian*, 23 July 2010.
3. Matuma Letsoalo and Charles Molele, 'Ex spy-boss slams Cwele over Guptas', *Mail & Guardian*, 17 May 2013.
4. Jacques Pauw, 'Cwele's spy war', *City Press*, 11 September 2011.
5. Ibid.
6. George Matlala and Moffet Mofokeng, 'NIA boss forced out?', *Sunday Independent*, 12 September 2011.
7. Ranjeni Munusamy, 'The top spooks' Gupta warning – which cost them their jobs', *Daily Maverick*, 6 May 2013.
8. 'Did the state security minister stop an investigation into the Gupta family?', statement by David Maynier MP, 6 May 2013.
9. Babalo Ndenze, 'Cwele: I didn't stop Gupta probe', *IOL*, 15 May 2013.
10. Letsoalo and Molele, 'Ex spy-boss slams Cwele over Guptas'.
11. 'Full text: MK generals, veterans call for Zuma to step down', *News24*, 23 March 2016.
12. Carien du Plessis, 'Ex-spy bosses to spill beans on Guptas', *Mail & Guardian*, 24 March 2016.
13. Ibid.
14. Ranjeni Munusamy, 'Captura continua: Guptas triumph as ANC shuts down state capture probe', *Daily Maverick*, 1 June 2016.
15. Thanduxolo Jika and Qaanitah Hunter, 'Mantashe "ignored" spy report on Guptas' influence', *Sunday Times*, 5 June 2016.
16. Thulani Gqirana, 'Inspector general candidate gets National Assembly nod', *News24*, 29 November 2016.
17. Luyolo Mkentane, '"Whitewash" jibe at ANC Gupta probe', *The Star*, 2 June 2016.

CHAPTER 10: THE DAWN OF A NEW AGE

1. 'UK and US see heaviest newspaper circulation declines', *The Guardian*, 17 June 2010.
2. Chantelle Benjamin, 'Newspapers and magazines still showing decline in circulation', *Business Day*, 20 May 2010.
3. 'History of "New Age" newspaper', South African History Online, 22 March 2011.
4. Andy Rice, 'Good luck Guptas – *The New Age* is gonna cost you, big time', *Daily Maverick*, 9 July 2010.
5. Sam Sole and Stefaans Brümmer, 'Zuma in talks over ANC paper', *Mail & Guardian*, 30 April 2010.
6. Rowan Philp, 'Essop Pahad, Guptas sever business ties', *TimesLive*, 7 August 2011.
7. Mandy Rossouw, 'Welcome to the Gupta club', *Mail & Guardian*, 23 July 2010.
8. Andy Rice, '*The New Age* launches; underestimate it at your peril', *Daily Maverick*, 23 July 2010.
9. 'Media transformation, ownership and diversity', ANC discussion document prepared for the National General Council, 20–24 September 2010, Durban, *Politicsweb*, 29 July 2010.
10. Sapa, '*New Age* garners government ads', *Mail & Guardian*, 23 September 2010.
11. Mandy de Waal, 'As *The New Age* enters the world, Atul Gupta enters new controversy', *Daily Maverick*, 27 September 2010.
12. Sapa, '*New Age* garners government ads'.
13. '*The New Age* postpones launch', *The Marketing Site*, 14 September 2010.
14. Sapa, '*New Age* rocked by resignations of senior staff', *Mail & Guardian*, 20 October 2010.
15. 'Senior editorial team members at *The New Age* resign', *The Marketing Site*, 20 October 2010.
16. Sapa, '*New Age* rocked by resignations of senior staff'.
17. Henry Jeffreys, 'Dawn of *The New Age*', *The New Age*, 6 December 2010.
18. Sapa, 'Zuma says *New Age* "a breath of fresh air"', *Mail & Guardian*, 9 January 2011.
19. Henry Jeffreys, 'In defence of the Guptas', *Moneyweb*, 21 February 2011.
20. Sapa, 'Jeffreys calls it quits as Fisher takes over at "New Age"', *Mail & Guardian*, 31 May 2011.
21. 'New editor for *New Age*', *News24*, 31 July 2012.
22. Mandy de Waal, 'Editor no. 4 for *The New Age*, but still no ABC', *Daily Maverick*, 2 August 2012.
23. *The New Age* rate card – advertisement rates effective September 1, 2010, available at http://www.tnamedia.co.za/rates/rates.pdf (last accessed 3 February 2017).
24. De Waal, 'Editor no. 4 for *The New Age*, but still no ABC'.
25. 'In defence of the *New Age* – Nazeem Howa's reply to the attacks by *City Press* and others', *Politicsweb*, 22 January 2013.
26. Sarah Evans and Lionel Faull, '*New Age*: Dawn of advertising riches with no circulation figures', *Mail & Guardian*, 25 January 2013.
27. 'Telkom splurges R34m on *New Age* ads', *City Press*, 10 February 2013.
28. AmaBhungane, 'Parastatals "bullied" into supporting the "New Age"', *Mail & Guardian*, 25 January 2013.
29. Matthew le Cordeur, 'SAA spends nearly R10m with the *New Age*', *Fin24*, 12 October 2015.
30. Donwald Pressly, 'Blade Nzimande pumps R2m into *New Age*', *Fin24*, 16 April 2015.
31. Stephan Hofstatter, Mzilikazi wa Afrika and Rob Rose, 'Massive looting at SABC exposed', *Sunday Times*, 7 October 2012.
32. Loyiso Sidimba, 'R25m for breakfast', *City Press*, 20 January 2013.

33. Lionel Faull and Sam Sole, 'Row over Eskom's R43m Gupta breakfast deal', *Mail & Guardian*, 24 October 2014.
34. Kgothatso Madisa, 'SABC resources used to fund ANN7: Vuyo Mvoko', *Sowetan*, 13 December 2016.
35. AmaBhungane, 'Parastatals "bullied" into supporting the "New Age"'.

CHAPTER 11: GUPTA TV

1. Sapa, 'DSTV to launch new channel', *IOL*, 7 February 2013.
2. Glynnis Underhill, 'Duduzane Zuma to be Gupta news channel's BEE partner', *Mail & Guardian*, 9 August 2013.
3. Africa News Network 7, 'About us', available at http://www.ann7.com/about-us/ (last accessed 3 February 2017).
4. Piet Rampedi, 'Zuma's "secret" visit to Gupta TV channel', *The Star*, 21 August 2013.
5. Vuyo Mkize, '"Gupta TV" to show "no fear, no favour"', *IOL*, 22 August 2013.
6. Gabi Mbele, 'Amateur hour at Gupta TV', *Sunday Times*, 25 August 2013.
7. Rebecca Davis, 'ANN7: Car-crash viewing, but no laughing matter', *Daily Maverick*, 26 August 2013.
8. Mbele, 'Amateur hour at Gupta TV'.
9. Glynnis Underhill, 'ANN7's Sundaram back in Delhi, still fearful', *Mail & Guardian*, 7 September 2013.
10. 'Gupta TV boss flees', *City Press*, 1 September 2013.
11. Underhill, 'ANN7's Sundaram back in Delhi, still fearful'.
12. 'Gupta TV boss flees'.
13. 'ANN7 flouts visa laws', *EWN*, 16 September 2013.
14. Advance information for *Indentured: Behind the Scenes at Gupta TV*, Jacana Media, available at http://www.jacana.co.za/downloads/submaterial/0.%202014/ SUB_1_MARCH_2014/JACANA/PDFs/C1_Indentured%20AI.pdf (last accessed 3 February 2017).
15. Thinus Ferreira, 'ANN7 explosive tell-all book, *Indentured: Behind the Scenes at Gupta TV*, from Rajesh Sundaram moving to a possible new publisher', *TV with Thinus* (blog), 5 June 2014.
16. Verashni Pillay, 'ANN7's Asanda Magaqa "escorted" off the premises', *Mail & Guardian*, 24 November 2014.
17. 'Journalist Asanda Magaqa wins CCMA case against ANN7', *Sowetan*, 9 October 2015.
18. Matthew le Cordeur, 'Guptas' staff appeal to banks to save their Oakbay jobs', *Fin24*, 20 April 2016.
19. 'Why did ANCYL's Collen Maine visit Oakbay employees?', 702.co.za, 20 April 2016.
20. Lizeka Tandwa, 'ANCYL's Maine chased away by Gupta employees', *News24*, 20 April 2016.
21. AmaBhungane, 'Guptas "backed" Oros R140k monthly bond', *City Press*, 1 May 2016.
22. Tandwa, 'ANCYL's Maine chased away by Gupta employees'.
23. Thando Kubheka, 'Sanef concerned about dismissal of 8 ANN7 employees', *EWN*, 26 June 2016.
24. Eduard de Kock, 'More journalists fired from ANN7, Sanef may start legal fees fund', *EWN*, 4 August 2016.
25. BEMAWU, 'ANN7 workers dispute settled', bemawu.org.za, 12 September 2016.
26. Matthew le Cordeur, 'Guptas and Duduzane Zuma resign from Oakbay', *Fin24*, 8 April 2016.

27. Mahlatse Gallens, 'All MK veterans must read and watch Gupta newspaper, channel – Van Rooyen', *News24*, 16 December 2016.
28. Lizeka Tandwa, 'We are proudly in business with the Guptas – MKMVA', *News24*, 30 March 2016.
29. Ranjeni Munusamy, 'ANC at 105: Succession endorsement grabs spotlight as Zuma dances off the stage', *Daily Maverick*, 12 January 2017.

CHAPTER 12: THE R75-MILLION WEDDING SPLURGE
1. Marida Fitzpatrick, 'My 4 dae by die Guptas', *Netwerk24*, 17 March 2016.
2. *Top Billing* Gupta wedding insert, SABC 3, 9 May 2013.

CHAPTER 13: ZWANE'S GUEST
1. For the full statement, see http://www.gov.za/media-statement-plane-which-landed -waterkloof-air-force-base-minister-justice-and-constitutional (last accessed 24 November 2016).
2. Phillip de Wet and Sarah Evans, 'Free State government gave Gupta guests an "alibi"', *Mail & Guardian*, 10 May 2013.
3. For the full report, see http://cdn.mg.co.za/content/documents/2013/05/22/waterkloof _report.pdf (last accessed 24 November 2016).
4. Confidential AFB Waterkloof VIP flying programme, 29–30 April 2013.

CHAPTER 14: CLUSTERFUCK
1. Peter Bruce, 'Thick end of the wedge: How to buy a mine for next to nothing', *Business Day*, 11 March 2016.
2. JCPS Cluster Report, 'Landing of a chartered commercial aircraft at Air Force Base Waterkloof', 17 May 2013, p. 6.
3. Ibid.
4. Ibid.
5. Ibid., p. 7.
6. Ibid.
7. Ibid., p. 8.
8. Ibid.
9. Ibid.
10. Ibid., p. 9.
11. Ibid.
12. Ibid., p. 10.
13. Ibid.
14. Ibid., p. 11.
15. Ibid.
16. Ibid., pp. 12–13.
17. Ibid., p. 13.
18. Ibid., p. 14.
19. Ibid.
20. Ibid.
21. Ibid., p. 9.
22. Ibid., p. 10.
23. Babalo Ndenze, 'Cops blow up Gupta gift', *IOL*, 15 May 2013.

24. JCPS Cluster Report, 'Landing of a chartered commercial aircraft at Air Force Base Waterkloof'.
25. Ibid., p. 11.
26. Ibid., p. 14.
27. Ibid., p. 15.
28. Ibid.
29. Ibid.
30. Ibid., p. 16.
31. Ibid.
32. Ibid.
33. Ibid., p. 17.
34. Ibid.

CHAPTER 15: POINTING FINGERS

1. JCPS Cluster Report, 'Landing of a chartered commercial aircraft at Air Force Base Waterkloof', 17 May 2013, p. 18.
2. Ibid.
3. Ibid.
4. Ibid., p. 20.
5. Ibid.
6. Ibid., p. 7.
7. Ibid., p. 18.
8. Ibid., p. 19.
9. Ibid.
10. Ibid., p. 20.
11. Ibid.
12. Ibid., p. 22.
13. Ibid.
14. Ibid., p. 25.
15. Ibid.
16. Ibid., p. 29.
17. Ibid., p. 27.

CHAPTER 16: THE SCAPEGOATS

1. JCPS Cluster Report, 'Landing of a chartered commercial aircraft at Air Force Base Waterkloof', 17 May 2013, pp. 25, 26.
2. Glynnis Underhill, 'Gupta saga: Vusi Koloane hung out to dry', *Mail & Guardian*, 10 May 2013.
3. Mogomotsi Magome, 'Guptagate: Top official demoted', *Sunday Independent*, 25 August 2013.
4. Nathi Olifant, 'Guptagate official rewarded', *Sunday Tribune*, 17 August 2014.
5. SANDF Board of Inquiry, Convening order no. 01/2013, 3 May 2013.
6. Letter from Captain Prashant Chowdhary to SANDF Chief of Defence Foreign Relations, 28 February 2013.
7. Letter from Department of Defence: Foreign Relations to SSO SAAF Foreign Relations, 5 March 2013.
8. Lieutenant Colonel Christine Anderson sworn affidavit, SANDF Board of Inquiry, 27 May 2013.

9. Warrant Officer Thabo Ntshisi sworn statement, SANDF Board of Inquiry, 31 May 2013.
10. Letter from SANDF Board of Inquiry to Warrant Officer Thabo Ntshisi, 24 June 2013.
11. Warrant Officer Thabo Ntshisi written response to letter from SANDF Board of Inquiry, 28 June 2013.
12. Sarah Ramotlalane sworn affidavit, Kliptown SAPS, 27 June 2013.
13. Erika Gibson, 'Guptas: Klag erg verwater', *Beeld*, 30 October 2013.
14. Erika Gibson, 'Beskuldigde in Gupta-sage nou staatsgetuie', *Beeld*, 24 January 2014.
15. Media statement by the SA National Defence Union, 'Condemning the SANDF's delay in finalising a trial date in the Guptagate matter', 24 January 2014.
16. Letter from Colonel F.J. Botha (SANDF) to the SA National Defence Union, 19 January 2015.
17. Erika Gibson and Jan-Jan Joubert, 'Guptas: Regering skarrel', *Beeld*, 2 May 2013.

CHAPTER 17: HORSESHOES AND GRAVY TRAINS

1. 'Transnet launches R300bn plan which will create thousands of jobs', Transnet media release, 10 April 2012.
2. Sapa, 'Molefe appointed new Transnet CEO', *Mail & Guardian*, 16 February 2011.
3. 'Molefe tipped to be Transnet CEO', *The New Age*, 7 December 2010.
4. Stefaans Brümmer and Sam Sole, 'Zuma "meddled in mine buyout"', *Mail & Guardian*, 14 May 2010.
5. Peter Bruce, 'Chairmen of Transnet, Eskom and Denel to go', *Business Day*, 9 June 2011.
6. 'Transnet awards largest-ever locomotive supply contract in South Africa's history', Transnet media release, 17 March 2014.
7. Lionel Faull, Vinayak Bhardwaj, Matuma Letsaolo, Sam Sole and Stefaans Brümmer, 'Transnet tender boss's R50-billion double game', *Mail & Guardian*, 4 July 2014.
8. VR Laser Services website, vrlaser.co.za.
9. Faull, Bhardwaj, Letsaolo, Sole and Brümmer, 'Transnet tender boss's R50-billion double game'.
10. BuaNews, 'Denel wins R8bn Armscor order', Brand South Africa, 18 May 2007.
11. 'More inertia on Hoefyster', *defenceWeb*, 24 August 2011.
12. Guy Martin, 'Hoefyster production contract on the way', *defenceWeb*, 1 July 2013.
13. Erika Gibson, 'Denel: Guptas pantser voort', *Rapport*, 17 April 2016.
14. 'Denel reinforces commitment to good governance', Denel press statement, 23 April 2016.
15. 'Denel partners with VR Laser to form Denel Asia', *defenceWeb*, 29 January 2016.
16. 'Denel Asia will expand business into South East Asia', *Denel Insights*, First Issue 2016.
17. Ibid.
18. 'Statement on reports that Denel established a joint venture', National Treasury media statement, 13 April 2016.
19. Stephan Hofstatter, 'Treasury "taking Denel to court" to halt Gupta deal', *Sunday Times*, 28 August 2016.
20. AmaBhungane, 'How Denel was hijacked', *Daily Maverick*, 29 May 2016.
21. Matuma Letsoalo, Lionel Faull and Mmanaledi Mataboge, 'Veterans' official in private deals', *Mail & Guardian*, 1 April 2011.
22. AmaBhungane, 'How Denel was hijacked'.
23. 'Denel tears into Gordhan, defends Guptas', *Fin24*, 30 August 2016.
24. AmaBhungane, '"Kickback" scandal engulfs Transnet', *Mail & Guardian*, 31 July 2015; Stefaans Brümmer, Susan Comrie and Sam Sole, 'Exclusive: Guptas "laundered" kickback millions – here's the evidence', *Mail & Guardian*, 8 December 2016.

25. AmaBhungane, 'State capture – the Guptas and the R250 million "kickback laundry"', amaBhungane.co.za, 29 October 2016.

26. Sabelo Skiti and Thanduxolo Jika, 'Transnet deals fall into Gupta man's lap', *Sunday Times*, 22 May 2016.

27. AmaBhungane, 'State capture – the Guptas and the R250 million "kickback laundry"'.

28. Brümmer, Comrie and Sole, 'Exclusive: Guptas "laundered" kickback millions – here's the evidence'.

29. Litha Mveliso Nyhonyha sworn affidavit, *Eric Anthony Wood and Marinus Johannes Hesselink vs Litha Mveliso Nyhonyha and Others*, South Gauteng High Court, Johannesburg, 7 November 2016.

30. Brümmer, Comrie and Sole, 'Exclusive: Guptas "laundered" kickback millions – here's the evidence'.

31. Litha Mveliso Nyhonyha sworn affidavit, *Eric Anthony Wood and Marinus Johannes Hesselink vs Litha Mveliso Nyhonyha and Others*.

32. Ibid.

33. Craig McKune, Stefaans Brümmer and Sam Sole, 'Transnet's shady Gupta loan deal', amaBhungane.co.za, 18 September 2016.

34. Sam Sole, Stefaans Brümmer and Craig McKune, 'Gupta-linked firm's R167m Transnet bonanza', amaBhungane.co.za, 28 August 2016.

CHAPTER 18: DIRTY MONEY

1. Department of Health and Human Services, Centers for Disease Control and Prevention, National Institute for Occupational Safety and Health, 'Coal mine dust exposures and associated health outcome: A review of information published since 1995', *Current Intelligence Bulletin* 64, April 2011.

2. Earthlife Africa, 'An action plan for acid mine drainage', earthlife.org.za, 5 April 2011.

3. Greenpeace International, 'Coal power plants', greenpeace.org, 15 April 2010.

4. 'Oakbay's Tegeta Resources expands production at Brakfontein colliery', *Mining Review Africa*, 19 November 2015.

5. Oakbay Resources & Energy Integrated Annual Report 2016, available at http://www.oakbay.co.za/wp-content/uploads/2015/10/Oakbay-5-September.pdf (last accessed 13 February 2017).

6. Bobby Jordan, '"The mine is in an environmentally sensitive wetland region"', *Sunday Times*, 6 November 2011.

7. Bobby Jordan, 'State ignores illegal Zuma-Gupta mining', *Sunday Times*, 3 November 2013.

8. Jordan, '"The mine is in an environmentally sensitive wetland region"'.

9. Jordan, 'State ignores illegal Zuma-Gupta mining'.

10. Sipho Kings, 'Illegal Gupta coal mine accused of polluting crop irrigation water', *Mail & Guardian*, 7 February 2014.

11. Matshela Koko, Group Executive for Generation at Eskom, 'How Eskom is transforming the R100bn-plus coal mine industry', Eskom.co.za.

12. Terence Creamer, 'Brown wants high cost of coal to Eskom investigated', *Mining Weekly*, 26 April 2016.

13. Koko, 'How Eskom is transforming the R100bn-plus coal mine industry'.

14. 'Medupi, Kusile to be completed by 2021', *EWN*, 22 April 2015.

15. 'Guptas strong-arm Eskom to back illegal mine', *News24*, 6 July 2014.

16. Chantelle Kotze, 'Cabinet makes major changes to state-owned company boards', *Engineering News*, 11 December 2014.
17. Sam Sole, Craig McKune and Stefaans Brümmer, 'The "Gupta owned" state enterprises', *Mail & Guardian*, 24 March 2016.
18. Ibid.
19. Loni Prinsloo, Stephan Hofstatter, Mzilikazi wa Afrika and Piet Rampedi, 'Former Eskom boss "bent the rules" to favour Gupta mines', *Sunday Times*, 19 April 2015.
20. Sabelo Skiti, 'How Eskom bowed to Guptas', *Sunday Times*, 13 September 2015.
21. Ibid.
22. Eugenie du Preez, 'Glencore blames Eskom deal for Optimum woes', *Fin24*, 5 August 2015.
23. Carol Paton, 'Eskom paying a "mind-boggling" price for Gupta coal', *Business Day*, 14 June 2016.
24. 'BHP Billiton announces sale of Optimum Colliery', BHP Billiton news release, 14 May 2008.
25. Optimum Coal 2011 Integrated Annual Report.
26. 'Glencore consortium completes acquisition of controlling interest in Optimum Coal Holdings Limited', Glencore media statement, 27 March 2012.
27. Barry Sergeant, 'Something nasty in the coalshed', *Noseweek*, 202, 1 August 2016.
28. Public Protector South Africa, 'State of capture: Report on an investigation into alleged improper and unethical conduct by the president and other state functionaries relating to alleged improper relationships and involvement of the Gupta family in the removal and appointment of ministers and directors of state-owned enterprises resulting in improper and possibly corrupt award of state contracts and benefits to the Gupta family's businesses', Report No: 6 of 2016/17, 14 October 2016.
29. Matthew le Cordeur, 'Transnet CEO Brian Molefe now acting CEO of Eskom', *Fin24*, 17 April 2015.
30. Public Protector South Africa, 'State of capture' report, p. 148.
31. Sapa, 'Optimum Coal Mine to cut operations', *IOL*, 29 January 2015.
32. 'Glencore to cut 380 jobs at SA coal mine', *Fin24*, 22 July 2015.
33. Martin Creamer, 'Optimum mine right suspended, penalties may force R1/t coal supply', *Mining Weekly*, 4 August 2015.
34. 'Optimum Coal commences business rescue proceedings', Glencore media statement, 4 August 2015.
35. Mazars (Wils Raubenheimer), 'Companies Act – business rescue', Mazars.co.za, September 2012.
36. Public Protector South Africa, 'State of capture' report.
37. Ibid., p. 162.
38. Ibid., pp. 163–165.
39. Vicus Bürger, 'Guptas se VS-bande ontbloot', *Volksblad*, 22 May 2013.
40. Sam Sole, Tabelo Timse and Stefaans Brümmer, 'Free State dairy project damned in Treasury investigation', *Mail & Guardian*, 7 February 2014.
41. Andisiwe Makinana and Setumo Stone, 'How new mineral resources minister was sneaked in', *City Press*, 27 September 2015.
42. AmaBhungane, 'Gupta past haunts new mines minister', *Mail & Guardian*, 24 September 2015.
43. Thanduxolo Jika, Piet Rampedi and Sibongakonke Shoba, 'Zuma's allies in revolt against Guptas', *Sunday Times*, 31 January 2016.

44. Matthew le Cordeur, 'Zwane denies joining Guptas on trip to Switzerland', *Fin24*, 25 May 2016.
45. Andre Janse van Vuuren, Bloomberg, 'Minister denies Gupta favours in Glencore talks', *Moneyweb*, 5 February 2016.
46. Public Protector South Africa, 'State of capture' report, p. 126.
47. 'Oakbay's Tegeta to acquire Glencore Optimum companies for R2.15 billion', *Mining Review Africa*, 11 December 2015.
48. Susan Comrie, 'Zuma Jnr benefits from coal deals', *City Press*, 15 February 2016; Susan Comrie, 'How Eskom bailed out the Guptas', *City Press*, 12 June 2016; Tegeta's major shareholders include the Gupta family's Oakbay Investments (29 per cent), Duduzane Zuma's Mabengela Investments (28.5 per cent), Gupta associate Salim Essa's Elgasolve (21.5 per cent) and two unknown investors in Dubai.
49. Public Protector South Africa, 'State of capture' report, p. 310.
50. Ibid.
51. Sole, McKune and Brümmer, 'The "Gupta owned" state enterprises'.
52. Public Protector South Africa, 'State of capture' report.
53. Comrie, 'How Eskom bailed out the Guptas'.
54. 'Report in terms of section 34(1)(a) of the Prevention and Combating of Corrupt Activities Act 12 of 2004', drafted by Piers Marsden and Peter van den Steen, 1 July 2016, and reproduced in Public Protector South Africa, 'State of capture' report, pp. 182–187.
55. Susan Comrie, 'Eskom prepaid Guptas R586m for coal', *City Press*, 12 June 2016.
56. 'Report in terms of section 34(1)(a) of the Prevention and Combating of Corrupt Activities Act 12 of 2004'.
57. Public Protector South Africa, 'State of capture' report, p. 326.
58. Ibid., p. 315.
59. Ibid., pp. 300–303.
60. Ibid., p. 302.
61. 'Watch: Molefe gets emotional during Eskom briefing', eNCA.com, 3 November 2016.
62. Brendan Ryan, 'Guptas' Oakbay sells Optimum Coal export rights for R3.6bn', *miningmx*, 5 September 2016.
63. Public Protector South Africa, 'State of capture' report, p. 341.
64. Matthew le Cordeur, 'Guptas, Eskom still not budging on R2bn coal fine payment', *Fin24*, 30 November 2016.

CHAPTER 19: PANDORA'S BOX

1. 'Guptas have business link to mine minister Zwane', *Fin24*, 19 February 2016.
2. Franz Wild and Paul Burkhardt, 'Zuma son got stake in Tegeta weeks before it bought Optimum', *Bloomberg*, 7 March 2016.
3. Alec Hogg (ed.), 'Nenegate: Zuma's R500 billion blunder', *Biznews* Special Report, December 2015.
4. 'Pravin Gordhan new finance minister – Jacob Zuma', *Politicsweb*, 13 December 2015.
5. Floyd Shivambu, 'South Africa is under the management of Guptas', *Daily Maverick*, 17 December 2015.
6. Stefaans Brümmer, 'Nuclear price tag set Nene against Jacob Zuma', *Mail & Guardian*, 18 December 2015.
7. Jan de Lange, 'Des van Rooyen se besems was reg om te véé', *Rapport*, 19 December 2015.
8. 'Zuma bows to business', *Africa Confidential*, 57(4), 12 February 2016.

9. Sam Mkokeli, '"Being Indian doesn't make me a Gupta"', *Business Day*, 17 February 2016.
10. George Matlala, 'ANC hauls Gupta family over the coals', *Sowetan*, 17 February 2016.
11. George Matlala, '"No Gupta capture of ANC"', *Sowetan*, 11 January 2016.
12. Andrew England, 'South Africa: The power of the family business', *Financial Times*, 8 March 2016.
13. Thanduxolo Jika, Qaanitah Hunter and Sabelo Skiti, 'How Guptas shopped for new minister', *Sunday Times*, 13 March 2016.
14. 'Statement from Oakbay Investments, on behalf of the Gupta family in response to *The Sunday Times* article "How Guptas shopped for new minister"', Oakbay Investments press release, 13 March 2016.
15. 'Statement by Deputy Minister of Finance Mr. Mcebisi Jonas (MP)', Treasury media statement, 16 March 2016.
16. 'Gupta family respond to false allegations', Oakbay Investments media statement, 16 March 2016.
17. Ferial Haffajee, 'How Guptas asked Jonas to "work with us"', *City Press*, 16 March 2016.
18. 'Social media comment by former member of Parliament', Presidency media statement, 15 March 2016.
19. 'Claims by ex-MP of Gupta offer trashed', *The New Age*, 16 March 2016.
20. Ibid.
21. Anna Majavu, 'Transnet paid for Vytjie Mentor', *Sowetan*, 7 December 2010.
22. 'Presidency maintains no recollection of Ms Mentor', Presidency media statement, 16 March 2016.
23. Vytjie Mentor Facebook post, 16 March 2016.
24. Barbara Hogan speaking to John Robbie on Talk Radio 702, 17 March 2016.
25. Leanne George, 'Guptas hét belang in dié lugdiens', *Netwerk24*, 26 April 2016.
26. Sabelo Skiti, 'Guptas tried to "buy" SAA boss with R500k', *Sunday Times*, 17 March 2013.
27. Vytjie Mentor interview with J.J. Tabane on Power FM, 17 March 2016.
28. Jan-Jan Joubert, 'Vytjie Mentor tearfully opens up about Guptas', *Sunday Times*, 20 March 2016.
29. Vytjie Mentor interview with J.J. Tabane on Power FM.
30. 'President Zuma announces changes to the National Executive', Presidency media statement, 31 October 2010.
31. 'Zuma announces cabinet reshuffle', *IOL*, 31 October 2010.
32. Vytjie Mentor interview with J.J. Tabane on Power FM.
33. Moipone Malefane, 'Zuma sold SA for plate of curry', *Sunday World*, 5 May 2013.
34. 'SONA: Transcript of Julius Malema's speech', *Politicsweb*, 24 February 2016.
35. Thomas Holder, 'Mbalula: I don't dance to the Guptas' chorus', *EWN*, 17 March 2016.
36. 'Oakbay, Guptas release details of meeting with ANC top brass', *The New Age*, 18 March 2016.
37. Transcript of proceedings in the National Assembly, 17 March 2016.
38. Qaanitah Hunter and Sibongakonke Shoba, '"Zuma told me to help Guptas"', *Sunday Times*, 20 March 2016.
39. Ibid.
40. Ruwaydah Harris, 'Jimmy Manyi: Gupta TV's Oprah', *Mail & Guardian*, 23 August 2013.
41. Stephen Grootes, 'Manyi: Guptas never interfered with my dept', *EWN*, 23 March 2016.
42. 'Gupta family: The inconvenient truth', Oakbay Investments advertisement, *The New Age*, 18 March 2016.

43. 'Another Gupta-inspired cabinet reshuffle?', SACP media statement, 17 March 2016.
44. Govan Whittles and Alex Eliseev, 'Senior SACP member downplays Gupta "political influence"', *EWN*, 16 March 2016.
45. Govan Whittles, 'Zuma to take the hot seat at ANC NEC meeting', *EWN*, 18 March 2016.
46. 'Full text: Letter from stalwarts' foundations to ANC NEC', *News24*, 20 March 2016.

CHAPTER 20: CLIPPED WINGS AND FAILED PROBES
1. 'Full text: ANC NEC statement', *News24*, 20 March 2016.
2. 'Full text: Guptas welcome ANC NEC review', *News24*, 22 March 2016.
3. 'Ramaphosa on Guptas and state capture: "We will stop you in your tracks"', *Rand Daily Mail*, 23 March 2016.
4. Ntsakisi Maswanganyi, 'Business urges ANC to widen Gupta probe', *Business Day*, 24 March 2016.
5. 'Stopping state capture starts at Parliament, chief whip', DA media statement, 27 March 2016.
6. African News Agency, 'ANC: DA's claims of support for Gupta probe "delusional"', *Mail & Guardian*, 29 March 2016.
7. Rapule Tabane, 'Former DGs seek Gupta probe', *City Press*, 16 May 2016.
8. 'Statement of the African National Congress following the National List Conference and National Executive Committee meeting held from the 27th to the 30th May 2016', ANC media statement, 31 May 2016.
9. Mpho Raborife, 'ANC only got 1 written complaint on state capture – Mantashe', *News24*, 31 May 2016.
10. Ranjeni Munusamy, 'Captura continua: Guptas triumph as ANC shuts down state capture probe', *Daily Maverick*, 1 June 2016.
11. Natasha Marrian, 'Why Mantashe's Gupta probe flopped', *Financial Mail*, 10 June 2016.
12. Luyolo Mkentane, '"Whitewash" jibe at ANC Gupta probe', *The Star*, 2 June 2016.
13. 'DA lays criminal charges against Guptas', DA media statement, 17 March 2016.
14. Phumzile Mlangeni, 'COPE opens treason case against Zuma and Guptas', *SABC News*, 17 March 2016.
15. 'Zuptagate corruption charges referred to the Hawks', DA media statement, 22 March 2016.
16. 'Police on Gupta family investigations process: Hawks to investigate DA's matter against the Guptas', SAPS media statement, 24 March 2016.
17. Jan-Jan Joubert, 'Mentor accuses ministers over Guptas', *Sunday Times*, 19 June 2016.
18. Philda Essop, 'Vytjie Mentor calls for an independent probe into "state capture"', *City Press*, 24 March 2016.
19. Joubert, 'Mentor accuses ministers over Guptas'.
20. 'Vytjie Mentor's Gupta files', *City Press*, 10 July 2016.
21. Ibid.
22. Piet Rampedi, Mzilikazi wa Afrika, Stephan Hofstatter and Malcolm Rees, 'SARS bugged Zuma', *Sunday Times*, 12 October 2014.
23. 'Taxman's rogue unit ran brothel', *Sunday Times*, 9 November 2014.
24. 'Commissioner Thomas Moyane's statement on SARS committee recommendations', SARS media statement, 5 December 2014.
25. Piet Rampedi, Mzilikazi wa Afrika and Stephan Hofstatter, 'Call to probe Pravin over SARS spy saga', *Sunday Times*, 4 October 2015.

26. Abram Mashego, 'Spooks get Gordhan docket', *City Press*, 29 May 2016.
27. Letter from Gildenhuys Malatji Inc. to Lt General B.M. Ntlemeza, Treasury press release, 2 March 2016.
28. 'Minister of finance responds to the Hawks', Treasury media statement, 30 March 2016.
29. See Press Council rulings: Pravin Gordhan vs *Sunday Times* (15 December 2015), Ivan Pillay vs *Sunday Times* (16 December 2016) and Johann van Loggerenberg vs *Sunday Times* (16 January 2016), available at presscouncil.org.za.
30. Bongani Siqoko, 'SARS and the *Sunday Times*: Our response', *Sunday Times*, 3 April 2016.
31. Nathi Olifant, Qaanitah Hunter and Thanduxolo Jika, 'Pravin Gordhan faces "imminent arrest"', *Sunday Times*, 15 May 2016.
32. Ranjeni Munusamy, 'Gupta hidden hand behind Gordhan "arrest" and how Zuma could be co-accused on SARS "rogue unit" case', *Daily Maverick*, 16 May 2016.
33. Siyabonga Mkhwanazi, 'Gordhan arrest talk just "rumours"', *IOL*, 16 May 2016.
34. Marianne Thamm, 'Breaking: SARS Wars endgame – Hawks order Pravin Gordhan and others to "present" themselves', *Daily Maverick*, 23 August 2016.
35. Xola Potelwa, 'Rand plunges on report Hawks circling Gordhan', *Fin24*, 23 August 2016.
36. Thamm, 'Breaking: SARS Wars endgame – Hawks order Pravin Gordhan and others to "present" themselves'.
37. Angelique Serrao and Adriaan Basson, 'Guptas are attacking me, Gordhan tells Treasury staff', *News24*, 26 August 2016.
38. Qaanitah Hunter, 'Pravin pulls plug on Guptas' breakfast cash cow', *Sunday Times*, 21 February 2016.

CHAPTER 21: BATTLE WITH THE BANKS AND CLOSING SHOP
1. Erika Gibson and Ferial Haffajee, 'Why Guptas left SA'/'Eksklusief: Guptas verlaat SA permanent', *City Press/Rapport*, 10 April 2016.
2. Susan Comrie, 'The Guptas' R445m Dubai mansion', *City Press*, 8 May 2016.
3. Matthew le Cordeur, 'KPMG cuts ties with Gupta business empire', *Fin24*, 1 April 2016.
4. Ibid.
5. Justin Brown, Dewald van Rensburg and Susan Comrie, 'Gupta ship abandoned', *City Press*, 3 April 2016.
6. 'JSE Limited listing requirements', available at https://www.jse.co.za/content/JSERulesPoliciesandRegulationItems/JSE%20Listings%20Requirements.pdf (last accessed 6 January 2017).
7. SENS announcement, 'Oakbay Resources and Energy Limited – update regarding change in auditor and sponsor', *Moneyweb*, 5 April 2016.
8. Brown, Van Rensburg and Comrie, 'Gupta ship abandoned'.
9. 'FNB dumps Guptas' Oakbay Investments', *Fin24*, 6 April 2016.
10. Sipho Jack, 'Oakbay demands answers from FNB', *ANN7*, 6 April 2016.
11. Tiisetso Motsoeneng and James Macharia, 'Update 2: Gupta-owned firm hopes to restore relations with South African banks', *Reuters*, 11 April 2016.
12. SENS announcement, 'Oakbay Resources and Energy Limited – changes to the board of directors of the company and the board of a major subsidiary', *Moneyweb*, 8 April 2016. Varun Gupta is the nephew of the Gupta brothers, the son of their sister Achla. He is the brother of Vega Gupta, who got married at Sun City after the Waterkloof debacle.
13. Justin Brown, Susan Comrie and Avantika Seeth, 'Oakbay loses R6bn in value', *City Press*, 17 April 2016.

14. SENS announcement, 'Oakbay Resources and Energy Limited – update regarding banking relationships', *Moneyweb*, 8 April 2016.
15. 'Exclusive: Oakbay calls on Zuma and cabinet ministers for help in leaked letter', *TimesLive*, 8 April 2016.
16. Liesl Peyper, 'Radebe opens Oakbay can of worms', *Fin24*, 21 April 2016.
17. 'Withdrawal of banking services by individual banks from Oakbay Investments', BASA media statement, 14 April 2016.
18. Nazeem Howa full unedited interview, *Carte Blanche*, 19 June 2016, available at https://www.youtube.com/watch?v=etAM4uyfmlA (last accessed 6 January 2017).
19. Sikonathi Mantshantsha, 'Everything but the truth', *Financial Mail*, 15 September 2016.
20. Qaanitah Hunter, '"Gupta minister" on mission impossible', *Sunday Times*, 1 May 2016.
21. 'South Africa's mines minister says in talks with banks over Gupta firm', *Reuters*, 18 May 2016.
22. Matthew le Cordeur, 'Ministers stall on banks intervention over Gupta blacklisting', *Fin24*, 25 May 2016.
23. 'Update 1: South Africa still pursuing banks on Oakbay accounts closures – mines minister', *Reuters*, 3 June 2016.
24. 'Statement of the chairperson of the inter-ministerial committee set up by cabinet to consider the implications of the decisions of certain banks and audit firms to close the accounts of and/or withdraw auditing services from Oakbay Investments', Department of Mineral Resources media statement, 1 September 2016.
25. 'Statement of minister of mineral resources is not government position', Presidency media statement, 2 September 2016.
26. Kaveel Singh, 'Zwane statement reckless – ANC', *News24*, 3 September 2016.
27. Matthew le Cordeur, 'Exclusive: Gupta PR firm knew about bank probe weeks before Zwane dropped bomb', *Fin24*, 22 September 2016.
28. Ibid.
29. Emsie Ferreira, 'Zwane insists he has backing for Gupta bank saga probe', *IOL*, 28 September 2016.
30. Matthew le Cordeur, 'Gupta-owned Oakbay finds new auditors', *Fin24*, 21 April 2016.
31. SENS announcement, 'Oakbay Resources and Energy Limited – change of sponsor', *Moneyweb*, 1 September 2016.
32. Bank of Baroda South Africa, http://www.bankofbaroda.co.za.
33. Thanduxolo Jika, Sabelo Skiti and Sibongakonke Shoba, 'Guptas' mystery cash trail probed', *Sunday Times*, 12 June 2016.
34. Angelique Serrao and Adriaan Basson, 'Guptas are attacking me, Gordhan tells Treasury staff', *News24*, 26 August 2016.
35. 'Gupta family responds to alleged comments', Oakbay Investments media statement, 27 August 2016.
36. 'Guptas to sell shareholding in all South African businesses', Oakbay Investments media statement, 27 August 2016.

CHAPTER 22: PRAVIN'S BOMB

1. 'What Oupa Magashula, Ivan Pillay & Pravin Gordhan are charged with', *Politicsweb*, 11 October 2016.
2. Cathleen Powell, 'Charges against finance minister show misuse of South African law', *The Conversation*, 17 October 2016.

3. Alec Hogg, 'Zuma v Gordhan: The end-game – Treasury considers "nuclear bomb" option', *BizNews*, 30 August 2016.
4. Pravin Gordhan founding affidavit, *Minister of Finance vs Oakbay Investments and Others*, North Gauteng High Court, 14 October 2016. The court application and all annexures are available at https://www.dropbox.com/sh/caqypypdq29ip98/AACMKQ VQRa2ZWjwKDla2WH8Oa?dl=0&preview=161014_gordhan+v+oakbay.pdf (last accessed 7 February 2017).
5. Letter from Nazeem Howa to Pravin Gordhan, 8 April 2016.
6. Pravin Gordhan founding affidavit.
7. Letter from Nazeem Howa to Pravin Gordhan, 17 April 2016.
8. Letter from Pravin Gordhan to Nazeem Howa, 24 May 2016.
9. Pravin Gordhan founding affidavit.
10. Letter from Nazeem Howa to Pravin Gordhan, 24 May 2016.
11. Ibid.
12. Letter from Stephan Nel to Pravin Gordhan, 28 June 2016.
13. Letter from Nazeem Howa to Pravin Gordhan, 25 July 2016.
14. Letter from Pravin Gordhan to Nazeem Howa, 10 August 2016.
15. Letter from Nazeem Howa to Pravin Gordhan, 9 September 2016.
16. Susan Comrie, Stefaans Brümmer and Sam Sole, 'Gordhan blows whistle on Guptas' R6.8bn "suspicious and unusual payments"', amaBhungane.co.za, 15 October 2016.
17. 'Live broadcast to FSPs – FIC overview', Stellenbosch, 19 October 2011.
18. Financial Intelligence Centre website, www.fic.gov.za.
19. Pieter-Louis Myburgh, 'Here it is: The full list of 72 "dodgy" Gupta transactions', *News24*, 15 October 2016.
20. Letter from Pravin Gordhan to Murray Michell, 28 July 2016.
21. Letter from Murray Michell to Pravin Gordhan, 1 August 2016.
22. Letter from Murray Michell to Pravin Gordhan, 4 August 2016.
23. 'Certificate in terms of section 39 of Financial Intelligence Centre Act, 2001 (Act no 38 of 2001)', signed by Murray Stewart Rodon Michell, 4 August 2016.
24. Oakbay Resources & Energy Integrated Annual Report 2015, available at http://www.oakbay.co.za/images/ORE%20Annual%20report%202015%20LR.pdf (last accessed 15 February 2017).
25. Pravin Gordhan founding affidavit.
26. Letter from Werksmans Attorneys to the South African Reserve Bank, 27 June 2016.
27. 'Oakbay Investments sets the record straight on Optimum Rehabilitation Fund', Oakbay Investments media statement, 17 October 2016.
28. 'CEO resignation due to health reasons', Oakbay Investments media statement, 17 October 2016.
29. 'Ajay Gupta and Oakbay Investments delighted at affidavit from Pravin Gordhan', Oakbay Investments media statement, 18 October 2016.
30. 'Oakbay responds to application by minister of finance', Oakbay Investments media statement, 19 October 2016.
31. Ronica Ragavan respondents' affidavit, *Minister of Finance vs Oakbay Investments and Others*, North Gauteng High Court, 20 January 2017.

CHAPTER 23: THULI'S LAST TANGO

1. 'Public Protector Thuli Madonsela on request to investigate Gupta family in state affairs', Public protector media statement, 18 March 2016.

2. 'DA calls on public protector to investigate Zuma over Guptagate scandal', DA media statement, 18 March 2016.
3. Zandi Shabalala, 'South African watchdog wants more resources to probe family with Zuma links', *Reuters*, 7 June 2016; Greg Nicolson, 'State capture: Madonsela needs funds to investigate as Jonas speaks out again', *Daily Maverick*, 8 June 2016.
4. Matthew le Cordeur, 'Madonsela gets funding boost to probe Guptas and state capture', *Fin24*, 7 July 2016.
5. 'Gordhan gives Madonsela money to investigate the Guptas but not white capital', *Black Opinion*, 12 July 2016.
6. 'Public protector shocked, appalled by rascals that invaded her office on Monday', Public protector media statement, 19 July 2016.
7. Susan Comrie, 'How Eskom bailed out the Guptas', *City Press*, 12 June 2016.
8. 'Media exposed, Guptas cleared', *Black Opinion*, 13 June 2016.
9. PTI, '"We are being unfairly targeted," say South Africa's scandal-hit Guptas', NDTV.com, 30 August 2016.
10. Lizeka Tandwa, 'Gupta report to be ready before Madonsela says final goodbye', *News24*, 14 September 2016.
11. 'Public protector meets with the president', Public protector press release, 6 October 2016.
12. 'President Zuma requests the public protector to provide him with names of witnesses interviewed and the transcripts of testimony', Presidency media statement, 10 October 2016.
13. Public Protector Act 23 of 1994, section 7(9)(b)(ii).
14. 'President Zuma requests the public protector to provide him with names of witnesses interviewed and the transcripts of testimony'.
15. 'Public protector notes Presidency statement', Public protector media statement, 10 October 2016.
16. 'We speak to outgoing Public Protector Thuli Madonsela', *News24*, 11 October 2016.
17. Letter from Van Der Merwe and Associates Incorporated to Public Protector South Africa, 11 October 2016.
18. Ibid. Text italicised and in bold as in original letter.
19. 'Public protector report', Parliament of the Republic of South Africa statement, 14 October 2016.
20. Thulani Gqirana, 'Mkhwebane won't oppose "state capture" interdict', *News24*, 21 October 2016.
21. 'Busisiwe Mkhwebane bares claws towards Thuli Madonsela', *TimesLive*, 20 October 2016.
22. 'Minister Zwane launches urgent application to interdict Public protector's report', Department of Mineral Resources media statement, 31 October 2016.
23. Lizeka Tandwa, 'Opposition parties win bid to intervene in state capture case', *News24*, 1 November 2016.
24. Gia Nicolaides and Barry Bateman, 'Public protector ordered to release state capture report by 5pm today', *EWN*, 2 November 2016.

CHAPTER 24: STATE OF CAPTURE

1. Nomahlubi Jordaan, 'State capture report release could be held up by Zwane's application: Public protector', *Sunday Times*, 2 November 2016.
2. Public Protector South Africa, 'State of capture: Report on an investigation into

alleged improper and unethical conduct by the president and other state functionaries relating to alleged improper relationships and involvement of the Gupta family in the removal and appointment of ministers and directors of state-owned enterprises resulting in improper and possibly corrupt award of state contracts and benefits to the Gupta family's businesses', Report No: 6 of 2016/17, 14 October 2016. The full report is available online at http://cdn.24.co.za/files/Cms/General/d/4666/3f63a8b78d2b495d88f10ed060997f76.pdf (last accessed 9 February 2017).

3. Sarah Evans, 'Judge Seriti has left the building', *Mail & Guardian*, 2 July 2015.
4. 'Read: President Zuma's full statement on the release of the arms deal report', *TimesLive*, 21 April 2016.
5. Public Protector South Africa, 'State of capture' report, p. 25.
6. Ibid.
7. Ibid., p. 343.
8. Ibid., p. 92.
9. Ibid., p. 93.
10. Ibid.
11. Ibid., p. 94.
12. Ibid.
13. Ibid., p. 95.
14. Ibid., p. 102.
15. Ibid., p. 104.
16. Ibid., p. 95.
17. Ibid., p. 107.
18. Ibid.
19. Ronica Ragavan respondents' supplementary affidavit, *Minister of Finance vs Oakbay Investments and Others*, North Gauteng High Court, 10 February 2017.
20. Naledi Shange, 'Jonas slams Ajay Gupta over Saxonwold meeting: I was offered R600-million to bring business to the family', *TimesLive*, 17 February 2017.
21. Public Protector South Africa, 'State of capture' report, p. 90.
22. Ibid., p. 97.
23. Ibid., p. 89.
24. Ibid., p. 108.
25. 'The Presidency lodges a complaint with the Office of the Public Protector', Presidency press statement, 7 November 2016.
26. Nomahlubi Jordaan, 'Zuma audio recording legitimately released, not leaked, says Madonsela', *TimesLive*, 9 November 2016.
27. 'Adv Madonsela must step back and allow processes to unfold', Presidency press statement, 11 November 2016.

CHAPTER 25: ENDGAME

1. 'Finance investment roadshow', Presidency media statement, 27 March 2017.
2. Matthew le Cordeur, 'Gupta-owned Sahara files papers over Gordhan attorney', *Fin24*, 27 March 2017.
3. Matuma Letsoalo, 'ANC top brass reject JZ's "badly-written"' spy files on Gordhan', *Mail & Guardian*, 29 March 2017.
4. 'Breaking: Zuma about to fire ministers', *News24*, 30 March 2017.

5. 'President Zuma to make special announcement', Presidency media statement, 30 March 2017.
6. 'President Zuma appoints new ministers and deputy ministers', Presidency media statement, 31 March 2017.
7. Pieter-Louis Myburgh, 'Deputy finance minister linked to Prasa malfeasance', *News24*, 31 March 2017.
8. 'Full statement: SACP calls for Zuma's resignation', *The Citizen*, 31 March 2017.
9. Tshidi Madia, 'Gigaba will do Guptas' bidding – SACP', *News24*, 31 March 2017.
10. 'Malema alleges Guptas gave Gigaba cash, house in Cape Town', *The Citizen*, 31 March 2017.
11. 'Parliament must not be found wanting', DA press statement, 2 April 2017.
12. Ahmed Kathrada's letter to President Jacob Zuma, 31 March 2016, available at http://www.iol.co.za/news/special-features/kathrada/kathradas-letter-to-zuma-8399164 (last accessed 3 April 2017).
13. Mahlatse Gallens and Tshidi Madia, 'Zuma the elephant in the room at Kathrada's funeral', *News24*, 29 March 2017.
14. Masego Rahlaga, 'Ramaphosa says he is firmly opposed to Gordhan's removal', *Eyewitness News*, 31 March 2017.
15. Rob Rose, 'Zuma's bogus intelligence in the spotlight', *Financial Mail*, 31 March 2017.
16. Koketšo Motau, 'Gordhan again rubbishes "unintelligent" intelligence report', *Eyewitness News*, 1 April 2017.
17. Getrude Makhafola, '#Malema: Zuma's intelligence report compiled by Gupta associate', *IOL*, 30 March 2017.
18. Sicario, 'State capture term is abused by politicians', *Berea Mail*, 9 November 2016.

EPILOGUE
1. Dineo Tsamela and Sabelo Skiti, 'Zuma's friend now SA's richest black businessman', *Sunday Times*, 11 December 2016.
2. James de Villiers, 'Very disturbing that Atul Gupta on rich list: Save South Africa', *News24*, 11 December 2016.

Index

Do you have any comments, suggestions or feedback
about this book or any other Penguin titles?
Contact us at **talkback@penguinrandomhouse.co.za**

Visit **www.penguinrandomhouse.co.za** and subscribe
to our newsletter for monthly updates and news